THE STATE OF THE STATES

THE STATE OF THE STATES
SECOND EDITION

Edited by

Carl E. Van Horn
Rutgers University

A Division of Congressional Quarterly Inc.
1414 22nd Street N.W., Washington, D.C. 20037

Library of Congress Cataloging-in-Publication Data

The State of the states / edited by Carl E. Van Horn. -- 2nd ed.
     p. cm.
   Includes index.
   ISBN 0-87187-720-1
   1. State governments--United States. I. Van Horn, Carl E.
JK2408.S825 1992   92-435
353.9--dc20   CIP

To Christy

CONTENTS

PREFACE

Hard economic times nationwide now are testing the mettle of state leaders and institutions like never before. When the first edition of *The State of the States* was published in 1989, state governments arguably were the most responsive, innovative, and effective level of government in the American federal system. How skillfully the states manage the current crisis will determine whether that characterization will be retained.

In the 1980s, state governments moved to the center of American domestic politics. Because of the Reagan administration's efforts to reduce the role of the federal government and the constraints imposed by huge federal budget deficits, states came to carry out more of the public business and to provide more political and policy leadership for the nation. State political and governmental institutions strengthened their capacity to address problems through the election of better qualified individuals, the expansion of professional staff, and the raising of more revenues. States advanced ambitious legislative agendas and offered pioneering public policies in a host of areas.

New challenges were awaiting state government institutions and their leaders in the 1990s, when a long and deep national recession resulted in an increased demand for government services while revenues dropped. The spending sprees of the 1980s ended. States cut back programs and raised taxes just to stay afloat. Public anger at American political institutions rose, and state government elected officials often became targets of voter wrath. Incumbent legislators and governors found getting reelected harder. States struggled to adapt to their new role.

The second edition of *The State of the States* brings together many leading observers of state politics and government to describe and assess the performance of state political institutions in the difficult and hostile environment of the early 1990s. Chapters on federalism, governors, legislatures, courts, bureaucracies, budgeting, political parties, and campaigns and elections highlight the profound changes that state governments are undergoing. The book includes a new chapter on state tax and spending policy, reflecting the dominant role of these issues. The other chapters have been updated to reflect current political and policy trends.

The essays that appeared in the first edition were commissioned by the Eagleton Institute of Politics at Rutgers University as part of the State of the States Project, which was funded from the estate of Charles and Inez Howell. The National Governors' Association, the National Conference of State Legislatures, the Council of State Governments, the National Center for State Courts, and the Advisory Commission on Intergovernmental Relations served as cosponsors of the project. I received and appreciated the support of the members of the State of the States Advisory Committee: Geoff Callas, Barry Van Lare, Neal Peirce, William Pound, Larry Sabato, Raymond Scheppach, Carl Stenberg, and Carl Tubbesing.

In helping to prepare the second edition, several colleagues commented on the first edition and made suggestions for improvements, including Jeffrey Henig, Burdett Loomis, and Carl Stenberg. Undergraduate and graduate students enrolled in courses on state politics and several government practitioners provided valuable feedback. Richard P. Nathan expresses his appreciation to Paul Page for help in making revisions. Lawrence Baum wishes to thank Karen Laderman for research assistance on his chapter. Joanne Pfeiffer, my secretary at the Eagleton Institute, handled her duties with dispatch and good cheer.

Working again with CQ Press also was a pleasure. Brenda Carter helped me through the revision, and Colleen McGuiness served as project editor.

I am especially grateful to Jim Florio, governor of New Jersey, for giving me the opportunity to serve as his policy director while on leave from Rutgers University. As I practiced the art of governance, I deepened my understanding of and appreciation for state politics and government in incalculable ways.

The book is dedicated to my wife, Christy Van Horn. In helping me sort out what I have experienced, she endured more than her share of conversations about state politics over the last twelve years.

THE STATE OF THE STATES

1 ▰▬▬

The Quiet Revolution

Carl E. Van Horn

For more than two generations, from the 1930s through the 1960s, state governments languished in relative obscurity—overshadowed by a burgeoning national government responding to the crises of depression, war, and internal strife and overseeing an unprecedented and extended period of economic prosperity. Americans turned to Washington, D.C., for leadership and for their share of a growing federal pie.

In the first two-thirds of the twentieth century, sweeping national and international events and a cadre of political leaders shifted governmental activism to the federal level. State governments were bypassed as the federal government expanded beyond the limited role envisioned by the framers of the Constitution. State governments were scorned by many as racist, incompetent, inflexible, and politically and economically anemic.[1]

State governments have changed profoundly since the early 1960s. Responding to the pressing concerns of their residents, states pioneered solutions to some of the country's most difficult problems and demonstrated effective leadership.[2] States reformed and strengthened their political and economic houses and, as a result, came to occupy a more important role in American life.

In the 1980s and 1990s, states were capable and willing to tackle tough problems. Governors, legislators, judges, and bureaucrats were setting national agendas. Innovative economic development, education, and health care programs laid the foundations for federal statutes. States were handling a wide range of vexing problems, from homelessness and Acquired Immune Deficiency Syndrome (AIDS) to fostering competitive industries and reducing automobile pollution. Increasingly, federal government officials expected state governments to assume greater policy and administrative responsibilities. States increased their commitment to manage and pay for such traditional local government services as law enforcement and education.

States became more politically significant, too. Several strong and

1

effective governors rose to prominence. Lamar Alexander, former governor of Tennessee and secretary of education under President George Bush, helped galvanize a nationwide education reform movement. Arkansas governor Bill Clinton and Oregon governor Barbara Roberts advanced pathbreaking policies on behalf of children and families. Two former governors—Jimmy Carter of Georgia and Ronald Reagan of California—occupied the White House from 1977 to 1989. And the 1988 Democratic presidential nominee was Massachusetts governor Michael S. Dukakis.

The rise of state governments came via a quiet revolution in American politics. The transformation was not always smooth, and it took several decades to reach full maturity. In the 1990s, state governments were struggling to meet their new responsibilities. The boom years of increasing state revenues were replaced by the gloomy years of budget deficits, tax increases, and program reductions. Federal officeholders passed the buck but not the bucks to handle a broad array of public problems—cleaning up the air, providing health care for the poor, and delivering services for the disabled. State officials and institutions now are being tested like never before.

The Tidal Wave of Reform

Powerful and effective state governments did not emerge overnight. A series of reforms in the structure and process of state government—some carefully planned, others accidental—has come about since the 1960s. Cumulatively, these reforms enhanced the capacity of state governmental institutions and encouraged state government officials to broaden their responsibilities.

State government reform was not exclusively the accomplishment of enlightened state politicians. Two landmark federal policies—the reapportionment of state legislatures and the enactment of national civil rights laws—provoked much of the upheaval in state capitals. Initially, state officials regarded these policies as slaps in the face. Ultimately, they helped transform state politics and propelled state governments into a new era of growth.

In a sweeping 1962 decision, the U.S. Supreme Court mandated in *Baker v. Carr* that state legislatures be reapportioned so that political representation would be based on the principle of "one person, one vote." [3] Up until that time, many state legislatures were dominated by rural and suburban lawmakers, intent on preserving the status quo of local government control, low taxes, and limited government. Over time, legislatures evolved into modern, representative institutions more accurately reflecting the broad range of interests and needs in their states. [4] Reformed legislatures then expanded the reach of government in accordance with the wishes of newly represented voters.

The enactment and implementation of landmark civil rights legislation—including the Civil Rights Act of 1964 and the Voting Rights Act of 1965—extended the influence of federal law throughout the federal system. Overt discrimination in education, employment, business, and government was sharply reduced.[5] Gradually, the composition of the electorate, the membership of legislatures, and the direction of public policy more accurately reflected the citizenry of each state.

Prior to the civil rights statutes, federal lawmakers argued that state governments could not be trusted with the stewardship of the disadvantaged and minorities.[6] Within less than a decade, the critical argument against giving state governments more power, and in favor of greater federal control, essentially evaporated from political discourse. In the early 1970s, southern governors such as Lester G. Maddox of Georgia and George C. Wallace of Alabama were symbols of state government intransigence when they refused black students admission to state universities. In the 1980s, Ray Mabus, Jr., of Mississippi, with a coalition of support that included prominent blacks and members of other minorities, came to represent the new breed of progressive southern governors.

Pressure for modern and effective political and governmental institutions also came from state officials. Since the 1960s, nearly forty states ratified new constitutions or significantly amended existing ones.[7] The office of governor has been enhanced by allowing for longer terms and increasing opportunities for succession, which have brought in better qualified individuals.[8] Statewide elections for many governmental positions, such as secretary of state, attorney general, and chief state school officer, have been eliminated. As a result, the governor's visibility and power increased; appointment and removal of important policy makers became the governor's responsibility. Chief executives took a greater role in the budget process, expanded planning and personal staffs, and turned the National Governors' Association into an advocate for stronger state governments.

Legislatures also became better prepared for governing. For decades, state legislatures were ridiculed as "inefficient and corrupt." [9] During the 1960s and 1970s, "legislatures undertook to rebuild themselves practically from scratch," according to political scientist Alan Rosenthal.[10] They devoted more time to lawmaking, streamlined rules and procedures, and tightened rules governing campaign financing and conflicts of interest. Turnover declined as legislators became careerists. Professional staff were hired to prepare legislation, review state budgets, and oversee program administration. By 1990, more than fifteen thousand people worked for legislatures on a full-time basis—an increase of more than 200 percent since the mid-1960s.[11]

State courts and state bureaucracies also have increased their ability to carry out the public's business. State courts have been strengthened through reforms that unified the judicial system and enhanced their administrative resources.[12] State bureaucracies have grown in size. During the 1980s, the U.S. population grew by 9 percent, while state government employment increased by 19 percent. Some states doubled their workforces in the 1980s, largely because of the need to monitor rapidly growing social service programs, such as Medicaid, and to guard convicts in state prisons. State government workers now are much more likely to be recruited on a merit system, and state employees are better trained and educated than ever before. The structure of state government also has changed in nearly all the states.[13] Almost two dozen states have experienced comprehensive reorganizations since 1965, and the rest have been partially reorganized.[14]

Fiscal Squeeze Play

State governments were the fiscal stepchildren of the federal system in the 1950s and 1960s. They depended heavily on the sales tax and user fees, and most were required to balance their budgets—a constitutional restriction then regarded as a liability. In contrast, the federal government enjoyed the powerful and progressive income tax, which tapped the rapid income growth of the post-World War II era. When revenues slumped during downturns in the business cycle, the federal government could pull itself out by borrowing money.

State government spending for public purposes changed dramatically. In 1964, for example, state governments spent $24 billion; by 1990, more than $350 billion. During this same period, state spending increased at a slightly faster rate than federal government spending, somewhat faster than the rate of inflation, and considerably faster than local government spending.[15]

Federal aid to the states jumped sharply during the 1970s, then declined, as a percentage of total state spending, for more than a decade. Although often attributed to President Ronald Reagan, this trend actually started during Jimmy Carter's presidency and accelerated during the 1980s. In 1975, four out of every ten dollars spent by the states were passed down from the federal Treasury; by 1983, three out of every ten dollars.[16] Recently, federal aid has inched up again, but it has not reached the mid-1970s levels.[17] More important, federal aid has not kept pace with federal mandates to provide health care to the poor or to help deliver services for the disabled.

When federal officials halted the rapid increase in federal aid for states and localities, state governments picked up some of the slack. According to the Reagan philosophy, "federalism means that the central government speaks to the states and lets the states speak to the cities," said John Shannon, former executive director of the Advisory Commission on Intergovernmental Relations.[18] From 1980 to 1986, for example, total state spending for local government grew by 57 percent, from $83 billion to $130 billion. (Inflation over the same period was 32 percent.) Most state aid went to public elementary and secondary schools—five of every eight dollars. The balance was allocated for health and welfare, highways, public transit, housing, corrections, and general government support.[19]

The revenue raising power of states has been enhanced. Individual and corporate income taxes now are far more important than sales taxes and other fees. In 1967, only 22 percent of state government revenue derived from the income tax; by the 1980s, nearly 40 percent.[20] States also have found significant new sources of revenue in state lotteries, which have been created in twenty-two states. Setting up lotteries to raise funds thus far has not been considered a serious option by the federal government.[21]

State fiscal policy has followed five distinct paths.[22] From 1960 to 1977, state governments added new taxes and increased existing taxes to underwrite expenditure growth and to satisfy constituent demands for new and expanded services in health, education, environmental protection, and transportation.

During the late 1970s, many states experienced a tax revolt. Spurred by California's Proposition 13, which reduced property tax revenues by 57 percent and limited future increases to no more than 2 percent annually, citizens and legislators clamped down on the rapid growth in state spending. Between 1978 and 1984, only three of the nine states that voted on Proposition 13-type initiatives approved them. But voters in eleven states accepted moderate tax and spending limitation measures.[23] Legislatures in dozens of other states responded to the California message. No new taxes were added from 1978 to 1980, and taxes declined in dozens of states.[24]

Between 1981 and 1983, states imposed substantial tax increases to cope with an economic recession and deep reductions in federal aid. Unlike the federal government, the states each year must raise sufficient revenues to cover the costs of operating state programs. States responded by jacking up the sales tax, increasing income tax rates, adding a penny or two to the gasoline tax, extending the concept of user fees for services, and creating state-sponsored lotteries.

When the economy rebounded in the mid-1980s, many states reaped a fiscal bonanza.[25] The income and sales tax increases levied earlier to stave off financial disaster became the driving force behind expansionary government spending programs. Not much of the unanticipated "windfall government profit" was returned to taxpayers. A few states in the energy-producing regions of the country, such as Texas and Louisiana, and states heavily dependent on single revenue sources or weak industries, such as

Oregon, did not experience a surge in financial horsepower, but many others did and they spent like mad.

In the 1990s, state governments were plagued with soaring deficits brought on by the spending of the 1980s and by sharp reductions in revenues that were received because of a deep national recession that lasted for nearly three years. In 1991, thirty-four states raised more than $16 billion in income, sales, and corporate taxes and cut more than $10 billion in programs just to try to keep their budgets in balance. California raised $7 billion in new revenues, cut $7 billion in programs, but still faced a $6 billion deficit the following year.[26]

The federal government's huge deficits and continuing appetite for mandating increases in state spending compounded the problem for state officials. Between 1981 and 1992, the total national debt quadrupled to more than $4 trillion.[27] Annual budget deficits rose from $25 billion in the $178 billion budget of 1968 to $200 billion in the $800 billion budget of 1983. By fiscal year 1991, the deficit had grown to $318 billion of the $1.4 trillion federal budget.[28]

The fallout from bloated federal deficits sent shock waves through state capitals. To pay for substantial increases in defense and entitlement programs, federal lawmakers sharply cut aid to state and local governments. Consequently, states received less money from the national government and more pleas for help from local governments.[29]

Federal officials now are reluctant or unable to mount new domestic program initiatives and pay for them with federal resources. Interest groups have turned up the heat on states to satisfy their demands. Unfortunately, state governments cannot "count on the federal cavalry to come charging over the hill with aid from Washington," said fiscal expert John Shannon. The states are operating in "an atmosphere of fend-for-yourself federalism." [30]

During the 1960s, new domestic policies were created through federally funded categorical aid programs. The assistance often bypassed state governments and went directly to local governments or community organizations. Federal officials specified the what, when, and how of program administration and tried to monitor closely program compliance, which was consistent with the underlying distrust of state government capacity and intentions.[31]

Although devolution of responsibility to state governments in the 1980s was supposed to be accompanied by deregulation of federal control, the federal government continued to imposed strict regulations. Federal mandates relating to health care for the poor, environmental protection, services for the disabled and senior citizens cost state governments billions of dollars annually. Congress and the president continued to satisfy constituent requests for assistance by imposing new demands on state capitals.[32]

Struggle and Innovation

For more than fifty years—from Franklin Roosevelt's New Deal to Jimmy Carter's Urban Policy—the national government created progressive public policies. With large federal budget deficits and conservative Republican presidents in the White House during the 1980s and 1990s, however, the federal government often took a back seat to state governments in devising domestic policy innovations. States offered new policy initiatives in a broad range of areas—natural resources and energy policy, human services and health care, economic development, education, business, and insurance regulation. State governments became deeply engaged in issues that affected state residents on a daily basis—the quality of schools, the supply of water, and the condition of roads and waterways. States also tackled some of the nation's most difficult problems—surrogate motherhood, the care and treatment of the medically indigent, drug abuse in the public schools, teenage pregnancy, pay equity, the liability insurance crisis, and the right to die.

The importance of state policy leadership recently has been demonstrated in economic development, education, welfare, and environmental protection policies. The states initiated successful policy experiments that were copied or endorsed by the national government. State governments provided the lion's share of the funds needed to carry out new public strategies, although progress has been slowed substantially by the lingering national recession of the early 1990s.

Economic development always has been an important responsibility of state governments. States fund bridge and highway construction; maintain ports, rivers, airline terminals, and mass transit systems; support the education and training of the workforce; and regulate basic financial institutions and utilities. During the 1980s and early 1990s, the states reconceived and expanded their economic development strategies. Facing double-digit unemployment and massive disruptions in communities, states initiated programs and policies to make their states economically competitive. States invested heavily in the development of new technologies, the retraining of workers, the development of small business opportunities, and the expansion of export markets. As journalist David Osborne noted: "While the national government debated whether it should develop a new industrial policy, the states were already implementing one." [33]

Clearly, however, state governments are limited in what they can accomplish when the national economy is not growing. New Jersey governor James J. Florio, for example, launched a major public works investment strategy to create 150,000 jobs over five years on projects designed to improve the state's roads, transit systems, airports, and ports. Despite this impressive commitment to capital spending, the state still lost more than 250,000 private sector jobs during the recession. Without the governor's program, the economy would have been in much worse shape, but state government policy alone cannot keep a state from sinking into a national recession.

Education reform has been another recurrent theme of state policy innovation since 1980. Governors and legislators increased the academic rigor of schools, upgraded the quality of teachers, and expanded the achievements of students. Remarkably, almost every state participated in reviewing and improving their educational systems. For example, forty-five states modified requirements for high school graduation, usually by making more math and science courses mandatory; and forty-six states created new techniques for assessing the quality of classroom teachers.[34] The national government was a "cheerleader on the sidelines," for nearly all of the changes were undertaken without federal mandates or appropriations. The so-called national goals for education, adopted in 1990, were fashioned by the National Governors' Association and subsequently approved by President Bush.

The issue of equity in school funding formulas again rose to prominence. According to a 1971 landmark California Supreme Court ruling, the state's system of financing schools denied equal protection to children living in property-poor school districts. Since then, school finance systems in Kentucky, Montana, Texas, and New Jersey were ruled unconstitutional and the states ordered to equalize spending between rich and poor districts.

In the early 1990s, lawsuits challenging the fairness of school funding formulas were filed in twenty-two states. In nearly every case, school districts with relatively small amounts of taxable property—often inner-city urban areas—argued that their students were unconstitutionally disadvantaged. The outcomes of these suits will depend upon the evidence presented and its relationship to the state's constitution. In states where decisions have been made, state governments will be required to raise and distribute more funds to the public school systems in an equitable manner, which will mean higher state taxes to replace local property taxes.[35]

Welfare reform commanded attention from state policy makers. For twenty-five years, federal lawmakers, administrators, and policy experts bemoaned the nation's ineffective welfare programs but failed to achieve significant improvements. State governments seized the initiative and restructured public assistance programs. Led by such diverse governors as liberal Democrat Michael Dukakis of Massachusetts and conservative Republican George Deukmejian of California, the states forged a new consensus: Welfare had to be changed from an entitlement program that fosters dependency to an education, training, and work program that promotes economic independence. The National Governors' Association, under the leadership of Arkansas governor Bill Clinton, focused on welfare reform and advocated changes in federal legislation. More than thirty states revised their welfare systems, and the federal government eventually adopted national policies already undertaken in the states.[36]

The national recession in the 1990s led many states to cut back on welfare assistance programs and dozens of other social service innovations mounted in the fiscally rich 1980s. In 1991, forty states cut or held stable Aid to Families with Dependent Children (AFDC)—the federal/state program that aids needy families. Fourteen states cut general assistance programs for needy adults, Michigan governor John Engler eliminated a program for able-bodied male welfare recipients, and California governor Pete Wilson suggested cutting welfare programs by 25 percent.[37]

Landmark environmental statutes mandating cleanup of the air, water, and land were enacted by the federal government in the 1960s and 1970s. The states were primarily responsible for the implementation of basic environmental statutes. Recent federal laws put the states in charge of some very tough problems, including dealing with the effects of automobile pollution. Decisions about where to dispose of toxic and low-level radioactive waste and how much Americans will be able to use their cars will be made by the states.[38]

Environmental policy innovations came from traditional sources—legislatures and governors—and from the voters, too. For example, Arizona governor Bruce Babbitt was able to break a forty-year deadlock over water conservation policy in his state with effective public and private leadership. The New Jersey legislature passed sweeping legislation that required industries to inform employees about the potential health effects of chemicals in the workplace. And California voters supported an initiative in 1986 that required the state government and industries to identify and stop the release of toxic chemicals into the groundwater.

More Power, More Conflict

Several underlying forces affected the ability, willingness, and need to enlarge the state governments. The expanding role of state governments came at a high price. Conflict accompanied their growth in influence. State legislators and governors are much less likely to be reelected. California voters imposed limitations on the number of terms state legislators may serve, and by 1992 twelve states were considering term limitation amendments to their constitutions.

Reformed, modernized, and more capable governmental institutions filled a void left by a financially strapped and politically conservative federal government. Six years of sustained economic growth throughout much of the nation in the 1980s expanded state treasuries and emboldened state elected officials to take on greater responsibility for meeting the needs of their constituents. When growth turned to recession in the 1990s, state governments were hard pressed to keep their fiscal heads above water.

This roller coaster of federal government expansion and decline increased pressure on state political institutions and processes. The chapters that follow describe and assess how states cope with their new power and authority. Some of the nation's leading students of state government and politics trained their skillful eyes on important trends in state political institutions and political processes. They provide perspectives on the impact of major changes that have taken place since the early 1960s, characterize the status of state politics and government today, and identify the challenges facing state political leaders in the late 1990s.

In Chapter 2, "The Role of the States in American Federalism," Richard P. Nathan describes the paradox of Reagan administration-inspired devolution during the 1980s. The conservative dream of reducing government actually fostered governmental activism at the state level. According to Nathan, a cyclical pattern exists in the roles played by state governments. During liberal periods, the 1930s through the 1970s, for example, those who favored increased governmental activity concentrated their energies on the federal government. During conservative periods, those seeking governmental action turned to the states. State governments have been the centers of activism and innovation in domestic affairs in conservative periods in U.S. history, according to Nathan.

In Chapter 3, "State Budgeting in the Nineties," Henry J. Raimondo traces in detail the conflict-ridden landscape of state fiscal policy in the 1990s. The sustained period of economic growth in the 1980s enabled states to avoid the trap of budget deficits. When the recession arrived in the 1990s, states were caught in a vice of shrinking revenues and increasing demands for services. States responded by raising taxes, cutting services, and passing costs on to local governments, college students, and school districts. The "go-it-alone federalism" of the 1990s turned the United States into fifty small countries.

In Chapter 4, "The Transformation of State Electoral Politics," Stephen A. Salmore and Barbara G. Salmore describe the rise of candidate-centered campaigns, in which personal qualities and issues communicated directly to voters compete with party labels and organizations as the principal voting cues in state elections. With the rise of state governments as policy makers, more state elections are considered important, more political players are interested in their outcomes, and more resources are available to wage campaigns. The trend toward candidate-centered campaigns is most pronounced in gubernatorial elections because of the rise in split-ticket and cross-party voting, the use of direct primaries, the effective use of incumbency, the decoupling of federal and state elections, and the increases in spending on elections.

These same trends have made legislative races—especially in the larger states—more like races for the U.S. Congress than ever before.

In Chapter 5, "Being Governor," Thad L. Beyle traces the strengthened role of governors, examines their growing significance on the national policy scene, and describes the difficulties of being a governor in the recession-plagued 1990s. As governors exercised more power in their respective states, they came into conflict with courts, legislatures, and other members in the executive branch. The mounting deficits that bring on program cuts and tax increases made life in the governor's office harder. Governors usually got their way on major policy initiatives, but they paid a high price at the polls and in public opinion surveys. Beyle considers the diverse legacies that governors leave their states when they leave office.

Chapter 6, "The Legislative Institution—In Transition and at Risk," by Alan Rosenthal, documents the "rise of the legislative institution" from the rural-dominated political backwaters of the 1950s to the modern, more representative institutions of today. New-generation legislators are unwilling to take a back seat to the governors, the courts, and the bureaucracy. Instead, they are exercising greater influence on the allocation of money and the direction of state policy. Despite these positive developments, Rosenthal argues that careerism among state legislators, increased politicization of legislatures, greater fragmentation of decision making, and an unfriendly political environment are subtly undermining America's legislatures.

Chapter 7, "Making Judicial Policies in the Political Arena," by Lawrence Baum, examines the institutions that often are called upon to referee conflicts between governors and legislatures or between governors and other executive branch agencies—the courts. State courts, however, also make policy and thus generate conflict with other governmental actors. In recent years, state courts have become more liberal in their policy making. In tort law, they expanded the rights of people who suffered personal injuries or property damage. In civil liberties, they relied upon provisions in the state constitutions to expand individual rights. This increased activism has not gone unchallenged. State legislatures have tried to overturn or modify court decisions. Initiatives and referendums have been used to overturn court decisions, especially those that expanded the rights of criminal defendants. Voters removed liberal justices from office in several states. Incumbent judges are rarely defeated, but they have become more vulnerable and more accountable for their actions.

In Chapter 8, "Accountability Battles in State Administration," William T. Gormley, Jr., summarizes the proliferation of controls intended to curb the power of state bureaucracies to make and carry out policy. As state governments, and hence state administrative agencies, took on greater responsibility for the implementation of public policy, other politicians, judges, and citizens began to demand more accountability from them. States have responded by increasing legislative oversight and executive management techniques and by involving citizens in a wider range of bureaucratic decisions. At the same time, federal agencies and federal and state judges increased their control over the functions of state bureaucracies. As the competition for control increased, accountability battles emerged. These pitted various state political institutions against one another in a bitter struggle over authority, with state bureaucracies as the ultimate prize.

Chapter 9, "The Persistence of State Parties," by Samuel C. Patterson, argues that political parties remain important participants in state politics. Careful observation of state political parties "belies the view that the state parties have been enervated—nationalized, swamped by political action committees (PACs), decimated organizationally, overcome by media technology or modern 'snake oil' public relations." Instead of becoming relics of the past, they are adapting to the new politics of the 1990s. State parties vary enormously across the nation, but on balance, they have profound influence over who runs for state office, who is elected, and what the nature of political participation in American politics will be.

In Chapter 10, "The New Storm over the States," I provide a summary of the essays. Some of the major problems facing state governments in the 1990s are considered, as well as how states are coping with the strains created by their new responsibility as central players in the federal system and by a national recession that brought abruptly to an end the golden years of expansion state governments experienced in the 1980s.

The quiet revolution in state governments has touched every state political institution and political actor. The stakes are higher than ever before. Competition for the exercise of power—a permanent feature of politics—has grown more intense. Conflict over questions of governance and political leadership has spread within and across political institutions. How well state political institutions and leaders handle these difficult challenges will determine how the nation is to be governed and how its citizens are to be served in the coming decades.

Notes

1. Terry Sanford, *Storm over the States*, (New York: McGraw-Hill, 1967).
2. Ann O'M. Bowman and Richard C. Kearney, *The Resurgence of the States* (Englewood Cliffs, N.J.: Prentice-Hall, 1986).
3. Timothy O'Rourke, *The Impact of Reapportionment* (New Brunswick, N.J.:

Transaction Books, 1980).

4. Alan Rosenthal, *Legislative Life* (New York: Harper and Row, 1981).

5. Charles S. Bullock III and Charles M. Lamb, eds., *Implementation of Civil Rights Policy* (Monterey, Calif.: Brooks/Cole, 1984).

6. Carl E. Van Horn, *Policy Implementation in the Federal System* (Lexington, Mass.: D.C. Heath and Co., 1979), 155-161.

7. Albert L. Sturm and Janice C. May, "State Constitutions and Constitutional Revisions: 1980-1981 and the Past Fifty Years," in Council of State Governments, *The Book of the States, 1982-1983* (Lexington, Ky.: Council of State Governments, 1982), 115-133.

8. Larry J. Sabato, *Goodbye to Good-time Charlie: The American Governor Transformed* (Washington, D.C.: CQ Press, 1983).

9. Sanford, *Storm over the States*, 39.

10. Rosenthal, *Legislative Life*, 3.

11. National Conference of State Legislatures, *Legislative Staff in the Fifty States* (Denver, Colo.: National Conference of State Legislatures, 1986).

12. Robert A. Kagan, Bloos Cartwright, Lawrence M. Friedman, and Stanton Wheeled, "The Evolution of State Supreme Courts," *Michigan Law Review* 76 (1978): 961-1005.

13. Deil S. Wright, *Understanding Intergovernmental Relations*, 2d ed. (Monterey, Calif.: Brooks/Cole, 1982).

14. Council of State Governments, *The Book of the States, 1982-1983*, 145-147; *The Book of the States, 1984-1985* (1984), 44-45; *The Book of the States, 1986-1987* (1986), 45-47; and *The Book of the States, 1988-1989* (1988), 47-48.

15. Advisory Commission on Intergovernmental Relations, *Significant Features of Fiscal Federalism, 1984* (Washington, D.C.: Advisory Commission on Intergovernmental Relations, 1984), 10.

16. Ibid., 62.

17. "Measuring Federal Aid: Whose Straw Is Shortest?" *Governing*, prototype, 1987, 48.

18. Ibid., 49.

19. "More State Dollars for the Localities," *Governing*, May 1988, 60-61.

20. Advisory Commission on Intergovernmental Relations, *Significant Features of Fiscal Federalism*, 51.

21. Steven D. Gold, Brenda Erikson, and Michelle Kissell, *Earmarking State Taxes* (Denver, Colo.: National Conference of States Legislatures, 1987), 6.

22. Advisory Commission on Intergovernmental Relations, *Significant Features of Fiscal Federalism*, 71.

23. Patrick B. McGuigan, *The Politics of Direct Democracy in the 1980s*, (Washington, D.C.: Free Congress Research and Education Foundation, 1985), 52, 54, 55.

24. Advisory Commission on Intergovernmental Relations, *Significant Features of Fiscal Federalism*, 71.

25. Steve D. Gold, ed., *Reforming State Tax Systems* (Denver, Colo.: National Conference of State Legislatures, 1986).

26. Earl C. Gottchalk, Jr., "Across the Country, Increased State Levies Hit Incomes Harder," *Wall Street Journal*, November 11, 1991, C1.

27. *Economic Report of the President* (Washington, D.C.: U.S. Government Printing Office, 1991), 375.
28. U.S. Congress, Joint Economic Committee, *The 1985 Joint Economic Report*, 99th Cong., 1st sess., 1985, 47; and Executive Office of the President, *Budget of the United States for Fiscal Year 1987* (Washington, D.C.: U.S. Government Printing Office, 1986). See also, *Budget of the United States, Fiscal Year 1992* (Washington, D.C.: U.S. Government Printing Office, 1991).
29. Richard P. Nathan and Fred C. Doolittle, *Reagan and the States* (Princeton, N.J.: Princeton University Press, 1987).
30. David Shribman, "Governors of Fiscally Strapped States, Seeing No Sign of Relief, Yearn for the Good Old Days," *Wall Street Journal*, August 19, 1991, 10.
31. James L. Sundquist, *Making Federalism Work* (Washington, D.C.: Brookings Institution, 1969).
32. Nathan and Doolittle, *Reagan and the States.*
33. David Osborne, *Laboratories of Democracy* (Cambridge, Mass.: Harvard Business School Press, 1988).
34. Susan Fuhrman, *State Politics and Education Reform* (New Brunswick, N.J.: Center for Policy Research in Education, Rutgers University, 1988).
35. Roberto Suro, "Equality Plan on School Financing Is Upsetting Rich and Poor in Texas," *New York Times*, October 9, 1991, 1.
36. National Governors' Association, *Making America Work: Productive People, Productive Policies* (Washington, D.C.: National Governors' Association, 1987).
37. Paul Taylor, "Little to Soften Squeeze of Recession and State Cuts on the Poor," *Washington Post*, January 30, 1992, 1; and Jason DeParle, "California Plan to Cut Welfare May Prompt Others to Follow," *New York Times*, December 18, 1991, 1.
38. National Conference of State Legislatures, *State Issues 1987* (Denver, Colo.: National Conference of State Legislatures, 1987), Chapter 2.

2 ▬▬▬

The Role of the States in American Federalism

Richard P. Nathan

British political scientist Kenneth C. Wheare's seminal work on federal government, published in 1946, stated that the modern idea of federalism was determined by the United States.[1] Before 1787, the term "federal" referred to a league in which the constituent states were members of a polity, like a club. In the United States, by contrast, both the central government and the regional governments operated directly upon the people; "each citizen is subject to two governments," said Wheare.[2] The central and regional governments should be "co-ordinate" in a federal system and must have "exclusive control" in some areas of activity, according to Wheare.[3] In a similar vein, American political scientist Arthur W. Macmahon in 1955 said, "The matters entrusted to the constituent governments in a federal system (whether their powers are residual or delegated) must be substantial and not trivial." [4] This is the traditional theory of federalism found in the writings of many political scientists.

A newer theory, which rejects both Wheare's idea about "co-ordinate" governments and Macmahon's idea about substantial powers being entrusted to the state governments, stresses a dynamic concept of shared powers or what is often called "cooperative" federalism. This theory is most closely associated with the writing of University of Chicago political scientist Morton Grodzins, whose famous essay on "marble cake" federalism was published in 1960.

> The American form of government is often, but erroneously, symbolized by a three-layer cake. A far more accurate image is the rainbow or marble cake, characterized by an inseparable mingling of differently colored ingredients, the colors appearing in vertical and diagonal strands and unexpected whirls. As colors are mixed in the marble cake, so functions are mixed in the American federal system.[5]

Much of the contemporary scholarship on federalism reflects Grodzins's view. For example, British political scientist M. J. C. Vile described

15

"a gradual slide away from what was felt to be the excessive legalism and rigidity of Wheare's definition to the point where the definitions that are offered are almost totally vacuous." [6] Likewise, G. F. Sawyer in 1969 said attempts to define federalism were "futile," [7] and Michael D. Reagan and John G. Sanzone in 1981 referred to "the bankrupt quality of federalism as an operational concept." [8] In an earlier study of American federalism, published in 1970, Richard H. Leach concluded, "Precisely what 'federalism' means is now and never has been clear." [9]

A challenge can be made to the constant-change, nothing-is-clear view of American federalism. True, relationships between the federal government and the states in American federalism are complicated, and over the long haul the national government has become more powerful. Nonetheless, a lasting geographical division of power exists between the central and regional governments in the American governmental system and in other federal systems that makes them different from nonfederal countries.

Federalism is a governmental form in which regional governments have a consequential role in the political system and process. This applies to many federal nations in which regional governments are called by different names: "states" in the United States, India, and Australia; "provinces" in Canada; "cantons" in Switzerland; and "Laender" in West Germany. Understanding the character and strength of the role of regional governments is the key to understanding modern federalism.

Also important to understanding is that the role of state governments in the United States and other federal countries is cyclical and changes on the basis of political ideology. [10] In conservative periods, state governments are activist, while in liberal periods, when the federal government becomes more assertive, they are subdued. In liberal times, proponents of increased governmental activity find it efficient to lobby for their interests at one place—the center. In conservative times, however, they have less clout and must try to get changes adopted wherever they can. Not surprisingly, therefore, pro-government lobbying activities focus on those progressive or liberal states that support a strong role for the public sector. The states—not all of them, but many of them—have been active and innovative in domestic affairs in conservative periods such as the one that began in the 1980s in the United States and continued into the 1990s.

In the early years of the twentieth century, the states of the United States were the source of liberal policy initiatives, including workers' compensation, unemployment insurance, and public assistance. According to Michael B. Katz, "Between 1917 and 1920, state legislatures passed 400 new public welfare laws; by 1931, mothers' pensions in all states except Georgia and South Carolina supported 200,000 children; and in constant dollars, public welfare expenses, fueled especially by mothers' pensions, increased 168 percent between 1903 and 1928." [11] In a similar vein, James

T. Patterson noted that the states "preceded the federal government in regulating large corporations, establishing minimum labor standards, and stimulating economic development," although, he added, "the most remarkable development in state government in the 1920's was the increase in spending." [12] In the 1920s, when the United States was "Keeping Cool with Coolidge," state initiatives planted the seeds of what would become Franklin D. Roosevelt's New Deal. From them grew many of the major national government programs adopted over the next four decades.

Rising Role of the States in the 1980s

Five factors contributed to the rising role of the states in the 1980s and 1990s. One was the conservative and devolutionary domestic policies, adopted by the Reagan and Bush administrations, that restrained and cut federal domestic spending and resulted in a heavier reliance on the states. A second and long-term factor supporting state activism was the modernization movement in state government. Basic reforms in governmental structure adopted by state governments since the mid-sixties increased their capacity to take on new and expanded functions. In a 1985 report, the Advisory Commission on Intergovernmental Relations said that "state governments have been transformed in almost every facet of their structure and operations." [13] A third factor was the effect of the 1962 U.S. Supreme Court reapportionment decision in *Baker v. Carr.* The Court asserted jurisdiction in cases in which the federal courts could require state governments to reduce the rural-urban imbalance in state legislatures. As a result, cities have been more willing to work with state governments. A fourth factor underlying the rising role of the states in American federalism was what Martha Derthick called "the end of southern exceptionalism." She wrote in 1987 that integration in the South created a situation in which "the case for the states can at last begin to be discussed on its merits." [14] Finally, the rapid recovery of the U.S. economy from the recession at the beginning of Reagan's first term made an important contribution to the resurgence of the states in the 1980s. The economic recovery interacted in an ironic way with Reagan's federalism policy stressing decentralization. Typically, state governments overreact to national recessions, battening down their fiscal hatches by cutting spending and raising taxes to balance their budgets. The strong recovery from the 1981-1982 recession meant that state coffers were filling just as Reagan's retrenchment policies for domestic programs were beginning to be felt. State governments were in a position in 1982 and 1983 to spend more and do more in the functional areas of government, where the federal government under Reagan was pulling back. Reagan said the states should do more, and they did. Their added spending, however, undercut Reagan's overall goal of reducing the size and role of government.

From 1983 to 1986, as the Reagan retrenchment and federalism policies took effect, state aid to localities increased by an average of 5.6 percent a year in real terms (that is, adjusted for inflation). Total state spending rose by nearly the same percentage. From the mid-1970s to 1983, both state aid to localities and total state spending were level in real terms.

According to Steven D. Gold, as the federal government disentangled itself from alliances with local governments, states asserted an increased leadership role. Throughout the country, they took on realignment issues. The basic questions involved were who provides particular services, who pays for them, and how. Referring to the recommendations of the Task Force of the National Conference of State Legislatures on State-Local Relations, Gold argued that states should assume the costs associated with major poverty-related programs such as Medicaid and welfare.[15] Some states completely finance these programs; others—principally the most populous, urban states—require local government to share the costs. The trend now is toward centralization at the state level. Such a realignment of state-local functions could increase accountability, enhance the targeting of state aid, and promote efficiency. Although in the early 1990s the recession and fiscal pressures could slow the transfer of responsibilities to states, Gold found evidence that states were moving ahead to redefine responsibilities shared with counties and municipalities. In 1990, New Jersey assumed responsibility for a number of local programs, including the costs of 95 percent of Aid to Families with Dependent Children (AFDC), all general assistance and Supplemental Security Income payments, a much larger share of supporting mental hospitals, serving clients in centers for the developmentally disabled, and caring for children under the jurisdiction of the Division of Youth and Family Services.[16]

In the field of education, reform initiatives were launched, for example, to mandate early childhood education, strengthen instruction in the basics, and upgrade the performance of teachers through merit pay. According to Denis P. Doyle and Terry W. Hartle, writing in 1985, "The last two years have witnessed the greatest and most concentrated surge of educational reform in the nation's history. Indeed, the most surprising aspect of the 'tidal wave of reform' is that it came from state governments." [17] Commenting on the overall resurgence of activism emanating from state capitals, Timothy J. Conlan observed, "Governmental activism has flourished during the 1980s as state after state has aggressively addressed issues of educational reform, economic development and welfare dependency." [18]

The argument that the role of U.S. state governments changes on a cyclical basis differs from much of the scholarly writing on federalism.

The dominant view in the literature is that over time the American governmental system has become steadily, unrelenting, more centralized. Part of the reason is that the United States has always been a country in a hurry that lives in the present. During the long period of growth in the power of the federal government, from Roosevelt's New Deal through the late 1970s, observers, however, forgot that states were the engines of innovation and governmental leadership during conservative times.

Several types of national government action influenced the relative roles of the national and state governments in American federalism: grants-in-aid, federal mandates, and judicial decisions.

Grants-in-Aid and Federal Mandates

Reagan and Sanzone wrote in 1981 that the sharing of functions in American federalism is "most clearly and dramatically seen in the explosive growth of federal grants-in-aid." [19] This was true in the three decades following World War II. Federal spending under grants-in-aid tripled as a percentage of federal outlays from 1950 to 1978, the peak year for federal aid (see Table 2-1).

Nineteen seventy-eight was pivotal for state and local governments for two reasons: (1) Proposition 13 was approved by California voters, sparking a tax revolt in many other states. Proposition 13 cut local property taxes in half and caused a rapid rise in state aid. (2) President Jimmy Carter began reversing the long-term trend of increased federal aid to state and local governments. President Reagan went further and faster in cutting federal aid and divesting the federal government of functions. [20]

Another way in which federal aid programs changed in the 1980s involved the recipient jurisdictions. According to Morton Grodzins's marble cake theory of federalism, the steadily expanding role of the national government involved not only the federal-state relationship but also the federal-local relationship. Beginning under President Harry S. Truman, direct federal grants-in-aid to local governments increased dramatically. This direct relationship between the national government and local governments, described as "the expanded partnership" by Roscoe Martin, [21] challenged the older tradition of "Dillon's rule." John F. Dillon, an expert on municipal government and an Iowa State Supreme Court justice in the late nineteenth century, argued that local governments were "creatures" of the state. Dillon said the state legislature gave local governments "the breath of life without which they cannot exist." [22] This two-level view still has its strong supporters who often point out that the U.S. Constitution nowhere mentions local governments; they are the province of the states.

As federal grants-in-aid grew and proliferated through the 1970s,

Table 2-1   Federal Grants-in-Aid, 1955-1989

Fiscal year	Federal grants (in billions of constant 1982 dollars)	Percentage of real increase or decrease
1955	12.7	4.1
1956	13.9	9.4
1957	14.8	6.5
1958	17.6	18.9
1959	23.0	30.7
1960	24.7	7.4
1961	24.8	0.4
1962	27.1	9.3
1963	28.7	5.9
1964	33.6	17.1
1965	35.4	5.4
1966	40.6	14.7
1967	46.0	13.3
1968	53.4	16.1
1969	54.8	2.6
1970	61.2	11.7
1971	66.8	9.2
1972	77.2	15.6
1973	88.9	15.2
1974	84.6	−4.8
1975	87.1	3.0
1976	96.2	10.4
1977	103.6	7.7
1978	109.7	5.9
1979	106.7	−2.7
1980	105.9	−0.7
1981	100.7	−4.9
1982	88.2	−12.4
1983	88.8	0.7
1984	90.2	1.6
1985	94.0	4.2
1986	97.0	3.2
1987	90.6	−6.6
1988	92.4	2.0
1989	93.4	1.1

Source: Advisory Commission on Intergovernmental Relations, *Significant Features of Fiscal Federalism* (Washington, D.C.: Advisory Commission on Intergovernmental Relations, 1984), Table 21, 42.

they had a major effect on power relationships in American federalism. Nevertheless, a tendency exists to exaggerate their role. Research by political scientists shows that federal grants, despite their requirements, often end up reinforcing state and local priorities and programs already in place. State and local officials are a cagey lot. They can bend the rules of federal grants to fit their particular purpose. Grants often have less effect on state programs and activities than is widely assumed.

While overall spending for federal grants is a good barometer of American federalism, all grants are not the same. The revenue sharing and block grants that Republicans support are generally broader and less conditional than the more specific and narrower categorical grants favored by Democrats. Although types of grants can be classified in many different ways, usually the more general their purposes the less intrusive they are likely to be.

Mandates from Washington need not be tied to grants. Sometimes the national government seeks to influence state and local behavior through mandates without money, which has obvious appeal in periods of fiscal stringency. In the Reagan-Bush years, mandates without money were a frequently preferred strategy that caused consternation among state and local government officials. Joseph F. Zimmerman argued that this role of the federal government increased recently in what he called "the preemption revolution." [23] He stated that Congress has been "employing its delegated powers frequently to supersede state and local law- and regulation-making authority totally or partially in an effort to achieve greater national regulatory uniformity." [24] According to Zimmerman, the effect has been an increase in total governmental power.

> Extensive use of coercive powers by the Congress paradoxically has increased and not reduced the exercise of political power by the States. The general theory must explain that political power in the national-state context in the United States is not a "zero-sum" system with an increase in the exercise of preemption powers by the Congress automatically resulting in a corresponding decrease in the exercisable reserved powers of the States. With the exception of total preemption statutes with no provisions for a turnback of regulatory authority, exercise of a preemption power generally has encouraged utilization of latent powers by all or most States. [25]

When money was in short supply (as in the Reagan-Bush period), Congress was more heavy handed in establishing mandates by requiring states to expand programs and regulations without supplying additional federal funds. Not surprisingly, widespread opposition from states and localities resulted.

Judicial Decisions

Another major influence on the role of state governments is the actions of the federal courts. In America's early history, the courts were a centralizing force. In the nineteenth century, they shifted to a pro-state position. However, since the Roosevelt reforms of the mid-1930s, the courts again have been a nationalizing force.[26] In the 1985 ruling in *Garcia v. San Antonio Metropolitan Transit Authority*, the Supreme Court held to a centralizing view, claiming that no intrinsic divisions of power and responsibility existed in American federalism. Writing for the majority, Justice Harry A. Blackmun said that efforts by the courts to impose limits on the power of Congress in relation to the states ultimately fall short because of "the elusiveness of objective criteria for 'fundamental' elements of state sovereignty." [27] Not all of the justices agreed, however. Justice Lewis F. Powell, Jr., in his dissent said that the Court's decision in *Garcia* "reduces the Tenth Amendment to meaningless rhetoric when Congress acts pursuant to the Commerce Clause." [28] (The Tenth Amendment reserves to the states and to the people powers not enumerated as those of the national government in the Constitution.) Even more striking than Powell's dissent, Justice William H. Rehnquist predicted a reversal: "I do not think it incumbent on those of us in the dissent to spell out further the fine points of a principle that will, I am confident, in time again command the support of a majority of this Court." [29] With conservatives on the Supreme Court holding a strong majority by the 1991-1992 term, Rehnquist's prediction may come true.

The role of the courts in increasing the authority of the national government has been selective. The expansion of the federal role has been greatest in matters involving rights (for example, civil rights and voting rights) but less so in areas that affect state and local finances directly. The courts, particularly the U.S. Supreme Court, have tended to stay out of the fiscal thicket. When pressed, for example, to equalize school spending between rich and poor districts or to set standards for welfare payments (decisions that would have large effects on state budgets), the Supreme Court has been more cautious than in areas of rights. This is less true of lower federal courts. District courts have asserted the rights of prisoners and patients in state mental institutions in a way that has caused major increases in state spending. The prison systems of more than forty states currently operate under federal court orders.

The Sorting-Out Theory

The history of American federalism can be seen as involving two theories that have competed for attention—the Grodzins marble cake theory and the traditional theory. Liberals have tended to favor the Grodzins theory; conservatives, the traditional theory.

A more complex theory occupying a middle ground is the "sorting-out" theory, which emerged in the late 1960s. In part, its rise was a reaction to the growth of the federal role under Lyndon B. Johnson's Great Society programs.[30] The sorting-out theory holds that the functions of American federalism need to be rationalized so that major areas of governmental activity are assigned to different levels of government. The responsible governments then could be more easily held accountable for their actions. Proponents of the theory criticized many federal grants for undermining accountability and causing political confusion and inefficiency. The Advisory Commission on Intergovernmental Relations has been a leading proponent of the sorting-out theory.[31] President Nixon's New Federalism program of the 1970s, which included welfare reform, revenue sharing, and block grants, reflected this theory.

Economists in the 1970s came to play a larger part in shaping theories of American federalism. Conventional economic concepts of public goods, spillovers, and externalities were considered when defining the functions that should be assigned to the national government because their costs and benefits extended beyond state political boundaries. This reasoning was said to apply, for example, to air and water pollution control and income maintenance. Functions such as police and fire protection, mass transit, and elementary and secondary education, however, were areas in which the national government should have a limited role, if any.

Another way in which economists became participants in intergovernmental relations involved the distribution of grants. Much of the recent scholarly literature on U.S. intergovernmental relations deals with equalization among the states. The underlying concern has been with differences in wealth and industrial capacity and the ways in which the national government should compensate for them. The subject is an important one, but an interest in equity among regions is not exclusive to federal systems of government. Equalization schemes are found both in federal and unitary political systems.

Different Brands of New Federalism

Most modern presidents have expressed ideas about federalism. While Nixon supported the sorting-out theory, Reagan took a more traditional position. As governor of California, he argued for the devolution of powers and functions from the national government to the states. In his first year as president, he pressed for policies reflecting this point of view. In 1981, Reagan won substantial cuts in federal grant-in-aid programs as a way to reduce both federal spending and the national government's overall role in domestic affairs. Also in 1981, Reagan successfully proposed the establishment of new federal block grants, which would reduce federal requirements and funding and increase the discretion available to state governments. Unlike the block grants enacted during the Nixon administration, no funds were provided under Reagan's block grants to local governments. All of these funds went to the states.

Reagan's biggest cuts in domestic spending came in 1981. The

Omnibus Reconciliation Act of 1981 reduced federal aid payments to states and localities by 7 percent, the first such cut in actual dollar terms in twenty-five years.[32] Research conducted at Princeton University on the effects of these reductions and changes in federal grants-in-aid revealed that state governments took on a larger role in areas that the federal government under Reagan decreased its aid or threatened to do so. The sample for the Princeton study included fourteen states and forty local governments within these states. The choice of sites was made on the basis of representativeness in size, location, and economic and social characteristics.

No ready calipers are available for measuring activism and innovation of the states. Research studies by political scientists Jack L. Walker and Virginia Gray indicate that, over time, the larger, older, and ideologically most liberal states were most innovative.[33] The Princeton-based research, however, suggested a broader distribution. Newer states and those that were changing ideologically toward a more liberal stance also enhanced the role of state government.[34]

Florida, Massachusetts, New Jersey, New York, and Oklahoma were classified as having made the "most pronounced" response to the Reagan cuts and changes in federal grants-in-aid. They replaced actual or threatened federal aid cuts out of state funds. They also took steps to play a stronger policy-making and administrative role in the functional areas of the Reagan federal aid cuts and block grants.

Eight states in the Princeton study were classified in "intermediate-response" groups. Three of these states—Mississippi, Ohio, and Texas—replaced some (though not appreciable) amounts of federal aid cuts out of state funds and also adopted a stronger policy-making and administrative role in the areas affected by the Reagan federal aid cuts and block grants. One state, Washington, voted to replace federal aid cuts but then was hard hit by the 1981-1982 recession and rescinded the restorations. It, however, did take advantage of the block grants created by the Reagan administration. The remaining four states in the intermediate-response group—Arizona, Illinois, Missouri, and South Dakota—did not replace any federal aid out of their own funds but took steps to exercise a stronger policy-making and administrative role in the functional areas in which the devolutionary policies of the Reagan administration were most pronounced.

California was classified as having made a minimal response to the Reagan changes. According to the field researchers, the enactment of referendums affecting state finances overwhelmed the effects of the Reagan federal aid policy shifts.

Forcing state governments to take on a larger role may have backfired on the administration. According to one analysis of the Reagan record, "Conservatives who gleefully assumed that shifting the responsibility for social programs to the states would mean the end of the programs have discovered that state governments were not as conservative as they thought." [35] The rising role of state governments in the 1980s can be seen in data on state taxation. Thirty-eight states increased taxes in 1983. Overall, the tax revenues of state governments rose by 14.8 percent from 1983 to 1984. Steven Gold noted that "real state general fund spending rose at a significant rate in 1984, 1985, and 1986." [36] Gold reported that total discretionary state tax increases were $4.5 billion in 1987, $0.6 billion in 1988, $3.5 billion in 1989, and $8.6 billions in 1990.[37] In 1987, states accounted for 26.1 percent of total tax revenue raised by all levels of government (excluding trust fund taxes such as Social Security). This represented an increase from 20.6 percent in 1970 to 23.9 percent in 1980. The most important change in state tax systems was the increased role of the personal income tax and state reliance on innovative forms of financing, such as charges, the taxation of interest and dividends, and natural resource royalties.[38]

While the Reagan administration was denouncing government, states were quietly raising governmental activity to higher levels of responsibility. This trend has continued under President Bush. The modesty of his domestic achievements partly reflected his style.[39] The main event under Bush was renewal of the Clean Air Act. On the whole, the budget crunch dominated the policy process and captured the attention of all players, just as it did at the end of the Carter years.

Under Bush, the national government became less of a big cheese. The Bush administration's federalism vision could be characterized as Swiss cheese—budgets with holes in domestic areas, debates dominated by confrontations over deficits. Meanwhile, however, state and local resilience continued. David Walker believed that state and local government activism would continue to dominate because of "the fiscal dilemmas confronting the national government, the public's demand for welfare programs and the better fiscal position of state and local governments." [40] In a similar vein, Bert A. Rockman, writing about the leadership style of George Bush, noted that the monumental budget deficits that Bush inherited from Reagan provided the "perfect cover for a president who did not mind being fiscally constrained." [41] According to Rockman, "The budget constraint could allow the Bush presidency to indulge in the symbols of ameliorative social policies without having to take direct responsibility for proposing any." [42]

Conclusion

All activities of government have three dimensions—policy making, financing, and administration. The assignment of governmental functions in a federal system can be analyzed by the level of government that has responsibility for them. Grants-in-aid affect the distribution of the three dimensions in important ways.

A federal grant may set policy for a program and increase the fiscal role of the national government, but not to the extent often advanced. Administration is likely to be unaffected, or much less affected, by grant programs. Administration of benefits or services is the responsibility of the recipient government, usually the states. Hence, even though the national government plays a policy and financial role in many functional areas, state and local governments retain more control than they often are credited with by those who highlight the intrusiveness of the national government in domestic affairs. Paying the piper does not always mean calling the tune. Under federal grants-in-aid, recipient governments retain substantial power. The Grodzins theory of federalism goes overboard.

While Grodzins's point about the sharing of functions in American federalism is important, it does not mean that the states have lost their individual standing and identity. For many functions of domestic affairs, the state role is dominant on all three dimensions of governmental activity. In public higher education, for example, the national government provides student aid and is instrumental in setting the research agendas of many universities. But the predominate role in chartering, structuring, locating, financing, and administering public institutions of higher education lies with the states. Much the same can be said for elementary and secondary education. The federal role has always been limited. States pay for well over half of public elementary and secondary education. Furthermore, the regulation of public utilities, insurance, marriage, adoption, foster care, divorce, as well as the licensing of drivers, animals, and professional practitioners, are all areas in which federal involvement is limited or nonexistent. In the same way, many of the hottest issues of social policy tend to be primary or at least heavy responsibilities of state governments: for example, laws and regulations relating to AIDS, surrogate parenthood, death with dignity, and the rights of homosexuals. American domestic government is less marbleized in the real world than portrayed in the academic literature.

The politics of American federalism involve both rhetoric and policy change. The rhetoric of Presidents Reagan and Bush was that the states should do more. The result was that they did. However, at the same time, another conservative aim was undercut—namely, reducing the role of government. The Reagan and Bush policies thus reinforced the traditional theory of federalism. A valuable lesson for both political theory and practice can be derived from the experience of Reagan and Bush. In a liberal period, conservative politicians are well advised to press for decentralization (strengthening states) as they did from the New Deal through the latter 1970s. But in a conservative period, such as in the 1980s and 1990s, they should employ the opposite strategy because states are likely to be the sources of activism and innovation. Advocating decentralization during conservative periods probably will stimulate the states to action instead of serving, as it often does in liberal periods, as a cover for budget and program reductions.

The role of the states as the broker of American federalism shifts as conditions change. In liberal periods, the relative role of state government tends to diminish. In conservative periods, the opposite is true. Then the American governmental system more strongly reflects the traditional state-focused model of American federalism. The state role in American federalism has not withered away.

Notes

1. K. C. Wheare, *Federal Government*, 4th ed. (New York: Oxford University Press, 1963; reprint, 1987), 1.
2. Ibid.
3. Ibid., 4-5.
4. Arthur W. Macmahon, "The Problem of Federalism: Survey," in *Federalism Mature and Emergent*, ed. Arthur W. Macmahon (New York: Doubleday, 1955), 4.
5. Morton Grodzins, "The Federal System," in President's Commission on National Goals, *Goals for Americans: The Report of the President's Commission on National Goals* (New York: Columbia University Press, 1960), 265.
6. M. J. C. Vile, "Federal Theory and the 'New Federalism,' " in *The Politics of "New Federalism,"* ed. D. Jaensch (Adelaide, Australia: Australian Political Studies Association, 1977), 1.
7. G. F. Sawer, *Modern Federalism* (London: C. A. Watts and Co., 1969), 2.
8. Michael D. Reagan and John G. Sanzone, *The New Federalism* (New York: Oxford University Press, 1981), 19. William Anderson also was wary of precise definitions of federalism, preferring to regard it as less a formal structure than "a concept of mind." See William Anderson, *Intergovernmental Relations in Review* (Minneapolis: University of Minnesota Press, 1960), 17.
9. Richard H. Leach, *American Federalism* (New York: W. W. Norton and Co., 1970), 9.
10. This point is suggested by Albert O. Hirschman in *Shifting Involvements: Private Interest and Public Action* (Princeton, N.J.: Princeton University Press, 1982).
11. Michael B. Katz, *In the Shadow of the Poorhouse* (New York: Basic Books, 1986), 208.
12. James T. Patterson, *The New Deal and the States: Federalism in Transition* (Princeton, N.J.: Princeton University Press, 1969), 4, 7.

13. Advisory Commission on Intergovernmental Relations, *The Question of State Government Capability* (Washington, D.C.: Advisory Commission on Intergovernmental Relations, January 1985).
14. Martha Derthick, "American Federalism: Madison's 'Middle Ground' in the 1980s," *Public Administration Review* 47 (January/February 1987): 72.
15. Steven D. Gold, *Reforming State-Local Relations: A Practical Guide* (Washington, D.C.: National Conference of State Legislatures, 1989), 22, 100.
16. Steven D. Gold and Sarah Ritchie, "State Policies Affecting Cities and Counties: Important Developments in 1990," *Public Budgeting and Finance* (Summer 1991): 33.
17. Denis P. Doyle and Terry W. Hartle, *Excellence in Education: The States Take Charge* (Washington D.C.: American Enterprise Institute for Public Policy Research, 1985), 1. Governors also have taken a leadership role in the field of public education. See National Governors' Association, *Time for Results: The Governors' 1991 Report on Education* (Washington, D.C.: National Governors' Association, August 1986), 7. Tennessee governor Lamar Alexander, while serving as chairman of the National Governors' Association, said, "The Governors are ready to provide the leadership needed to get results on the hard issues that confront the better schools movement. We are ready to lead the second wave of reform of American public education."
18. Timothy Conlan, "Conflicting Trends, Competing Futures," *Journal of State Government* (January/February 1989): 50.
19. Reagan and Sanzone, *The New Federalism*, 75.
20. Steven D. Gold, "Changes in State Government Finances in the 1980s," *National Tax Journal* (May 1991): 7.
21. Roscoe C. Martin, *The Cities and Federal System* (New York: Atherton Press, 1955), 171.
22. *City of Clinton v. Cedar Rapids and Missouri RR Co.*, 24 Iowa 475 (1868), as quoted in James A. Maxwell and J. Richard Aronson, *Financing State and Local Governments* (Washington, D.C.: Brookings Institution, 1977), 11.
23. Joseph F. Zimmerman, *Federalism in the United States: The Preemption Revolution*, presented at the Maxwell Graduate School, Syracuse University, October 25, 1990.
24. Ibid.
25. Ibid., 17.
26. *United States Supreme Court Reports*, 89 L. Ed. 2d., no. 9 (March 2, 1985), 1032.
27. Ibid., 1040.
28. Ibid., 1052-1053.
29. For a discussion of this position, see David B. Walker, *Towards a Functioning Federalism* (Cambridge, Mass.: Winthrop Publishers, 1981).
30. Nathan and Doolittle, *Reagan and the States*.
31. The commission, a nybrid agency, is federally chartered and funded, but state and local government officials constitute a majority of its members.
32. Nathan and Doolittle, *Reagan and the States*.
33. Jack L. Walker, "The Diffusion of Innovation among the American States," *American Political Science Review* 63 (1969): 880-899. Walker's analysis is for the period 1870-1969. See also Virginia Gray, "Innovation in the States: A

Diffusion Study," *American Political Science Review* 67 (1973): 1174-1185.
34. Nathan and Doolittle, *Reagan and the States*.
35. Jerry Hagstrom, "Liberal and Minority Coalitions Pleading Their Cases in State Capitals," *National Journal*, February 23, 1985, 426.
36. Steven D. Gold, "Developments in State Finances, 1983 to 1986," *Public Budgeting and Finance* 7 (Spring 1987): 15.
37. Gold, "Changes in State Government Finances in the 1980s," 7.
38. Gold, *The Changing Face of Fiscal Federalism*.
39. Ibid., 11.
40. David Walker, "American Federalism: Past, Present and Future," *Journal of State Government* (January/February 1989): 10.
41. Bert A. Rockman, *The Bush Presidency: First Appraisals* (Washington, D.C.: Brookings Institution, 1991), 11.
42. Ibid., 11.

3 ■■■■■■

State Budgeting in the Nineties

Henry J. Raimondo

When the national economy boomed in the eighties, growth in state spending soared. As the national economy went bust in the nineties, growth in state spending slowed. State governments were caught in a fiscal squeeze. During a recession, state revenues fall, but the pressure for increased spending intensifies as people turn to the state government for relief from their economic distress. An economic slowdown depresses sales as well as personal income and business income tax collections. At the same time, service costs in education, health care, welfare, and corrections escalate. The fiscal consequences of a recession—revenues down and costs up—are recurring budget shortfalls.

By January 1992, the national economy was in a recession that had lasted longer than most economists predicted. The national unemployment rate climbed to a five-year high of 7.1 percent, which translated into 8.9 million Americans out of work. Economists estimated that another 1 million were "discouraged" workers—those who lost hope of finding work and dropped out of the labor market. Many Americans were working part time because they could not find full-time employment. A sample of state jobless rates across the country told the economic tale of woe: 8.9 percent in Michigan, 8.7 percent in Florida, 8.4 percent in New York, 8.2 percent in Illinois, 8.1 percent in California, 7.9 percent in Massachusetts, 7.8 percent in Texas, 6.8 percent in New Jersey, and 5.7 percent in North Carolina.[1]

The fallout from the stagnant economy landed in every governor's office and every legislative chamber. Half the states could not fund their fiscal 1992 budget even though states increased taxes by more than $16 billion in fiscal 1991.[2] On the spending side of the budget, some states had to eliminate programs and cut state financial assistance to local governments ("local aid") to cover an overall estimated $6 billion shortfall. On the revenue side of the budget, some states had to increase fees or raise taxes again. Public employees were fired or furloughed (temporarily laid off).

State budget scrambling did not go unnoticed on Wall Street. Budget imbalances mean that states are viewed as poor credit risks. When a state that is a poor credit risk wishes to raise money by selling bonds, it must pay higher interest for the loan. High interest payments or debt service mean less available money for state services. Of the forty-one states rated by the bond rating agencies in 1991, only ten (including New Jersey and California) had the best rating, Aaa. Massachusetts had the worst rating, Baa. New York and Louisiana were one notch up from the worst, Baa1.[3]

Fundamentals of State Government Finances

State governments suffer from an image problem. Many people do not know what they do or why they are necessary. The federal government spends money on national defense and transfer programs for individuals (for example, Social Security, Medicare, Medicaid, and food stamps). Local governments educate children, police communities, put out fires, pick up trash, and plow streets. What do state governments do under this arrangement?

Public services that state governments provide are seemingly invisible because people have become so accustomed to having these services available when they need them: the road and rail system, state courts and prisons, welfare payments, subsidized health and nursing home care, moderately priced and accessible public colleges and universities, affordable housing, and financial aid to local governments.

Data on the amounts state governments spent on direct services in fiscal years 1981 and 1990 are presented in Table 3-1. State governments in fiscal 1990, compared with fiscal 1981, spent less for education, highways, and in the 'other' category, and more for corrections, debt service, and human services. As in fiscal 1981, education and human services dominated state direct spending (61 cents of every dollar). States in fiscal 1990 spent relatively less on investment services (education and highways) and more on current consumption needs (human services and corrections) and debt. These budget priorities do not enhance future national economic growth. In the nineties, a well-prepared workforce and a world-class transportation system will be prerequisites for successful world trade and require investment now.

States get the money to provide direct services from the federal government, a variety of taxes, and other sources. State government revenues for fiscal 1981 and fiscal 1990 are detailed in Table 3-2. State governments in fiscal 1990, as compared with fiscal 1981, raised less from federal aid, selective sales taxes, and business taxes, and more from general sales taxes, personal income taxes, and charges.

The total revenue for fiscal 1990 exceeded direct spending by $130.7 million. The difference is largely, although not entirely, attributable to

Table 3-1 Direct State Government Spending, Fiscal 1981 and Fiscal 1990

Expenditure category	Amount of each dollar directly spent by state government		Total spent in fiscal year 1990 (in thousands of 1982 constant dollars)
	Fiscal year 1981	Fiscal year 1990	
Corrections	$ .03	$ .05	$ 11,251.1
Debt service	.05	.06	15,238.4
Education	.25	.23	53,274.7
Highways	.13	.11	25,806.4
Human services	.36	.38	89,425.2
Other	.18	.17	40,516.4
Total direct spending	$1.00	$1.00	$235,512.2

Source: U.S. Bureau of the Census, *Census of Governments* (Washington, D.C.: Government Printing Office, 1982 and 1991).

Note: Education spending primarily was for higher education but also was for local schools. Human services included health care, hospitals, Medicaid, and public welfare. The 'other' category included environmental protection, housing, and administration.

Amounts expressed in 1982 constant dollars are calculated using 1982 figures. Comparisons, exclusive of inflation, then can be made across years.

state intergovernmental grants to local governments, especially school districts. These grants are often cash transfers from the state to subsidize local government activities. As such, they are not direct expenditures, but intergovernmental expenditures.

Twenty-nine states follow a one-year or annual budget cycle; twenty-one states, a two-year or biennial cycle. For forty-six states, the fiscal year extends from July 1st of one year to June 30th of the next year. Four states use different beginning and ending dates: Alabama and Michigan follow the federal government fiscal year (October 1st to September 30th); New York uses April 1st to May 31st; and Texas, September 1st to August 31st.[4]

The typical fiscal year (based on the July 1st to June 30th cycle) is divided into three intervals: preparation, adoption, and implementation.[5] During the preparation interval, from October to December, the executive branch prepares its budget based on accepted economic and fiscal forecasts of state spending and revenue collections. Inaccuracies in the revenue forecast are not uncommon. Democrats and Republicans often make different assumptions regarding revenue estimates. For example, Republicans might overestimate revenues to reduce taxes or underestimate revenues to cut spending. Democrats might overestimate revenues to expand human services programs or underestimate revenues to increase taxes. The governor presents a budget to the state legislature in January. During the adoption interval, from January to June, the state senate and house or assembly reviews and reworks the governor's budget. In June,

Table 3-2   State Government Revenues, Fiscal 1981 and Fiscal 1990

Revenue category	Amount of each dollar raised by state government		Total raised in fiscal year 1990 (in thousands of 1982 constant dollars)
	Fiscal year 1981	Fiscal year 1990	
Business income taxes	$ .05	$ .04	$ 15,393.6
Charges	.07	.08	30,264.6
Federal aid	.26	.23	83,759.9
General sales taxes	.18	.19	70,560.5
Personal income taxes	.16	.19	67,994.5
Selective sales taxes	.10	.09	33,522.6
Other	.18	.18	65,032.3
Total revenues	$1.00	$1.00	$366,202.0

Source: U.S. Bureau of the Census, *Census of Governments* (Washington, D.C.: Government Printing Office, 1982 and 1991).

Note: Charges were fees for service. Federal aid included grants for public welfare, education, health care, hospitals, and the environment. Selective sales taxes included taxes on motor fuel, alcohol, and tobacco. The 'other' category included nontax revenues and gambling revenues.

Amounts expressed in 1982 constant dollars are calculated using 1982 figures. Comparisons, exclusive of inflation, then can be made across years.

the governor signs the budget into law. The implementation interval, which runs the entire fiscal year, refers to the execution of the approved budget resolution.

The governor may veto the entire budget—requiring the legislature to reconsider it—or a portion of the budget. Governors in forty-three states have the line-item veto, which allows disapproval of individual lines in the budget or specific expenditure items. Whether the governor vetoes the entire budget or specific parts, the legislature can vote to override the veto.

In forty-nine states (Vermont is the exception), the state constitution or state statutes require a balanced budget; that is, expenditures must equal revenues. A budget surplus results if expenditures are less than revenues. A budget deficit occurs if expenditures are greater than revenues. When expenditure commitments routinely exceed forecast revenues, the state budget has a built-in deficit, or a structural deficit. Unless expenditures are cut or taxes raised, the structural deficit will persist. Because a budget may be in balance the day it is approved, but in deficit, for example, a month later, thirty-six states prohibit budget deficits being extended into the next fiscal year. Balancing a budget in deficit can be achieved through authorized spending cuts, rainy-day funds, and borrowing.

Most states authorize the executive branch (usually the governor) to take the lead in balancing the budget. Twenty states permit the governor to make selective and across-the-board cuts in spending; thirteen allow the governor to specify only across-the-board cuts; eight empower the governor to decide upon spending cuts up to some maximum (expressed in dollars or percentage); and eight require that the governor consult with the legislature on cutting expenditures.

A financially sound state budget sets aside a percentage of the revenues to be used to make up the shortfall for higher than anticipated expenditures or less than anticipated revenues. This rainy-day fund, formally installed by twenty-nine states, is insurance against a deficit. Some voters and legislators oppose the fund, believing that every dollar of public money should be spent or that the state government should not be holding taxpayers' money as surplus funds. In a recessionary cycle, a rainy-day fund is usually depleted or empty—a dry hole.

Borrowing to close a budget gap entails selling state bonds to raise money to cover the operating budget. However, the debt service on the borrowed money, as well as a repayment schedule to pay back the principle, would appear in subsequent state budgets. To help state executives and legislators maintain fiscal discipline, sixteen states place tight constitutional controls on the use of borrowing to balance state budgets. A recession increases the likelihood of a budget deficit. A budget deficit, in turn, sends bond ratings tumbling. Low bond ratings sour investors on purchasing state debt. As a result, borrowing can be a costly option, if available at all.

Prelude to the Budget Crisis in the Nineties

Two events of the 1970s foreshadowed the state budget shortfalls of the 1990s: the success of the tax revolt movement and the decline in federal aid (in real, per capita terms) to state governments. California's Proposition 13, approved in 1978, led the property tax revolt, which swept across the country. Bowing to the popular call for lower local property taxes, state governments—at first cautiously, then enthusiastically—bailed out local governments through substantial, rapid increases in local aid levels.[6] The action brought city hall's problems into the statehouse. Governors and legislators soon took on the overwhelmed look of mayors.

Meanwhile, the federal government began following a plan of "go-it-alone" federalism by limiting contributions to state government activities. Presidents John F. Kennedy through Gerald R. Ford had increased this assistance, but by midway through the Carter administration, federal grants to state and local governments declined in per capita, real dollar terms.[7] The Reagan and Bush administrations increased the pace of the federal government pull-out. Go-it-alone federalism became the new federalism of the 1990s.

Despite the loss of revenue from taxes and the federal government, many states managed to sprint through the 1980s with budget surpluses. For example, according to the National Income and Product Accounts, the fifty states had a combined surplus of $68.5 billion, which represented 12.7 percent of state government total receipts in 1984. State governments not only subsidized local governments, replaced some of the lost federal aid, and funded federal service mandates, but also increased spending on elementary, secondary, and higher education; corrections; health care; transportation; environmental protection; public welfare; and economic development campaigns. For a short time during the late 1980s, state governments across the country added to their reputations as "laboratories of democracy." [8]

Gross state product, a measure of economic activity in a state, grew almost without exception because of a booming national economy coupled with the state tax increases put in place during the 1981-1982 recession. The "great American job machine" created jobs in construction, finance, services, and high-tech industries at a record pace.[9] These additions more than offset the continued loss of manufacturing jobs to overseas competitors.

By 1990, the national economic boom was over, and the revenue windfall that made impossible financial times so easy for state governments to handle vanished. The onset of a long and deep recession brought new construction to a halt. The glut of office and residential buildings guaranteed that the construction industry would not rebound quickly. Bank failures and bankers' new-found caution translated into job layoffs in the finance industry. The growth in high-tech industries stalled when faced with intense overseas competition. The service industry responded with job cuts of its own. The continued job loss in manufacturing took on an even more ominous meaning.[10] Without a stable manufacturing base, state economies went into an economic free fall and took the state treasuries along with them. The drop in gross state product was sudden and steep. In many cases, individual states suffered far more than the national economy.

The slumping economy reduced state government revenues and increased the demands placed on entitlement programs such as Aid to Families with Dependent Children (AFDC), Medicaid, and general assistance. Budget deficits were inevitable unless revenues were increased or expenditures reduced or both.

Although the state treasuries were depleted, federal mandates obligated state government in previously unimagined ways. The president and Congress still needed to deliver public services to the people. State governments were told to do so but were not provided the necessary funds because the federal government did not have them. In the 101st Congress (1989-1991), federal mandates were found in such diverse legislation as the Affordable Housing Act, the Child Care Act, Medicaid Amendments, the Clean Air Act, the Americans with Disabilities Act, the Education of the Handicapped Amendments, the Drug Free Schools Communities Act, and the Older Workers Benefit Protection Act.

An Analysis of State Budgets

The structural budget deficits confronting state governments in the nineties have their origins in the eighties. An examination of the trends in state government spending, revenues, and employment from fiscal year 1981 to fiscal year 1990 reveals the different ways state governments had their budgets knocked out-of-balance. Some state governments were acting responsibly to replace lost federal aid; some were forced to spend more on schools and prisons on the orders of federal or state courts; some had to bear the burden of higher state employees' health and pension costs; and some were victims of ambitious executive and legislative branch officials who, to enhance their reelection, promised more to their constituents.

For the purpose of this analysis, the states were organized into two groups. The first group, labeled STABLE, consisted of the twenty-two states with fiscal year 1991 budgets in balance as of December 15, 1990.[11] The second, labeled DISTRESS, consisted of the sixteen states with fiscal year 1991 expenditures exceeding revenues by at least 4.0 percent. (Twelve states had budget deficits greater than zero and less than 4.0 percent.) The study covered the time period from fiscal 1981 to fiscal year 1990, which was divided into recession (fiscal 1981-1983 and fiscal 1989-1990) and recovery (fiscal 1983-1989) cycles. Because the fiscal data were converted into 1982 dollars, the trends in spending and revenues could be presented in real terms and meaningful comparisons could be made between the two groups of states. The analysis does not address the adequacy or the quality of state direct services but looks only at the growth in levels of state spending.

Expenditures

In addition to examining total direct spending, five expenditure categories were singled out for review: corrections, debt service, education, highways, and human services (see Table 3-3). For the recession years of fiscal 1981-1983, total direct expenditures in the DISTRESS states grew faster than in the STABLE states. The DISTRESS states increased their spending on redistributive human services activities faster than the STABLE states, while the STABLE states increased their direct spending on corrections, debt service, and education faster than the DISTRESS states.

Decisions made in the recovery years of fiscal 1983-1989 positioned the states for their budget problems in the nineties. The DISTRESS states continued to grow faster than the STABLE states in overall direct expenditures and virtually every component spending category. The

Table 3-3   Real Growth Rates for Selected State Expenditures,
Fiscal 1981-1990

	Percentage of direct spending growth					
	Fiscal 1981-1983 recession		Fiscal 1983-1989 recovery		Fiscal 1989-1990 recession	
Expenditure category	STABLE states	DISTRESS states	STABLE states	DISTRESS states	STABLE states	DISTRESS states
Corrections	+8.67	+7.17	+5.69	+9.12	+5.34	+5.85
Debt service	+16.44	+7.85	+5.38	+4.34	+2.75	+3.81
Education	+1.46	−.15	+1.37	+4.02	+5.48	+4.21
Highways	−8.15	−.14	+1.50	+6.44	+2.68	+3.49
Human services	+.51	+4.08	+2.43	+5.04	+10.13	+4.80
Total direct spending	+.45	+2.64	+2.17	+5.32	+5.12	+3.39

Source: U.S. Bureau of the Census, *Census of Governments* (Washington, D.C.: Government Printing Office, 1982 and 1991).

Note: STABLE states had fiscal year 1991 budgets in balance as of December 15, 1990: Alabama, Alaska, Arkansas, Hawaii, Idaho, Illinois, Kansas, Kentucky, Louisiana, Montana, Nebraska, Nevada, New Mexico, North Dakota, Oklahoma, Oregon, South Dakota, Texas, Utah, Washington, West Virginia, and Wyoming.

DISTRESS states had fiscal year 1991 expenditures that exceeded revenues by at least 4.0 percent: Connecticut, Delaware, Florida, Georgia, Indiana, Maine, Maryland, Michigan, New Hampshire, New Jersey, New York, North Carolina, Pennsylvania, Rhode Island, Vermont, and Virginia.

Education spending primarily was for higher education but also was for local schools. Human services included health care, hospitals, Medicaid, and public welfare. The 'other' category included environmental protection, housing, and administration.

Calculations of percentages were based on 1982 constant dollars.

DISTRESS states outpaced both the inflation rate and the STABLE states in education and human services activities. The higher growth rates can be traced to the level of economic activity in the various states and public choice or demand for particular services, as well as the legal requirements that mandate specific service levels and the funding for these services.

The DISTRESS states could not sustain the spending surge of the recovery years. The growth rates in total direct, education, human services, and corrections spending contributed to the fiscal problems that the DISTRESS states experienced. The STABLE states increased their direct spending faster than the DISTRESS states during the fiscal 1989-1990 recession. The areas of education and human services were the largest benefactors in the STABLE states. However, the growth rate in human services (10.13 percent), which accounts for one-third of the state direct spending, could lead the STABLE states to the fiscal edge that the DISTRESS states already have gone over.

The rate of increase in expenditures during the recovery cycle positioned the DISTRESS states for a fiscal crisis when the economy stalled in fiscal 1989-1990. Throughout the recovery, the DISTRESS states increased education spending, which represented 23 percent of state direct expenditures, by an average of 4 percent a year; human services, 38 percent of direct expenditures, by an average of 5 percent a year. Not surprisingly, redistributive human services activities and to a lesser degree education activities became the prime targets for the budget ax in the 1990s.

Revenues

Total revenues were studied as well as six individual revenue categories: business income taxes, charges, federal aid, general sales taxes, personal income taxes, and selective sales taxes (see Table 3-4). During the fiscal 1981-1983 recession, the DISTRESS states raised revenues faster than the STABLE states in about every category. The two exceptions—business income taxes and federal aid—experienced a slower rate of revenue loss in the DISTRESS states.

For the recovery years of fiscal 1983-1989, the DISTRESS states continued to grow faster than the STABLE states in total revenues. The pattern of rising revenue generally can be traced to tax increases that the state governments passed during the fiscal 1981-1983 recession. The DISTRESS states also outpaced both the inflation rate and the STABLE states in growth of business income taxes, general sales taxes, and personal income taxes. The STABLE states, meanwhile, increased their revenue raising faster than the DISTRESS states in the categories of selective sales taxes and user charges.

During the fiscal 1989-1990 recession, the STABLE states switched positions with the DISTRESS states. The STABLE states increased their revenues at a faster rate than the DISTRESS states in total revenues as well as charges, general sales taxes, personal income taxes, and selective sales taxes.

Throughout the eighties, all fifty states became more dependent on less progressive taxes. The growth in general and selective sales taxes, user charges, other miscellaneous revenues, and business income taxes—which together represent approximately 60 percent of total revenues—are regressive, or at best proportional, taxes.[12] As a result, lower and lower-middle income people paid a disproportionate share of the state tax increases.

The evolution of the state revenue system can be traced in part to the limited nature of revenue-raising measures and in part to economic development strategies. Real estate taxes, sales taxes, and user charges are all regressive or proportional at best. At the same time, personal and business income taxes are kept modest and at a flat rate to avoid the real or imagined fear of driving people and business out of the state.[13]

Table 3-4   Real Growth Rates for Selected State Revenues,
Fiscal 1981-1990

	Percentage of revenue growth					
	Fiscal 1981-1983 recession		Fiscal 1983-1989 recovery		Fiscal 1989-1990 recession	
Revenue category	STABLE states	DISTRESS states	STABLE states	DISTRESS states	STABLE states	DISTRESS states
Business income taxes	−22.13	−5.34	+4.01	+5.94	−15.39	−13.75
Charges	+3.95	+5.91	+4.13	+4.04	+8.08	+5.04
Federal aid	−7.00	−3.13	+2.89	+3.20	+4.73	+2.80
General sales taxes	+.63	+2.85	+4.30	+5.85	+4.19	+1.70
Personal income taxes	+.80	+4.67	+4.56	+5.24	+6.18	+2.58
Selective sales taxes	+.57	+1.21	+3.07	+1.52	+2.08	+1.15
Total revenues	−1.70	+1.74	+2.50	+4.83	+3.84	+1.65

Source: U.S. Bureau of the Census, *Census of Governments* (Washington, D.C.: Government Printing Office, 1982 and 1991).

Note: STABLE states had fiscal year 1991 budgets in balance as of December 15, 1990: Alabama, Alaska, Arkansas, Hawaii, Idaho, Illinois, Kansas, Kentucky, Louisiana, Montana, Nebraska, Nevada, New Mexico, North Dakota, Oklahoma, Oregon, South Dakota, Texas, Utah, Washington, West Virginia, and Wyoming.

DISTRESS states had fiscal year 1991 expenditures that exceeded revenues by at least 4.0 percent: Connecticut, Delaware, Florida, Georgia, Indiana, Maine, Maryland, Michigan, New Hampshire, New Jersey, New York, North Carolina, Pennsylvania, Rhode Island, Vermont, and Virginia.

Charges were fees for service. Federal aid included grants for public welfare, education, health care, hospitals, and the environment. Selective sales taxes included taxes on motor fuel, alcohol, and tobacco. The 'other' category included nontax revenues and gambling revenues.

Calculations of percentages were based on 1982 constant dollars.

Employment

Entering the 1990s, state workers found their jobs increasingly vulnerable. Workers were being furloughed or fired, and wages were being frozen and cost-of-living adjustments denied. State government hiring practices in the 1980s explain the circumstances that state employees confronted in the 1990s. The analysis of employment rates covered all noneducation employees and six separate subcategories: corrections, health, highways, hospital, public welfare, and other (see Table 3-5).

For the recession years of fiscal 1981-1983, employment in the DISTRESS states grew faster than in the STABLE states, highlighted by increases in corrections and public welfare. Both the DISTRESS

Table 3-5 Real Growth Rates for Selected State Full-Time Equivalent Employment, Fiscal 1981-1990

	Percentage of real employment growth					
	Fiscal 1981-1983 recession		Fiscal 1983-1989 recovery		Fiscal 1989-1990 recession	
Employment category	STABLE states	DISTRESS states	STABLE states	DISTRESS states	STABLE states	DISTRESS states
Corrections	+6.33	+7.46	+8.15	+6.95	+.97	+11.89
Health	−.63	−.30	+5.82	+4.89	+5.14	+.45
Highway	−.46	−1.89	+.50	+1.45	+.74	+.26
Hospital	−1.73	−3.19	+.20	+.08	+3.63	+.32
Public welfare	+.40	+1.87	+2.39	+2.96	+6.00	+5.54
Other	+1.16	+1.16	+1.10	+2.54	+7.29	+.39
Total noneducation employment	+.43	+5.67	+1.95	+2.51	+4.63	+2.42

Source: U.S. Bureau of the Census, *Census of Governments* (Washington, D.C.: Government Printing Office, 1982 and 1991).

Note: STABLE states had fiscal year 1991 budgets in balance as of December 15, 1990: Alabama, Alaska, Arkansas, Hawaii, Idaho, Illinois, Kansas, Kentucky, Louisiana, Montana, Nebraska, Nevada, New Mexico, North Dakota, Oklahoma, Oregon, South Dakota, Texas, Utah, Washington, West Virginia, and Wyoming.

DISTRESS states had fiscal year 1991 expenditures that exceeded revenues by at least 4.0 percent: Connecticut, Delaware, Florida, Georgia, Indiana, Maine, Maryland, Michigan, New Hampshire, New Jersey, New York, North Carolina, Pennsylvania, Rhode Island, Vermont, and Virginia.

Education employees were excluded from the study.

and STABLE states reduced employment in the health, highway, and hospital categories.

In the fiscal 1983-1989 recovery years, the DISTRESS states continued their total noneducation growth relative to the STABLE states, which reflects increases in public welfare and the 'other' category. The STABLE states significantly increased their employment, as compared with the DISTRESS states, in the areas of corrections and health.

During the fiscal 1989-1990 recession, the STABLE states increased their total employment at a faster rate than the DISTRESS states, as well as in the categories of health, hospital, public welfare, and other. The slowdown in employment growth during fiscal 1989-1990, especially in the DISTRESS states, anticipated the workforce reductions, the payless paydays, and the wage freezes that would become routine for state employees. The difficult employment climate for state employees was in part a result of their success in the late eighties, when they received cost-of-living wage increases, comprehensive health insurance coverage with a minimal employee copayment, and generous pension benefits.

This review of state government expenditures, revenues, and employment during the eighties provides the setting for the fiscal crisis in state budgeting that would take place during the nineties. State governments raised substantial amounts of revenue and spent much of their tax dollars on education, public welfare, health and hospitals, highways, and corrections. In undertaking these responsibilities, state governments increased their workforce. With the ensuing budget crunch, some or all of those activities had to be jettisoned.

Fiscal Crisis in the Nineties

By comparing the growth rates for total direct spending, total revenues, and total noneducation employment, the threat of recurring budget shortfalls throughout the nineties for all states—STABLE and DISTRESS—becomes apparent. During the fiscal 1981-1983 recession, the growth in direct spending outstripped the growth in revenues for both STABLE and DISTRESS states. During the fiscal 1983-1989 recovery, the growth in direct spending and revenues converged for STABLE and DISTRESS states. An imbalance returned during the fiscal 1989-1990 recession, when DISTRESS states authorized direct spending increases of 3.39 percent while revenues grew at a rate of 1.64 percent. STABLE states authorized direct spending increases of 5.12 percent while revenues grew at a rate of 3.84 percent, portending the fiscal squeeze that would be experienced in the nineties.

Extending the expenditure, revenue, and employment analysis beyond fiscal 1990, a report prepared by the National Governors' Association and the National Association of State Budget Officers took stock of how thirty-two states dealt with the fiscal debris that they faced in fiscal 1991.[14] States used combinations of expenditure, revenue, and employment actions to balance their budgets. On the expenditure side, twenty-eight states cut specific programs, eleven reduced or delayed aid to local governments, and fourteen used across-the-board program cuts. On the revenue side, twenty-six increased taxes. Twenty-five states enacted a hiring freeze, twelve fired workers, and seven used a furlough program to cut payrolls.[15] Not one of the thirty-two states studied expected the budget picture to brighten in the near term. Their expectations were met in fiscal 1992. Eighteen states eliminated programs, seventeen reorganized programs to cut costs, and thirteen cut state financial assistance to local governments ("local aid"). Thirteen states increased fees, and four raised taxes. Public employees were fired in fourteen states and furloughed in six.[16] Whether state governments are "downsizing"—or the more popular and less downbeat term, "rightsizing"—they will grow more slowly, if they grow at all, in the nineties.

Beyond the simple count of how many states put an ax to their programs, the story of specific program cuts is one of the retrenchment of state government services that benefit the lower and middle classes. States have more government than their citizens are willing or able to pay for. The dramatic cuts in general assistance in California, Illinois, and Michigan captured newspaper headlines, but cuts in redistributive activities were widespread.[17] Maine, New Hampshire, New York, North Carolina, and Rhode Island, for example, reduced human services spending.[18]

A report published by the Center on Budget and Policy Priorities and the Center for the Study of the States at the State University of New York at Albany found that forty states froze or cut benefits under the AFDC program; fourteen cut general assistance programs (half of those that had such programs) intended for poor single people and childless adults; eleven cut programs that granted payments to people to avoid homelessness; and nine cut programs to benefit the homeless.[19]

Medicaid spending also was under fire. A 1990 U.S. Supreme Court decision encouraged hospitals and nursing homes to sue state governments to force them to increase Medicaid payments to levels that reflected actual patient costs.[20] Meanwhile, states across the country—including Arkansas, Colorado, Indiana, Louisiana, Michigan, Oklahoma, Pennsylvania, Utah, Virginia, and Washington—were having trouble meeting their current Medicaid obligations. The pressure to pay more for health services collides with the diminishing amounts of revenue from which payments are made. The outcome likely will be less access to health care and fewer health care options.

The services that make life tolerable for low income people—income transfers, health care, education, and transportation—were being scaled back. In addition, cuts in kindergarten through twelfth grade (K-12) education, higher education, and transportation spending meant that middle income families saw their young children attending larger classes, their older children paying higher tuition at state colleges and universities, and their road tolls and transit fares increasing dramatically. Reductions in state services made life less satisfying, more costly, and less manageable.

Twenty-eight state legislatures enacted tax increases in fiscal 1992. The National Conference of State Legislatures reported that net state tax increases totaled more than $16 billion, of which personal income, business income, general, and selective sales taxes accounted for 88.8 percent (see Table 3-6).

In fiscal 1992, twenty-one states increased and five stated decreased personal income taxes, which tend to be proportional (or at most modestly progressive). A proportional personal income tax collects the same percentage of a taxpayer's income regardless of income level. Personal income taxes accounted for 40.1 percent of the net tax increases. The bulk of the revenue came from California, Connecticut, New York, and

Table 3-6   Net State Tax Increases and Tax Incidence, Fiscal 1992

	Number of states			
Tax	Increased tax	Decreased tax	Amount raised (in millions)	Type of tax
Business income	22	4	$1,690.1	Regressive
General	17	8	5,061.9	Regressive
Personal income	21	5	6,494.9	Proportional
Selective sales				
Alcohol	3	0	219.9	Regressive
Motor fuel	15	1	716.4	Regressive
Tobacco	12	0	216.6	Regressive

Source: Figures are from Corina Ecki, Anthony Hutchinson, and Ronald Snell, *State Budget and Tax Actions—1991: Legislative Finance Paper #79* (Denver, Colo.: National Conference of State Legislatures, 1991).

Pennsylvania. Twenty-two states increased and four states decreased business income taxes, which tend to be regressive if they are partially or completely passed on to consumers through higher prices. A regressive business income tax collects a decreasing percentage of a taxpayer's income as income rises. Business income taxes represented 10.4 percent of the net tax revenue increases. California and Pennsylvania relied heavily on the business income tax.

Seventeen states increased and eight states decreased general sales taxes, which usually are regressive (or at most proportional). General sales taxes raised 31.2 percent of net tax increases. States that recorded high general sales tax increases were California, Minnesota, North Carolina, and Pennsylvania. Selective sales taxes, largely regressive, accounted for 7.1 percent of net tax revenue increases.

Taxing people on the basis of their ability-to-pay was not the highest priority for state governments. For the sake of discussion here, ability-to-pay means a progressive tax structure; that is, tax payments increase as a percentage of a taxpayer's income as income rises. Combined state tax increases in fiscal 1992 were regressive (or at most proportional). States thus asked lower to lower-middle income people to make the greatest sacrifice to balance the state budget.

These same people often were the ones who lost state education, public welfare, and Medicaid services when the state government cut expenditures. And a disproportionate share is made up of people of color. Lower and lower-middle income earners play a far greater role in the state fiscal crisis than they should. They lose service benefits and pay more under an increasingly regressive state tax system. In the nineties, state governments took more and gave less to those who had the least.[21]

State employees also bore the burden of balancing state government budgets. Hiring freezes, dismissals, and furloughs were common in fiscal

1991. In fiscal 1992, states reduced or were likely to reduce their labor force and labor costs. For example, Connecticut, Georgia, Iowa, Maine, Ohio, and Washington were actively considering layoffs. Public sector layoffs are especially pernicious to people of color, who traditionally have found more employment opportunities in the public sector than in the private sector. So any job losses harm them more than their white co-workers as a group.[22] The same fate awaits women in the public sector workforce, especially at the senior level. Across the nation, women hold 31.3 percent of the high-level state-local government jobs. As states cut employees, the opportunity for women to gain equity with men in these positions is diminished.[23]

Lessons from a Crisis

Examining states under fiscal duress produces five worthy lessons.

1. A State Budget Breaks When the Economy Drops. State budgets are dependent on the performance of the national economy. Governors and legislatures have little power to influence national economic performance through state tax and expenditure policies. A sagging economy drags down state revenues and swells the demand for state assistance. Budget deficits become unavoidable. A booming economy reverses the process. State revenues rise while demand for state assistance lags. The eighties are a perfect illustration. State finances were in disarray during the fiscal 1981-1983 national recession. Only a series of tax increases saved many states from running budget deficits. With the increased revenue from taxes, state treasuries overflowed during the national boom of fiscal 1983-1989. New programs were initiated; existing programs were expanded; cash assistance, health care, housing, education, and transportation were revitalized. When the economy went sour and another recession hit beginning in fiscal 1989, state finances again were in crisis. Those activities that were expanded during the recovery were in jeopardy.

2. The Neediest People Lose the Most. Budget deficits and state redistribution activities do not mix. Public welfare and health and hospital services are among the hardest hit. Even K-12 education programs, which are investment programs for the states, are scaled back. With the federal government showing aggressive indifference to those most in need, the 1990s cuts in state government programs have a special sting for the low and middle income people, the biggest losers of service benefits. Meanwhile, the bottom fifth of the income distribution experienced a 10 percent drop in income during the 1980s.[24] So those who had less to begin with received less because of the budget cuts and paid more because of the regressive tax increases. Middle income people fared only marginally better. Cuts in K-12 education, higher education, and transportation reduced their standard of living.

3. It Is Better to Be Rich.   State governments generally have been unwilling or politically unable to raise taxes in a progressive fashion. The nature of a federal system of government may discourage progressive taxation at the state level. States fear interstate tax competition. If a state has a progressive tax structure, it believes people, jobs, and income will be lost to its neighbors with a less progressive tax structure.

State governments were forced to raise taxes in the fiscal 1981-1983 and 1989-1990 recessions. Taxes of all types went up—personal income taxes, business income taxes, general sales taxes, selective sales taxes, and user charges. Most of these taxes are regressive or, in some cases, proportional taxes. They come down hardest on low and middle income earners. People, especially those of color, who are caught between increases in regressive taxes and decreases in education and human services spending see the state government as contributing to, not alleviating, their economic misfortunes.

4. 'Bureaucrats' Is a Dirty Word.   State decision makers look with increasing frequency to state employees to help balance the budget. State payroll is a significant part of the budget, and bureaucrats are an easy political target. Most voters, jaded or not, view state employees as unproductive, incompetent, political hacks. Therefore, voters believe that firing or furloughing state employees will have little or no consequences on the quality of state direct services.

While worker inefficiency is, to some degree, a problem for all organizations—public and private—reducing the state workforce (and not replacing them with contracts for services delivered by the private sector) will more often than not adversely affect the quality of state direct services. Many state services—for example, education, health and hospital care, transportation repair and construction, and corrections—are labor intensive; that is, they rely heavily on people, not capital. Cutting personnel is tantamount to cutting the service. Over time, fewer health care providers in nursing homes, fewer guards in prisons, fewer teachers in the classroom, and fewer drivers operating public transit will lead to service deterioration.

A hidden by-product of state employee layoffs is that many more people of color will lose their jobs in proportion to white workers because minorities have found greater employment opportunities in the public sector than in the private sector.

5. The United States 'Are' a Collection of States Again.   The 1990s crisis in state budgeting can be traced to the national economic recession; generous state direct spending on education, human services, highways, and corrections; state revenue shortfalls; and state employment practices. Another major player that contributed to the creation of this crisis is the federal government.

Prior to the Civil War, "United States," thought of as a collection of states, took a plural verb. After the Civil War, "United States" became singular—reflecting its status as a unified country. The intergovernmental fiscal arrangements between the states and the federal government in the 1980s and 1990s harkened back to the pre-Civil War mentality. Go-it-alone federalism dominated policy discussions.

In the eighties, the federal government limited federal deductibility of state taxes in the Tax Reform Act of 1986, increased mandated services that the states must provide, and reduced real per capita federal grants to the states. Each action weakened the financial links that bind the federal government and the states together and encouraged interstate competition for existing jobs and income instead of creating new jobs and more income.

State governments reacted by cutting services and raising taxes. The services were not just redistributive activities, but also investment activities, such as education and public construction. The type of taxes raised were regressive, because they would not frighten off wealthy people and businesses in the state and they were less visible to low and middle income earners.

As the United States approaches the end of the twentieth century, the federal system is not well positioned to expand economic opportunity. The federal government has no coherent domestic agenda to enhance economic competitiveness. The states meanwhile are disinvesting in people and public infrastructure. Lack of planning and destructive activity do not form a combination that leads to economic growth and social justice.

Go-it-alone federalism has changed the nature of intergovernmental relations in the United States. The federal government and some income classes are neglecting their financial responsibilities to the society as a whole. Pre-Civil War thinking will not allow states to educate their people, rebuild their infrastructure, provide for their homeless, tend to their elderly and infirm, and still balance their budgets.

Notes

1. Peter Gosselin, "Jobless Rate Falls to 7.9 Percent in Bay State," *Boston Globe*, February 8, 1992, 1 and 20; and Robert Hershey, Jr., "7.1 Percent Rate for Jobless Unchanged," *New York Times*, February 8, 1992, 35 and 47.
2. Corina Ecki, Anthony Hutchinson, and Ronald Snell, *State Budget and Tax Actions—1991: Legislative Finance Paper #79* (Denver, Colo.: National Conference of State Legislatures, 1991).
3. Kevin Sack, "Rating for Bonds of New York State Downgraded Again," *New York Times*, January 7, 1992, A1 and B4.
4. Advisory Commission on Intergovernmental Relations, *Significant Features of Fiscal Federalism* (Washington, D.C.: Government Printing Office, 1986).

5. Paul Solano and Marvin Brams, "Budgeting," in *Management Policies in Local Government Finance*, ed. J. Richard Aronson and Eli Schwartz (Washington, D.C.: International City Management Association, 1987).

6. Henry J. Raimondo, *Economics of State and Local Government* (New York: Praeger, 1992).

7. Advisory Commission on Intergovernmental Relations, *Significant Features of Fiscal Federalism* (Washington, D.C.: Government Printing Office, 1989).

8. David Osborne, *The Next Agenda: Lessons from the Laboratories of Democracy* (Cambridge, Mass.: Harvard Business School Press, 1988).

9. Kenneth Johnson, John Kort, and Howard Friedenberg, "Regional and State Projections of Income, Employment, and Population to the Year 2000," *Survey of Current Business* (May 1990): 33-54.

10. Stephen S. Cohen and John Zysman, *Manufacturing Matters* (New York: Basic Books, 1987).

11. Michael Hinds with Erik Eckholm, "80's Leave States and Cities in Need," *New York Times*, December 30, 1990, A1 and A16.

12. Joseph Pechman, *Who Paid the Taxes, 1966-85?* (Washington, D.C.: Brookings Institution, 1985); and Donald Phares, *Who Pays State and Local Taxes?* (Cambridge, Mass.: Oelgeschlager, Gunn, and Hain, 1980).

13. Peter B. Doeringer and David G. Terkla, *Invisible Factors in Local Economic Development* (New York: Oxford University Press, 1990); and Robert J. Newman and Dennis Sullivan, "Econometric Analysis of Business Tax Impacts on Industrial Location: What Do We Know, and How Do We Know It?" *Journal of Urban Economics* 23 (March 1988): 215-235.

14. National Governors' Association and the National Association of State Budget Officers, *Fiscal Survey of the States* (Washington, D.C.: National Governors' Association and National Association of State Budget Officers, 1991).

15. Martin Tolchin, "Despite Billions in Tax Increases, States Cut Back," *New York Times*, October 30, 1991, A16.

16. National Association of State Budget Officers, *Looking for a Light at the End of the Tunnel* (Washington, D.C.: National Association of State Budget Officers, 1992).

17. Don Terry, "To Avoid Deficit, Michigan Ends Welfare to Some Adults," *New York Times*, October 7, 1991, A1 and A12; Jane Gross, "California Proposes Cutting Aid to the Poor," *New York Times*, December 11, 1991, A25; Jason DeParle, "California Plan to Cut Welfare May Prompt Others to Follow," *New York Times*, December 18, 1991, A1 and D21; and Paul Taylor, "A Meaner, Harsher Nation," *Washington Post National Weekly Edition*, January 5, 1992, 32.

18. National Conference of State Legislatures, *NCSL State Budget Update* (Denver, Colo.: National Conference of State Legislatures, 1991).

19. Center for Budget Policy Priorities and the Center for the Study of States, *The States and the Poor: How Budget Decisions of 1991 Affected Low Income People* (Washington, D.C.: Center for Budget Policy Priorities, 1991); and "States Slashed Aid to the Poor in 1991, Report Says," *New York Times*, December 19, 1991, A28.

20. Robert Pear, "Suits Force U.S. and States to Pay More for Medicaid," *New York Times*, October 29, 1991, A1 and A20.

21. Penelope Lemov, "The Axe and Its Victims," *Governing*, August 1991, 26-30.
22. Gary Orfield, *The Closing Door: Conservative Policy and Black Opportunity* (Chicago: University of Chicago Press, 1991); and Don Terry, "Cuts in Public Jobs May Hurt Blacks Most," *New York Times*, December 10, 1991, A1 and A26.
23. "Few Women Found in Top Public Jobs," *New York Times*, January 3, 1992.
24. Spencer Rich, "Rich Got Richer, Poor Got Poorer, Study Says," *Washington Post*, July 24, 1991, A4.

4 ■■■■■■

The Transformation of State Electoral Politics

Stephen A. Salmore and Barbara G. Salmore

A massive change in presidential and congressional campaigns has been caused by the emergence of candidate-centered campaigns. Candidates now use television, radio, and direct mail to communicate messages about themselves directly to voters. As a result, candidates' personal qualities and their records in office have become voting cues as significant as or more important than the party labels that traditionally determined most voters' decisions. Candidate-centered voting was slower to take hold in state gubernatorial and legislative elections because, being less visible and their victories seemingly less consequential, candidates for these offices were less able to get their message directly to voters. Party labels and organizations remained critical factors in determining election outcomes.

However, as state government has become more important and visible in policy terms, it attracts increasingly able and ambitious politicians. More is at stake in state-level elections, more political players are interested in their outcomes, and more resources are available to wage campaigns. Not surprisingly, therefore, party-line voting is declining, and candidate-centered campaigns are becoming more prevalent at the state level.[1]

Gubernatorial Campaigns and Elections

Three interrelated developments provide insight into the character of recent gubernatorial contests: the "presidentialization" of gubernatorial elections, the increased decoupling of partisan outcomes in state and national executive races, and trends in the financing of gubernatorial election contests.

Candidate-Centered Campaigns

Television transformed how presidents are elected in the United States. Voters, able to see and hear the candidates on the nightly news

51

programs as well as in political commercials, judge candidates on their character and values more than ever before. The personal, even intimate, problems of a Gary Hart, who sought the Democratic presidential nomination in 1984 and 1988, or a Bill Clinton, who sought it in 1992, can easily become the focus of voter attention. As a result, presidential candidates' images have become more salient than their party labels and substantive issue positions.[2] The net result is a style of campaigning that focuses almost exclusively on the candidate instead of the party.

Candidate-centered presidential appeals led to candidate-centered campaign organizations. Presidential candidates increasingly choose to separate their central campaign organizations from the national party organization. The campaign finance laws of the 1970s, providing for public funding of the general election and partial public funding of individual candidates in the nomination phase—funneled through individual campaign organizations and not the parties—reinforced this inclination. Many recent candidates not only separated themselves from their national party organizations, but also practically divorced themselves from their fellow partisans running for other offices.

Presidents seeking reelection try to stay above the partisan fray during the actual campaign season. Paid advertising emphasizes their accomplishments in office. Presidents proclaim themselves too busy to debate their opponents, making it difficult for voters to compare the candidates or get the idea that the challenger might be as accomplished as the current chief executive.

In short, both the presidential campaign and presidential office have become the province of individual entrepreneurs, relying on their own skills and their own resources more than those of their political parties. These developments are mirrored in the campaigns of many governors.

Split-Ticket and Cross-Party Voting

A variety of aggregate data suggests that split-ticket and cross-party voting has become rampant in recent gubernatorial elections.[3] During the 1950s, the governor's party on average controlled both houses of the state legislature in 68 percent of cases and neither house in only 20 percent of cases. This partisan homogeneity was a consequence of the state electorates' patterns of party identification. Usually, when split control did occur, it resulted from legislative gerrymandering and malapportionment. By the 1970s, although Supreme Court decisions had ended malapportionment and blatant gerrymandering, the governor's party controlled both houses only 53 percent of the time and neither 35 percent of the time. By 1990, 49 percent of the thirty-five states in which one party controlled both legislative houses had a governor of the other party.

Another indicator of candidate-centered voting in gubernatorial elections is the increase in partisan turnovers. In the 1950s, 24 percent of elections resulted in partisan turnovers in the governor's office, a figure that rose to more than one-third in the 1970s and 1980s. Moreover, party turnovers were much more likely in contests without incumbents. As party identification in the electorate and party organizations in campaigns became less important, candidates of either party had a better shot of winning. The races most likely to be competitive—those for open seats—were much more likely to attract strong challengers.

A popular and seemingly invulnerable incumbent, meanwhile, probably would attract only the weakest of challengers, particularly if the governor is of the majority party, but often even with more balanced party competition. Incumbent governors in such situations seem to barely acknowledge that a campaign is going on. Consider, for example, the 1990 race in Pennsylvania.

Ordinarily Republicans should be competitive in Pennsylvania. The Democratic governor, Robert P. Casey, had won only narrowly in 1986, ending eight years of GOP rule. The state's two U.S. senators had both been Republicans since 1962. Yet in 1990, Casey was seen as such a secure incumbent that the Republicans could not field a strong candidate. State auditor Barbara Hafer barely defeated a pro-life legislator in the Republican primary and was never able to mount a credible challenge to Casey. The governor's staunch pro-life position did not became an issue, and Hafer was never taken seriously. The *Philadelphia Inquirer* declared, after a lackluster debate performance, that she "pretty much disqualified herself with a halting 'uh'-sprinkled performance." [4] Casey went on to win by a ratio of better than 2 to 1.

Carroll A. Campbell, Jr., became the first Republican to be elected South Carolina's governor in modern times when he narrowly won in 1986. Yet in four years, he was able to become the dominant political figure in the state. He pushed through major educational reforms, reduced income taxes, successfully settled some nettlesome environmental problems, submitted the state's first-ever executive budget, and enforced it by using his line item veto 277 times. In 1990, his Democratic opponent was a black state senator who could not muster even 30 percent of the vote.

In contrast, less secure incumbents and candidates for open seats must fully engage their opponents. In 1990, after Connecticut's Democratic governor chose not to run, a three-way race developed that ultimately was won by former Republican U.S. senator Lowell P. Weicker, Jr., running as an independent. The Democratic nominee came in third with just 21 percent of the vote. In the same year, California and Texas both featured open seat races that closely resembled presidential contests. In both states, more than $50 million was spent on intensive television campaigns that went on for much of the year. The Texas race also included character issues involving charges of drug use and alcohol abuse on the part of the Democratic candidate and verbal gaffes and unethical business practices on the part of the Republican candidate. In Minnesota's gubernatorial contest, the Republican candidate withdrew nine days before the election in the face of charges of sexual misconduct. He was replaced by the candidate he had defeated in the primary—who went on to defeat a Democratic incumbent whose personal lifestyle earned him the sobriquet "Governor Goofy." [5]

Thus, campaigns for governor often come to be dominated by the candidates in a way that makes issues and party secondary, just as in presidential contests. Nationally, the Republicans have never surpassed the Democrats as the majority party in terms of voters' identification, but they have elected presidents in the majority of recent contests. Similarly, Republicans have been much more successful in electing governors than in winning control of state legislatures. When party becomes a secondary concern, the longstanding Democratic advantage in party loyalty can be more easily overcome.

The Rise of Direct Primaries

The spread of the direct primary has had the same negative effect on party control of gubernatorial nominations and campaigns that it had on presidential contests. Virtually all gubernatorial candidates have their own personal campaign organizations and personal band of political consultants. In only sixteen states have provisions been made for pre-primary endorsements by state parties in gubernatorial contests, and little evidence exists that they regularly count for much.[6] Primary elections can be remarkable free-for-alls, with the state party organization helpless to control events.

Massachusetts's 1990 gubernatorial race is a good example of the irrelevance of party organizations when nominations can be won in a direct primary by candidates who appeal directly to voters with strong and effective messages. After losing the presidency to George Bush in 1988, Gov. Michael S. Dukakis saw his job ratings plummet as the "Massachusetts miracle" he had touted in his presidential campaign turned into an economic nightmare. In 1989, with his negative job ratings soaring to 80 percent, Dukakis announced he would not seek reelection. The Democratic party selected former attorney general Frank Bellotti at its state convention. The Republican party threw its support to House minority leader Steven Pierce. Both party-endorsed candidates were defeated in the primary election by political outsiders, neither of whom had ever run for political office, and with the help of independent voters, who are allowed to vote in primary elections in Massachusetts. Bellotti lost to Boston University president John Silber; Pierce lost to former U.S. attorney William F. Weld. Weld went on to defeat Silber in a high-profile race in which the candidates' unusual political positions confounded many voters' images of the parties they represented. Republican Weld ran as a social liberal who supported a tax-cutting initiative. Democrat Silber ran as a social conservative who opposed the tax-cutting proposal as imprudent.[7]

Not all states exhibit such extreme candidate-centered campaigns, and the stronger state parties participate in other ways in gubernatorial elections, particularly in encouraging voter mobilization on election day. Republicans often mail absentee ballots to likely Republican voters. Both state parties make sizable contributions to various statewide races. State Democratic organizations, often in conjunction with Democratic congressional candidates, finance substantial get-out-the-vote efforts in heavily black (and Democratic) voting precincts. The Republican National Committee, in addition to contributing directly to some candidate campaigns, pays for full-page newspaper advertising the Sunday before the election.

The Powers of Incumbency

Part of the advantage of gubernatorial incumbency is related to structural enhancements of the office. The almost universal adoption of the four-year term (now enjoyed by forty-seven of the fifty governors, as opposed to only thirty-five in 1964) permits the building of stronger and more visible records. Additionally, more governors are eligible to run for multiple terms—also up to forty-seven currently, as opposed to thirty-five of the forty-eight governors as recently as 1950.

A clear correlation exists between the strengthening of the governor's position and the proportion of incumbents both seeking reelection and gaining it. Between 1900 and 1930, the percentage of governors (who were legally able to do so) seeking reelection ranged from under one-half to less than two-thirds; beginning in the 1960s, it rose steadily to almost four in five by the 1980s. And those who sought to stay in office were more successful. Whereas a third suffered defeat through the 1960s, three-quarters were successful in the 1980s.[8]

However, executive incumbency, because of its visibility, also can be fraught with dangers. Vincent Breglio, a consultant who worked in many gubernatorial contests, likened voters' views of governors to

> a microcosm of the presidential race. They see in that chair all the power to make good things happen or bad things happen. . . . For a governor it's meat and potatoes—what's his or her record? If the farmers haven't had rain, the governor's going to get blamed.[9]

In 1990, when the economy began to sag noticeably, many incumbents chose not to seek reelection. Many of those who decided to face the voters were either defeated or managed to survive very close contests. Only half of the thirty-three governors eligible to run in 1990 were still in office in 1991—ten declined to run and six were defeated in November.

Unlike legislators, who work in relative obscurity and are able to control most of their press coverage and other publicity, governors are more in the spotlight. Newspaper statehouse bureaus cover them intensively. Television does, too, particularly when the state capital is in a major media market. As a political consultant who works in many gubernatorial contests put it:

> In Mississippi, say, 50 percent of the people are in the Jackson media market, and they all know about state government. It's the same with Denver and Colorado. New York State is very well covered by TV, but state politics isn't because Albany is a jerkwater town. In a state like West Virginia, only about a quarter of the population lives in that [capital] media market. An incumbent has the opportunity to tell people what his record is during a campaign, whereas in other states they already know.[10]

But governors, like presidents, have learned to use media attention and official resources to their benefit. They are able to obtain extensive media coverage unfiltered by reporters. More and more governors appear in "nonpolitical" public service and tourism ads, often broadcast to their own constituents instead of to vacationers from other states—such ads, featuring incumbent Thomas H. Kean, ran in New Jersey throughout his 1985 reelection campaign.

An extraordinarily direct use of parallel state government "public service" advertising and gubernatorial campaign advertising occurred in the 1986 Illinois contest. Late that summer, incumbent James R. Thompson ran paid commercials showing him signing legislation committing state lottery profits to education (the ads did not mention that he previously had twice vetoed the same measure). Starting October 1, the State Lottery Commission spent $288,000 for statewide TV advertising on the same topic.

Additionally, the State Department of Commerce and Community Affairs bought $73,000 worth of radio advertising on the Chicago Bears' radio network during the football (and election) season for messages promoting Illinois's standing as the nation's third-ranking state for high-tech industry—another Thompson campaign theme. Referring to the state-financed television advertising, Thompson's outraged opponent complained, "The governor is trying to brainwash people with their own money. . . . This commercial is nothing more than a gift to Thompson's campaign from the taxpayers." Governor Thompson, acknowledging the parallel advertising themes in the "state" and "campaign" commercials responded, "That's true. Well, I'm the governor, and part of a governor's

campaign talks about what's going on in the state under his administration." [11]

The Decoupling of Federal and State Elections Outcomes

The ability of governors to run candidate-centered campaigns also
has been aided by the states' growing practice of holding gubernatorial
elections in nonpresidential election years. By 1992, only twelve states
held gubernatorial elections in presidential years, as compared with
thirty-four that did so in 1932. Three of these,[12] which still have two-year
gubernatorial terms, also are among the thirty-six states that elect their
chief executives in midterm years. An additional five states insulate state-
level elections from national ones even further by holding their gubernatorial contests in odd-numbered years, when no federal elections take
place at all.

The absence of a concurrent presidential election makes it easier
for gubernatorial candidates to focus voters' attention on their appeals.
Not only is actual coattail voting impossible in the thirty-eight states
where presidential and gubernatorial elections never coincide, but the
kinds of casual voters that traditionally come out in presidential years and
are most prone to engage in coattail voting also are absent from the
midterm and odd-year electorates. On average, in the eighteen states that
have held both midterm and presidential-year gubernatorial elections
since 1960, turnout is a full 18 percent lower in the former than
the latter.[13]

However, strong evidence exists that the effect of candidate-centered
appeals further transcends the mere structural changes of moving most
gubernatorial elections out of the presidential-year cycle. First, the 1986
elections broke an iron law of midterm gubernatorial elections since
1950—that the president's party tallies a net loss in gubernatorial seats in
the midterm. Between 1950 and 1982, the president's party lost gubernatorial chairs in every midterm election but 1962 (when no change
occurred). The average loss of 6.2 seats was heavier for Republicans (who
averaged 7.4) than Democrats (who averaged 4.7).[14] In 1986, however,
the president's Republican party gained eight governorships. In 1990,
both parties suffered a net loss of one governorship when two independents were elected.

The longstanding pattern of midterm losses for the president's party
has been attributed to national trends, particularly the state of the
national economy. For their own electoral purposes, presidents attempt to
manipulate the economy so that, as much as possible, good news comes in
presidential years and bad news, if unavoidable, in the off years, or
midterm. Voters attribute the state of the local economy more to the
president than to the governor, but they take it out on the governor in the

midterm anyway. The Republicans' heavy losses in the recession year of 1982 were widely ascribed to this tendency.[15]

However, in 1986, Republican governors did best in some of the places where the economy was in the worst shape. And in 1990, the weak economy took its toll on governors of both parties in almost equal measure—Republican lost governorships in seven states, Democrats in five, and independents won two, for no net change in partisan balance. For example, in New England, a region in particularly severe economic distress, three Democratic governors—Madeleine M. Kunin in Vermont, William A. O'Neill in Connecticut, and Michael Dukakis in Massachusetts—declined to seek reelection and were replaced by two Republicans and an independent. Two Republican governors—Judd Gregg in New Hampshire and John R. McKernan, Jr., in Maine—did stand for reelection and both won, although McKernan only barely survived. And in Rhode Island, Republican Edward DiPrete lost to Democrat Bruce Sundlun by the incredible margin of 74 percent to 26 percent, which perhaps was the worst showing of an incumbent governor ever.

The year 1990 offers another indicator of the decoupling of federal and state elections—in fourteen of the twenty-five states with contests for both governor and U.S. senator, candidates of opposite parties won. Furthermore, New Jersey's U.S. Senate race provided an example of state-level forces overwhelming national ones. Democrat Bill Bradley, seeking his third term, was considered the overwhelming favorite. A senator with a national reputation and often mentioned as a possible presidential candidate, he was almost defeated by a virtually unknown candidate who was outspent by a ratio of more than 10 to 1. What almost brought Bradley down was his refusal to comment on a tax increase pushed through the state legislature the previous year by Democratic governor James J. Florio. Thus, the process came full circle, with the unpopularity of a governor altering the electoral fortunes of a contest for a federal office.

A final indicator of the decoupling of partisan outcomes in national and state politics is evident in the minority of gubernatorial races that take place in presidential years. Both the 1936 Roosevelt Democratic and the 1952 Eisenhower Republican presidential landslide victories resulted in wins for 90 percent of their fellow partisans running for governor in the states they carried. The results were almost identical in presidential and gubernatorial elections from 1896 to 1908. Split presidential-gubernatorial outcomes were still less than 20 percent from 1912 to 1924. However, in the candidate-centered period since 1960, they have averaged around 40 percent.[16]

Thus, structural change—moving gubernatorial contests out of the presidential year—also helped to reinforce the increasingly candidate-centered nature of gubernatorial races, and the two together have notably decoupled presidential and gubernatorial partisan outcomes.

Campaign Finance

The growing advantages of gubernatorial incumbency generally resulted in more incumbents running, more winning, and more winning bigger victories. Three recent trends in gubernatorial campaign finance strengthened the incumbent advantage specifically and candidate-centered campaigning generally: dramatically higher campaign expenditures, increasingly heavy campaign contributions from the recipients of official patronage, and public financing in a few states.

The campaign "hyperinflation" (far exceeding increases in the general cost of living) that has struck U.S. Senate races is only too evident in gubernatorial contests. As recently as 1978, spending of $3 million by at least one of the gubernatorial candidates occurred in only three states— California, Florida, and Texas. Total expenditures were below $500,000 for both candidates in ten states that year.

In the following two election cycles, expenditures in the same three "leading" states approached or exceeded combined totals of $20 million, and the "$3 million candidate" became the norm in many states. In 1990, four states saw total campaign expenditures for governor exceed $20 million, with two topping $50 million. The average race cost almost $10 million. This figure rose to almost $17 million in the thirteen open seat contests. Only in Vermont did total expenditures remain below $1 million. But such contests are becoming positively quaint, as other relatively small states saw record multimillion-dollar media contests. Not surprisingly, the most expensive races occur in large states with many media markets and closely contested open seats (such as Texas, California, and Illinois in 1990) or potentially vulnerable incumbents (such as Florida and Alabama in 1990).[17]

The warchests of well-financed incumbents and candidates in hotly contested open seats bulge with the contributions of recipients of official state patronage. Finance reports document massive contributions by those seeking to get or keep state contracts, jobs, or favorable regulatory decisions. Attorneys, contractors, developers and realtors, the financial community, health interests, and unions figure heavily in every state, and agricultural interests in many. During New Jersey's midterm legislative elections in 1991, Democratic governor Florio, reeling from a tax revolt that had driven his performance ratings to near historic lows, still was able to raise $2.5 million in one evening at an affair largely attended by lawyers, contractors, builders, and others who had extensive business dealings with the state.

In the wake of the Watergate scandal, which brought taxpayer-funded presidential general election campaigns (and partially funded nomination contests), a number of states made some provision for public funding of state-level races. By 1992, nineteen states had some provision for public funding from either a state income tax checkoff or a small voluntary add-on, but in only four states did the sums involved approach significance—New Jersey, Michigan, Wisconsin, and Minnesota. All four use the checkoff provision to raise funds that are funneled directly to individual candidates. Gubernatorial elections (both primary and general) in New Jersey and Michigan are largely funded by public money, in systems similar to the federal procedure for presidential contests.[18]

Experience with public funding in the states reaches back barely fifteen years, but two principal effects are discernable: it holds down expenditures, and it likely advantages incumbents.

When the pioneering New Jersey system was first used in 1977, the sums provided seemed adequate for a state with no commercial television stations of its own and no tradition of media-based campaigns. However, the collapse of the traditional party organizations that year unleashed an escalating spiral of expenditures—which mostly were the result of having to depend on the expensive New York City and Philadelphia media outlets necessary to reach the state's voters. By 1985, gubernatorial candidates in New Jersey spent more than three-quarters of all their funds on television-related expenses.[19] However, the total of about $4.2 million allotted to both gubernatorial candidates in 1985 was less than what any one of the victorious U.S. Senate candidates spent in their three contests between 1982 and 1988. Similarly, Michigan's candidates in 1986 each spent less than $1 million in their contest, as compared with the more than $5 million expended by the two 1984 U.S. Senate candidates.

Unlike presidential campaigns, where major candidates receive extensive news ("free media") coverage for two years preceding the election, challengers in gubernatorial campaigns have had a difficult time running against better-known incumbents. In New Jersey, incumbents won in landslides in both of the races that took place in the public finance era.[20] In Michigan, incumbents also won two races in landslides, although, in 1990, Democratic incumbent James J. Blanchard was narrowly defeated by Republican John Engler.

New Jersey's experience also shows that public funding linked to a limit on total campaign expenditures can create problems similar to those that occur in presidential campaigns. In 1989, a higher limit of $5 million, with two-thirds publicly funded, was established. Florio, the Democratic candidate, however, helped raise an additional $5 million for the state party, which was used to finance a series of generic television ads urging voters to vote Democratic and using the same themes and issues that Florio was using in his campaign. Republican governor Kean had raised money for a generic ad campaign in his 1985 reelection bid. The money contributed to the state parties did not come under the contribution or expenditure limits imposed on gubernatorial candidates. In presidential campaigns, money similarly raised for state party activities is referred to as "soft money" by some, and "sewer money" by others.

Money is a major factor in gubernatorial campaign, as challengers usually have to spend more than incumbents to offset incumbents' greater recognition levels and electorally useful official resources. In all recent gubernatorial election cycles, the bigger spender won much more often and usually was the incumbent. Even in the relatively few cases where incumbents were outspent, they (particularly Democrats) still won more than half the time.

Thus the presidentialization of gubernatorial contests, the delinking of state and national politics, and trends in campaign finance all contribute to the growth of candidate-centered campaigns for state chief executives. Have their compatriots in the state legislatures followed the path of their legislative brethren in the U.S. Congress and also moved down the road to candidate-centered campaigns?

State Legislative Campaigns and Elections

If gubernatorial contests have become "presidentialized," state legislative races are becoming "congressionalized"; that is, taking on the attributes that federal congressional campaigns increasingly have exhibited.

The Dimensions of Congressionalization

The outcome of most congressional elections through the 1960s could be explained by a pattern of "surge and decline" related to presidential coattails and performance.[21] Beginning in the 1970s, this pattern substantially broke down, as more voters, with less and weaker identification with the political parties, began to do in legislative elections what they already were doing in presidential races—casting their vote more often for the candidate than the party. Because much less information usually was available about challengers to sitting legislators, voters often chose "the devil they knew"—the incumbent. To have any chance of winning, challengers had to become almost as well known and favorably regarded as their opponents.[22] Additionally, challengers found they had to disseminate unfavorable information about their opponents. Otherwise, voters faced with two equally acceptable choices tended to adopt an "If it ain't broke, don't fix it" mentality, resulting in incumbent victories.[23] Three closely interrelated developments contributed to incumbents' advantages and thus increasingly candidate-centered congressional races: more entrepreneurial behavior on the part of incumbents, an expansion of official resources, and the changing sources of congressional campaign money.

The entrepreneurial congressional candidate is a product of the decline of the party as vote-cue. When congressional candidates no longer could depend on their party labels to assure victory or the president's coattails to help them in marginal districts, they began to feel electorally insecure no matter how large their previous victories.[24] Thus, they began relying almost exclusively on their own efforts to win reelection. Furthermore, other candidates, who in the past could not expect party organizational support and hence did not run, now saw greater chances of success and were more likely to get into races. As one member of Congress observed in 1983:

> You can look around the floor of the House and see a handful—twenty years ago you saw a lot of them—today you can see just a handful of hacks that were put there by the party organization, and there are very, very few of them left. It is just mostly people that went out and took the election.[25]

"Taking the election" required that candidates make electorally effective use of official resources and raise their own campaign money.

Informational newsletters and targeted mailings enormously drove up the use and cost of the congressional postal frank. More staff and more staff time were detailed to constituency service, and district offices were established or expanded to provide it. A full-time press secretary, previously rare, became a fixture of the staff. Seeking committees for electoral instead of policy reasons became more commonplace. The House committee system was reorganized to make acquiring chairmanships and their attendant perks and publicity easier for more members, and more junior members. More time in session was spent on "position taking" than legislation.[26]

Federal legislators also acted to change the campaign finance laws in a variety of ways that, intentionally or not, served their electoral ends. Publicly financed presidential elections freed huge sums for contribution to legislative campaigns. The creation of political action committees (PACs) channeled much of this money in distinctive ways. Most came from pragmatic economic interests more interested in access than ideology. Thus legislators on committees overseeing or regulating particular economic sectors could expect large numbers of PAC contributions. Much of the rest of the money came from issue-oriented groups whose support could be had by judicious position taking.

The limits placed on political party contributions relegated them to third place behind individuals and PACs. Although able to contribute far more heavily than any single individual or PAC, parties were outweighed by a ratio of at least 4 to 1 when compared with individual and PAC contributions combined. Furthermore, because nonparty contributions are so much more dispersed and individually are such a small part of the total, incumbents are beholden to no one in particular.

Because PAC money went so overwhelmingly to "properly" placed incumbents and party money was not that important to them, the political parties increasingly targeted their funds to the relatively few open seats and strong challengers. Once the beneficiaries of their largess were elected, they became incumbents, too, and no longer beholden, to the extent they ever were, to their party organizations.[27]

Thus, congressionalization means making congressional incumbents relatively autonomous actors. Official resources build favorable recognition among constituents and give incumbents the ability to raise their own money from grateful individuals and political action committees. Challengers rely more on party money but need to demonstrate that they are among the small minority with a realistic chance of winning to get the party's limited resources.

What Encourages Congressionalization?

In the states, three sets of developments are parallel to those at the federal level: Legislative professionalization results in greater official resources that can be used for electoral purposes, incumbency is replacing party as a voting cue, and more and more campaign money comes from PACs. However, in most states none of these processes is as far advanced as in the U.S. Congress. Furthermore, the requirements of campaign finance, the campaign technology that money buys, and the need for that technology differ in important ways from the federal situation.

For much of the twentieth century, as the power and scope of the federal government grew, state government languished. However, the "new federalism" espoused by the Nixon and Reagan administrations made state government more important, more powerful, and more interesting to competent and ambitious politicians. The "one person, one vote" court reapportionment decisions that ended malapportionment and blatant gerrymandering also changed the nature of representation in the state legislatures, the possible levels of party competition, and the nature of the contestants.

As in Congress, stronger institutions produced more official resources, at least in the larger states. Staff, particularly partisan staff attached to new or stronger legislative caucus organizations, grew apace. Computers analyzed policy alternatives but also generated newsletters, form letters to constituents, and targeted mailing lists. The number of states holding annual legislative sessions to deal with increased official business grew from nineteen in 1962 to forty-four in 1990. Legislative salaries increased to the point that by 1979 in ten states they exceeded $30,000 a year.[28]

Larger state budgets and a heavier legislative workload also produced in many places further official perquisites—increased expense accounts, budgets for personal legislative aides and district offices, and the chance to gain more visibility (and still more official resources) through leadership positions and committee chairmanships. Not surprisingly, in the face of these developments, more legislators found staying in office attractive, and more people aspired to gain office. From the 1930s to the 1960s, average turnover in state lower houses dropped by half, to about a third, and fell below a third in the 1980s.[29]

Working harder at their jobs and having more interest in keeping them, incumbents not only chose to run for reelection more often, but also were more successful. In the 1960s and 1970s, typically fewer than a fifth of all legislative incumbents were defeated. In the 1980s, this number rarely approached a tenth and was frequently close to zero.[30] Nor do large numbers of incumbents have close races. Half or more of legislators in a sizable number of states run unopposed.[31]

All the things that incumbents do to solidify their positions is reflected, as at the federal level, in the increase in split-ticket voting in legislative elections. Although the heavily candidate-centered contests for governor are more responsible for the sharp rise in split partisan control than are individual legislative races, legislators themselves are responsible for the growing number of instances in which partisan control of the two legislative houses is split.

Between 1961 and 1983, the number of states in which different parties controlled the two legislative houses ranged from four to nine. This number rose to eleven in 1985 and fourteen in 1991. Split-ticket voting is by definition an indication of the waning power of party as a vote cue. Although incumbency and party effects are impossible to entirely disentangle, partisan turnover is more than twice as likely to occur when a legislative race is for an open seat.[32]

The growing role of PAC money in legislative campaigns is the way that they most resemble those for Congress. Even in states where professionalization has barely made a dent, turnover (mostly voluntary) still approaches a third, and campaigns are cheap, PACs are growing rapidly as a major source of campaign funds. Typically, about a third of all campaign contributions, and a majority of incumbents' warchests, come from PACs. This was the case in recent elections in, for example, Arizona, Iowa, Kansas, and Missouri.[33]

What Limits Congressionalization?

Congressionalization is not complete everywhere or, indeed, almost anywhere. A number of factors limit its development and require adjustments to achieve the same ends in state legislative elections. First, official resources that are useful for individual state legislative contests are fewer. Legislative districts—even those in the upper house—are much smaller than congressional ones. (California state senate districts, which are larger than U.S. House districts, are the only exception.) For example, a U.S. representative in a large state such as Illinois or Ohio serves about 550,000 constituents; the state assembly counterpart serves about 97,000 in Illinois and 110,000 in Ohio, which would be considered large assembly constituencies. Comparable figures are 45,000 in Wisconsin, 23,000 in Connecticut, and a mere 2,500 in New Hampshire—which has the largest lower house in the nation to serve the eighth smallest population.

Although many state legislative budgets are growing rapidly, nowhere do they resemble the commitment the federal government makes to the upkeep of its legislature. More than four times as many dollars are behind each member of the federal legislature as are behind those who serve New York state (by far the best financed legislature both absolutely and per capita in the nation), and ten times as many as those supporting the New Jersey legislature, still at the upper end of the national spectrum. California's senate staff allowance is comparable to that of a U.S. House member with a slightly smaller constituency, but, in the vast majority of states, an allowance one-tenth the size, to support perhaps one personal aide and a secretary, is extraordinarily generous. A Nevada legislator whose perks consist of $60 for postage and $1,000 for telephone calls over a two-year period or a New Hampshire representative who is paid $100 per year would find the California allowance unimaginable. And no state legislator enjoys the most prized of all congressional perks—the unlimited postal frank.

Although the advantages of incumbency are growing for state legislators, fewer official resources make incumbency less helpful than for those in Congress. The effects of coattails on state legislative outcomes diminished by half in the 1970s and 1980s as compared with the 1940s through 1960s, but they still are present to some extent.[34] With fewer official resources, state legislators also find achieving the recognition levels of their federal peers harder. Although systematic data are sparse, in New Jersey, for example, recognition levels of legislators have doubled in recent years but still are half those of members of Congress.[35] In the relatively low-information, low-turnout elections that now take place, party identification doubtless counts for more, too, as fewer of the casual independent voters bother to come out or they make their way to the bottom of the ballot when they do.

Individual candidates also do not have the money to tap into the high-cost, high-tech campaign techniques that are so crucial to nurturing candidate-centered voting. Accurate poll samples are no smaller for a legislative race than a congressional one. Media advertising depends on the size of a station's market, not the size of a candidate's constituency. Television, the best medium for building recognition quickly, is grossly cost-inefficient for almost all legislative candidates because stations cover so many legislative districts. News coverage is scarce enough for federal legislative candidates, let alone those for the state legislature, and the free "advertising" made possible by the federal frank is not available either.

Furthermore, although an entrepreneurially minded state legislator needs to build personal recognition just as much as a federal legislator does, the payoff is simply not the same in the vast majority of cases. The federal candidate is seeking more prestige, more perquisites, and a higher step on the ladder of political ambition. Despite the longer and more frequent state legislative sessions, most state legislators still will spend less time in the state capital than federal legislators spend in Washington, D.C.

Although campaign costs at the state level are rising steeply,[36] only in the largest states do spending levels even approach those in U.S. House contests. In 1990, House incumbents spent an average of $693,000 in seeking reelection. In California, the comparable figure for all incumbents was $495,000. In other large states such as Ohio, Pennsylvania, New Jersey, and New York, occasional races may cost in excess of $300,000. However, for the vast majority of state legislative candidates, their campaign spending levels are only a fraction of these high dollar races. The much smaller district sizes and much larger numbers of districts ensure that state legislative candidates will never have available the large warchests that most members of Congress routinely possess.

Congressionalization of state legislative elections are far from complete and are significantly less complete than the presidentialization of gubernatorial elections. However, state-level legislative candidates have been creative in devising ways to deal with the shortcomings.

The Role of Political Parties

The key difference between federal and state legislators is that members of Congress are better able to operate as independent entrepreneurs. Their ability to use official resources as campaign resources when party resources failed them led to the description of congressional offices as individual enterprises.[37] Almost all individual state legislators lack the access to such resources.

Therefore, the obvious solution has been for the state legislators to band together in some larger organization that has the resources they lack. That organization: the political party. In the past, incumbents seeking reelection benefited from voters' psychological attachments to the parties more than the work of party organizations. The state organizations were more interested in the governor's office, and county and local organizations more interested in positions at those levels. Both the governor and county officials had what legislators lack—access to the patronage jobs that are the lifeblood of traditional party organizations.

Some observers believe that revitalized state party organizations, particularly on the Republican side, now emulate the national party organizations and have a new interest in legislative races, given that governors have lost most of their patronage powers and no longer need the state parties to run their races. Elaborate studies detail growing state party budgets, larger staffs, and provision of campaign services to legislative candidates. In addition, in 1980 and 1990, the national Republican party mounted a major effort to aid state parties in their quest to capture more state legislatures and thus gain greater influence in the congressional and legislative redistricting process. However, it was no more successful in 1990 than in 1980 in helping to secure GOP victories in state legislative contests. Republicans lost a net of forty-three seats in 1990, and their hold on state legislatures dropped to a post-Watergate low.

A close look also casts some doubt on the state parties' efficacy. Although some are performing some "service bureau" functions, their budgets actually have decreased over the past few decades once inflation is taken into account. More importantly, no relationship exists between the state parties' organizational strength and either the number or closeness of legislative victories.[38] An inverse correlation has been present between Republican party efforts in the states and their performance in legislative elections. Republican control of the ninety-eight partisan state legislative houses dipped steadily from thirty-five in 1980 to twenty-three in 1990. Democrats, whose state party organizations often were bankrupt, performed better in legislative elections.

Many state legislative candidates favor a solution that already is in place in many cases—help not from the traditional party organizations, but from their fellow legislators in legislative party caucuses.

California pioneered the initiative and referendum, the use of political consultants, and the election of celebrities to office. California assembly leader Jesse Unruh also created, almost twenty years ago, the first legislative caucus devoted principally to the winning of state legislative elections. Now, legislative caucuses in more than thirty states raise funds to support legislative campaigns. In at least twelve of these (and most of the largest states), the amount of funds raised is enough to exert a significant effect on campaigns and, in at least fourteen, is a source of power for the legislative leadership that controls the caucuses' campaign activities.[39]

Although fund raising is carried on by both minority and majority party caucuses, the majority finds attracting contributors easier, particularly the political action committees that provide a large portion of such funds. Generally speaking, state PACs steer individual contributions heavily toward incumbents and anticipate that challengers will be supported by the large sums PACs also contribute to legislative caucus campaign committees. With the Democrats in control of about two-thirds of all statehouses throughout the 1980s, an important explanation of their electoral success emerges.

One advantage to candidates of funds controlled by the legislative leadership is that leaders want nothing more from the recipients than their vote to organize the chamber and reelect the leaders to their positions. Former Wisconsin house leader Tom Loftus was perhaps particularly candid when he described his criteria for disbursing caucus funds to promising assembly challengers:

> Our only test is that a candidate is in a winnable seat and he or she is breathing, and those two requirements are in order of importance. . . . We don't care if this person believes in the principles of the Democratic party or if he or she belongs to the Democratic party. We know if they make it they will vote with the Democrats to organize, and that's the goal we care about.[40]

Campaign money is not the only valuable resource the legislative leadership controls. Desirable committee assignments, which provide not only visibility but electorally useful staff and access to individual campaign contributions, also are within the power of many to dispense. California's Willie Brown described his use of this power in much the same way as Tom Loftus: "The Speaker in California has an awesome amount of power over House organization, and I don't use it based on party participation or party loyalty; I use it based on Speaker loyalty." [41]

In addition to the interests of the leadership and the rank and file in using campaign funds and organizational resources for mutual benefit, electorally useful government appropriations are available for the leadership to dole out. Besides the normal kinds of "pork barrel" legislation, a few legislatures specifically reserve discretionary funds that members, through the good offices of leaders, can use in their districts. Political scientist Alan Rosenthal noted the "worthy legislative projects" that comprised almost 5 percent of Maryland's legislative budget and the "special entries" awarding slush funds of $100,000 and $50,000 to North Carolina's senators and assembly members, respectively, in 1985. "Member items" in the New York state legislative budget have run as high as $1.8 million per member. Member items are sums that may be spent on district items entirely at a legislator's discretion.

Observers of the legislative caucuses often note the extent to which they have taken over the electoral functions of what is conventionally thought of as "the party organization." This usually occurs because of the weakness of those organizations. In New York, "the two houses of the legislature have in many ways assumed the functions of statewide party organizations" because "the influence of local political leaders has waned." [42] In other states, caucuses have acted because the parties offer no or minimal assistance. In Oregon, the majority of state party money goes for staff salaries and overhead, and "candidates in partisan contests are left in the lurch." [43] Of a state party role in Wisconsin legislative races, former Speaker Loftus said:

Let me assure you that the expression of that sentiment would be an alien formation from the lips of those controlling the Wisconsin Democratic party. You might get some agreement that the purpose of the party was to help the candidate for governor or president. But a blank stare would greet you should you suggest some relationship with the jerk on the ballot who has happened to run under the banner for the legislature.[44]

The caucuses therefore assume many of the electoral functions once carried out by party organizations. In Ohio, for example, the House Republican Campaign Committee holds a two-day "issues seminar" for all Republican House nominees immediately after the primary. It also sponsors, in conjunction with its Senate counterpart, a campaign management seminar covering video training, pointers on targeted mail, and the like. In 1991 and 1992, campaign organizations established by legislative leaders in Pennsylvania and New Jersey contracted directly with professional consultants to conduct polls, produce radio and TV advertisements, and create direct mail campaigns for targeted challenger and incumbent races.

However, just as congressionalization is more or less advanced in various states, so, too, is the electoral activity of the legislative caucuses. A few states do not have organized caucuses. They are mostly in the Deep South, where Democrats still are both the overwhelming majority of members and highly factionalized—to the point where leaders sometimes organize by getting votes from the minority Republicans and appointing them to committee chairmanships. And no party caucus exists in the unicameral and nonpartisan Nebraska legislature.

Varieties of Congressionalization

The shape of legislative campaign politics in a given state is related to the sometimes overlapping factors of state political culture, the level of party competition, and the presence of particularly entrepreneurial leaders.

A state's political culture affects the extent of congressionalization and activity by legislative caucuses. They almost always are advanced in states with a history of strong traditional party organizations.[45] The old "machine" states that stretch in a broad band across the northeast and the industrial midwest are precisely those states—New York, New Jersey, Pennsylvania, Ohio, and Illinois—with strong and active legislative caucuses.

In these states, the legislature has become the repository of many of the patronage jobs once provided elsewhere. In New York, local party officials often are paid staffers on the Albany legislative payroll but work at least part time out of county party offices, in legislative district offices, or in campaign organizations.[46] In New Jersey, the majority and minority partisan staffs provide employment for many campaign staffers in between elections. In Illinois, every professional legislative staff position is partisan, and many are deployed by the leadership to work in campaigns. One explains, "By the book partisan staff does campaign work on weekends and during leaves of absence—but everybody violates the rule.... There is a token effort made to prevent state resources from being turned into party resources." [47]

A second set of active legislative caucuses are found in the upper midwest, in states that also traditionally had strong party organizations, albeit based more on issues than patronage. Wisconsin and Minnesota's legislative caucuses and their fund raising coexist with partially public-financed elections and strict spending limits.

The Wisconsin caucuses are limited to raising only about $150,000 per election cycle and donating a maximum of $3,000 per campaign. Campaign spending is limited if public funds are accepted, and every dollar of PAC money a candidate takes reduces the amount of public money available.[48] Because of the limits on accepting PAC contributions and requirements that candidates raise a minimum on their own and have an opponent, the public money acceptance rate is lower in Wisconsin than in Minnesota, and the per capita expenditures in Minnesota are higher than in Wisconsin.[49] Yet within these limits, the Wisconsin and Minnesota caucuses are effective in using modern campaign technology to elect candidates, especially challengers.

In contrast, caucus activity is notably absent in small or heavily rural states with a tradition of localism and citizen legislatures. In a state such as New Hampshire, an expensive House campaign directed toward 2,500 constituents might cost $500, principally for lawn signs. Direct mail and radio advertising are unknown, and "the town dump is a good place to campaign." [50] As a result, in smaller states with less professionalized legislatures, such as Vermont, Idaho, and Montana, campaign expenditures have increased much more slowly, and direct voter contact by individual candidates remains the dominant mode of campaigning.[51]

The level of party competition is another factor affecting the extent of congressionalization and caucus activity. In states with a persistently low level of party competition, principally in the South, factionalism within the dominant party hampers the emergence of an effective party caucus. Members of the minority party are likely to do better working with factions of the dominant party. In a number of southern states, the governor appoints legislative leaders, and a tradition exists of rotating them rapidly out of office, making the development of an independent power base impossible.

High or increasing levels of party competition have the opposite effect. Connecticut, for example, was one state with truly strong state party organizations. State conventions, not primaries, chose all candidates for state office, including the governor.[52] Additionally, Connecticut was one of the few states in the nation that retained the party lever on voting machines. When Republicans, swept into legislative majorities for two years in the 1984 Reagan landslide, managed to get rid of the lever beginning in 1988, Democrats swung into action. A strong House leader and caucus operation emerged almost immediately, legislative salaries were raised somewhat, media campaigns dominated the 1986 governor's race for the first time, a new legislative complex was built, and partisan staff was increased.

In Wisconsin, both parties' legislative campaign committees were galvanized by the 1984 elections, which produced a seven-seat gain in the assembly for the Republicans and dangerously narrowed the Democrats' traditional margin. The Democrats faced the further disadvantage of an unpopular governor at the top of the ticket in 1986. Targeting of resources became almost total; safe and hopeless candidates for the first time were completely shut out. Money was spent on generic television advertising, individualized radio advertising, polls, and phone banks. Commenting on candidates' suspicion of the new technology, an architect of the efforts concluded, "If there weren't the real threat of losing, it would not have happened. They would never have changed if they could always win." [53]

Summary

State-level campaigns and elections have taken on many of the attributes of executive and legislative contests at the federal level. Certainly, differences remain that seem immutable. Governors do not face the organizational challenges of presidential candidates, do not receive the same degree of national media attention, and are not expected to have the same grasp of foreign policy. But increasingly, like presidents, they run as individuals, succeed or fail because of their retrospective or prospective records as leaders and economic managers, communicate their messages through television, and find party labels and organizations increasingly less important to their endeavors. Also like presidents, their personal popularity is less transferable to their fellow partisans, although they may, if they so choose, raise campaign money for them.

Legislators generally represent smaller constituencies than their federal peers, are less well known to their constituents, and cannot and need not raise the same sums to wage their campaigns. But like U.S. senators and representatives, they rely increasingly less on party labels or executive coattails to bring them victory and more on their own efforts, incumbency, official resources, and candidate-centered campaigns. The costs of modern campaign technology have made legislative campaigns in some of the larger states almost identical in style and form to congressional campaigns and as expensive as well-financed congressional contests were scarcely a decade ago. Even in capitals still populated with "amateur" citizen-legislators, candidates now raise much of whatever funds they need from political action committees, as do their federal brethren. And like congressional candidates, that fund raising is much easier for incumbents and leaders.

In the most recent elections, legislative campaign committees in many of the larger states, organized by caucus leaders, have come to resemble the Washington, D.C.-based congressional campaign committees. Instances of targeting resources to open seats, vulnerable incumbents, and strong challengers have grown. The campaign services the committees finance or provide also are similar—polling, direct mail production, strategic planning, and broadcast advertising.

As technology becomes more affordable and available—for example, personal computers, campaign software packages, and greater penetration of cable television—the similarities between contested legislative and congressional contests will grow even further. The major difference is that economies of scale, varying levels of official resources, and fund-raising capacity make most state legislative candidates, even incumbents, more dependent on mutual rather than individual resources than are their federal counterparts.

As state politics develops in the same directions as federal politics, the same concerns arise. One common fear is about campaign finance, particularly the role of special interest PACs and conversion of public funds. Newspapers and good government groups often inveigh against "the best legislatures that money can buy." Concerns are particularly strong in New York and California, where campaign costs and use of official resources for campaign purposes are highest. After several years of heated debate, California voters in 1988 approved a ballot measure on legislative campaign financing that banned intercandidate transfers, restricted PAC contributions to $2,500 per candidate, and limited political parties and "broad-based committees" to contributions of $5,000 per candidate.[54] In the same year, the New York state senate minority leader, his chief of staff, and two former or current state senators were charged with misuse of public money by keeping full-time campaign employees in "no show" jobs. Two years later, similar charges that legislative staffers were doing campaign work were investigated by New Jersey's attorney general. Ultimately, in both states, the judicial system decided that the legislatures had no clear rules defining proper conduct for staffers, and therefore no rules had been broken. However, the clear message was that the blurring of the lines between staff work and campaigning was an issue that needed to be addressed.

Although these may be extreme examples, they point out some of the difficulties. Campaign spending can be regulated in only four ways, listed in the order of their current use and future feasibility: disclosure requirements, contribution limits, spending limits, and public financing.

Disclosure of contribution sources gives the public some information and requires some accountability of the part of candidates. Contribution limits place some check on influence and encourage diversity of funding sources. Spending limits raise both legal and practical objections. In *Buckley v. Valeo*, the Supreme Court ruled that in elections, in the absence of public funding, expenditure limits constitute an abridgment of freedom of speech and are not permissible. Even when public funding is available, as is currently the case in presidential elections, candidates may opt not to take it, so long as they observe whatever contribution limits the law specifies. Many politicians argue that both spending limits and public funding discriminate against lesser-known challengers and serve as an "incumbents' protection act." Finally, as a practical matter, in the states as in Washington, the political parties are so split on the issue of public funding—with the majority of Republicans opposing it and the majority of Democrats favoring it—that it is not likely to make much further headway.

A second frequently voiced concern relates to the diminished role of the political parties. From a policy point of view, the argument has been made that a collection of entrepreneurially minded officeholders who owe nothing to their parties makes for incoherent policy and lack of accountability. Furthermore, the increasing number of long-term incumbents and seemingly "permanent majorities" are said to inspire smugness and arrogance. But others see immobilism and incoherence as a reflection of public opinion and believe that politicians can and do move rapidly and decisively when the public will is clear. The "permanent majorities" also are a great deal less institutionally permanent than were the malapportioned and gerrymandered legislatures that preceded them, when an aroused majority of voters often could not work its will.

Nevertheless, the public is increasingly disposed to seeing the full-time professional legislator as an arrogant and out-of-touch incumbent who uses the perquisites of office to win reelection without effectively dealing with the public concerns. One response has been a movement calling for term limitations. In 1990, California, Oklahoma, and Colorado passed initiatives that limited the number of terms legislators could serve. Some method of limiting terms is being pursued in as many as forty-five states.[55] The California initiative also called for reducing the legislature operating budget by 38 percent. Whatever impact term limitation measures might have on the operation of state legislatures, they serve as a warning that many citizens are uncomfortable with the idea of professional legislators.

Unless the term limitation movement broadly succeeds, the inexorable trend seems to be toward more, if not complete, presidentialization and congressionalization of state campaigns and elections. However, term limits, where they are enacted, are unlikely to result in the reemergence of the part-time citizen legislator. The new class of political entrepreneurs that has developed since the 1960s has proven to be very resourceful.[56] They have succeeded in making politics and elective office a career, and term limitations will be seen as just another change in the rules of the game. The policy role of the states is likely to continue to increase as power and policy initiative continues to flow to them. Governors and state legislators are growing more adept at using the resources at their disposal and acquiring the resources needed to run modern, technologically sophisticated campaigns. Multimillion-dollar media campaigns for the state legislature may never take place in New Hampshire or North Dakota, but plenty of room exists for expansion, particularly in a number of the larger southern states, such as Florida or Texas, that are likely to see more competitive partisan politics at the state level. If the system has imperfections and concern about it arises, the conclusion of a study of similar concerns about federal politics is well remembered: "That all does not work to perfection reflects fundamental tensions of political life, and fundamental contradictions in political institutions, not just human failing. We can't always have everything we want." [57]

Notes

1. This argument is elaborated upon in Barbara G. Salmore and Stephen A. Salmore, *Candidates, Parties, and Campaigns*, 2d ed. (Washington, D.C.: CQ Press, 1989).
2. Martin P. Wattenberg, *The Decline of American Political Parties, 1952-1984* (Cambridge, Mass.: Harvard University Press, 1986); and Martin P. Wattenberg, "The Reagan Polarization Phenomenon and the Continued Downward Slide in Presidential Candidate Popularity," *American Politics Quarterly* 14 (1984): 219-246.
3. Much of the aggregate data in this section appears in Larry J. Sabato, *Goodbye to Good-time Charlie: The American Governorship Transformed* (Washington, D.C.: CQ Press, 1983); and Malcolm E. Jewell and David M. Olson, *American State Political Parties and Elections*, 3d ed. (Homewood, Ill.: Dorsey Press, 1988).
4. Quoted in Michael Barone and Grant Ujifusa, *The Almanac of American Politics 1992* (Washington, D.C.: National Journal, 1991), 1046.
5. Ibid., 655-656.
6. Malcolm E. Jewell, *Parties and Primaries: Nominating State Governors* (New York: Praeger, 1984); and Sarah M. Morehouse, "Money versus Party Effort: Nominations for Governor" (Paper delivered at the annual meeting of the American Political Science Association, Chicago, September 3-6, 1987).
7. Paul Watanabe, "Where Independents Have Made a Difference: The Case of Massachusetts," *The Public Perspective* 2:1 (November/December 1990): 27-28.

8. J. Stephen Turett, "The Vulnerability of American Governors, 1900-1969," *Midwest Journal of Political Science* 15 (1971): 108-132; and Thad L. Beyle, "Gubernatorial Elections: 1977-1990," *Comparative State Politics* 12:2 (April 1991): 18-21.

9. Barbara G. Salmore and Stephen A. Salmore, *Candidates, Parties, and Campaigns* (Washington: CQ Press, 1985), 67.

10. Ibid., 66.

11. *Chicago Tribune*, October 27, 1986.

12. All three are in New England—New Hampshire, Rhode Island, and Vermont.

13. Malcolm E. Jewell and David M. Olson, *Political Parties and Elections in American States* (Homewood, Ill.: Dorsey Press, 1988), 209.

14. John S. Bibby, "Statehouse Elections at Midterm," in *The American Elections of 1982*, ed. Thomas E. Mann and Norman J. Ornstein (Washington, D.C.: American Enterprise Institute for Public Policy Research, 1983), 115.

15. See for example, ibid.; and John E. Chubb, "Institutions, the Economy, and the Dynamics of State Elections," *American Political Science Review* 82 (March 1988): 133-154.

16. Walter Dean Burnham, "The System of 1896: An Analysis," in *The Evolution of American Electoral Systems*, ed. Paul Kleppner (Westport, Conn.: Greenwood Press, 1981).

17. Thad L. Beyle, "The Costs of the 1990 Gubernatorial Elections," *Comparative State Politics* 12:5 (October 1991): 3-7.

18. The data in this discussion are drawn from Herbert E. Alexander and Michael Eberts, *Public Financing of State Elections* (Los Angeles: Citizens' Research Foundation, 1986).

19. New Jersey Election Law Enforcement Commission, *New Jersey Public Financing: 1985 Gubernatorial Elections* (Trenton: New Jersey Election Law Enforcement Commission, September 1986).

20. It was widely believed that incumbent Tom Kean intended to opt out of the public finance provisions in 1985 if the race showed any sign of becoming close. (He ultimately won with a record-setting 70 percent of the vote.)

21. The original statement of the "surge and decline" argument is from Angus Campbell, "Surge and Decline: A Study in Electoral Change," *Public Opinion Quarterly* 29 (1960): 397-418. An application to state elections is made by James E. Campbell, "Presidential Coattails and Midterm Losses in State Legislative Elections," *American Political Science Review* 80 (1986): 45-64.

22. See, for example, Gary C. Jacobson, *The Politics of Congressional Elections* (Boston: Little, Brown, 1987).

23. This explains the recent increase in negative advertising. If negative advertising were to disappear, even fewer challengers would be elected. Because persuasive negative advertising works, finding cases to test this hypothesis empirically is impossible. See Alan Ehrenhalt, "Technology, Strategy Bring New Campaign Era," *Congressional Quarterly Weekly Report*, December 7, 1985, 2559-2565.

24. This argument, advanced by Thomas Mann, got strong empirical confirmation from Gary Jacobson, who demonstrated that incumbents in recent

decades have had to increase their victory margins substantially to achieve the same probability of winning next time. See Thomas Mann, *Unsafe at Any Margin* (Washington, D.C.: American Enterprise Institute for Public Policy Research, 1978); and Gary Jacobson, *The Politics of Congressional Elections*, 2d ed. (Boston: Little, Brown, 1987).

25. Quoted in John F. Bibby, ed., *Congress off the Record* (Washington, D.C.: American Enterprise Institute for Public Policy Research, 1983), 43.
26. Among the most important of the many discussions of these developments are David Mayhew, *Congress: The Electoral Connection* (New Haven: Yale University Press, 1974); and Bruce Cain, John Ferejohn, and Morris Fiorina, *The Personal Vote: Constituency Service and Electoral Independence* (Cambridge, Mass.: Harvard University Press, 1987).
27. A point made by David Adamany, "Political Parties in the 1980s," in *Money and Politics*, ed. Michael Malbin (Chatham, N.J.: Chatham House, 1984), 110.
28. Chubb, "Institutions, the Economy, and the Dynamics of State Elections."
29. Alan Rosenthal, "And So They Leave: Legislative Turnover in the States," *State Government* 47 (1974): 148-152; and Richard Niemi and L. R. Winsky, "Membership Turnover in State Legislatures: Trends and Effects of Redistricting," *Legislative Studies Quarterly* 12 (1987): 115-124.
30. Jerry Calvert, "Revolving Doors: Volunteerism in State Legislatures," *State Government* 52 (1979): 174-181; Charles M. Tidmarch, Edward Lonergan, and John Sciortino, "Interparty Competition in the U.S. States: Legislative Elections, 1970-1978," *Legislative Studies Quarterly* 11 (June 1986): 353-374; Lucinda Simon, "The Mighty Incumbent," *State Legislatures* 18 (July 1986): 31-34; and Keith E. Hamm and David E. Olson, "The Value of Incumbency in Legislative Elections: Evidence from the 1982-1986 Elections in Five States" (Paper delivered at the annual meeting of the American Political Science Association, Chicago, September 3-6, 1987).
31. Some examples: In 1986, 75 percent of the candidates for the Massachusetts house, 73 percent of the candidates for the Tennessee senate, 72 percent of the candidates for the Georgia house, and 58 percent of the candidates for the New Hampshire senate ran unopposed. Tidmarch, Lonergan, and Sciortino found fourteen states in which at least one-third of the House seats were uncontested in 1978. See Tidmarch, Lonergan, and Sciortino, "Interparty Competition in the U.S. Senate," 366-369.
32. Jewell and Olson, *American State Political Parties and Elections*, 3d ed., 216.
33. See Bruce B. Mason, "Arizona: Interest Groups in a Changing State," *Interest Group Politics in the American West*, ed. Ronald J. Hrebenar and Clive S. Thomas (Salt Lake City: University of Utah Press, 1987), 28; Charles W. Wiggins and Keith E. Hamm, "Iowa: Interest Group Politics in an Undistinguished Place" (Paper delivered at the annual meeting of the Midwest Political Science Association, Chicago, April 9-11, 1987); Allan J. Cigler and Dwight Kiel, "Interest Groups in Kansas: Representation in Transition" (Paper delivered at the annual meeting of the Midwest Political Science Association, Chicago, April 9-11, 1987); and Greg Casey and James D. King, "Interest Groups in Missouri: From Establishment Elite to Classic Pluralism,"

in *Interest Group Politics in the Midwestern States*, eds. Ronald J. Hrebenar and Clive S. Thomas (forthcoming).

34. See Campbell, "Presidential Coattails and Midterm Losses in State Legislative Elections"; Chubb, "Institutions, the Economy, and the Dynamics of State Elections"; and Thomas M. Holbrook-Provow, "National Factors in Gubernatorial Elections," *American Politics Quarterly* 15 (1987): 471-484.

35. Stephen A. Salmore and Barbara G. Salmore, "Congressionalization of State Legislative Politics: The Case of New Jersey" (Paper delivered at the annual meeting of the American Political Science Association, Chicago, September 3-6, 1987).

36. Herbert E. Alexander, *Reform and Reality: The Financing of State and Local Campaigns* (New York: Twentieth Century Fund Press, 1991).

37. Robert H. Salisbury and Kenneth A. Shepsle, "U.S. Congressman as Enterprise," *Legislative Studies Quarterly* 6 (1981): 559-576; and Burdett Loomis and Elizabeth H. Paddock, "The Congressional Enterprise as Campaign" (Paper delivered at the annual meeting of the Midwest Political Science Association, Chicago, April 9-11, 1987).

38. The most eminent members of the school arguing that the state parties are more consequential are Cornelius Cotter, John Bibby, Robert Huckshorn, and James Gibson, who have published numerous works on the subject. The fullest explication of their views is Cotter, et al., *Party Organizations in American Politics* (New York: Praeger, 1984). The data presented here on party budgets come from this study, 39n, 88-89. The other major study of the role of state parties is considerably more restrained in its conclusions. See Advisory Commission on Intergovernmental Relations, *The Transformation of American Politics: Implications for Federalism* (Washington, D.C.: Advisory Commission on Intergovernmental Relations, 1986), Chapter 4.

39. Malcolm E. Jewell, "A Survey of Campaign Fundraising by Legislative Parties," *Comparative State Politics Newsletter* 7 (1986): 9-13.

40. Tom Loftus, "The New 'Political Parties' in State Legislatures," *State Government* 58 (1985): 109-110.

41. Quoted in *State Legislatures* 13 (November/December 1981): 26.

42. Ibid.

43. William H. Hedrick and L. Harmon Ziegler, "Oregon: The Politics of Power," in *Interest Groups in the American West*, 106.

44. Loftus, "The New 'Political Parties' in State Legislatures," 108-109.

45. For a survey of this subject, see David Mayhew, *Placing Parties in American Politics* (Princeton, N.J.: Princeton University Press, 1987).

46. Elizabeth Kolbert and Mark Uhlig, "Albany's Discreet Budget: A Tool for Political Ends," *New York Times*, July 14, 1987; and Ronald Sullivan, "Judge Retains 400 Charges for the Trial of Ohrenstein," *New York Times*, June 16, 1988.

47. Private communication, fall 1987. In the fall of 1987, the student fellows of the Eagleton Institute of Politics at Rutgers University conducted interviews with legislative officeholders, legislative partisan staff, lobbyists, and reporters in several states. This quote and others that follow come from interviews with persons who did not wish to be quoted with attribution.

48. However, in another example of the endless ingenuity of campaign fund-

raisers, this "PAC problem" can be bypassed. Company employees give donations of less than $20 (the limit for unidentified contributions) to a person designated as a "conduit," who then contributes the pooled money as an individual instead of as a PAC donation.

49. Frank J. Sorauf, *Money in American Politics* (Glenview, Ill.: Scott, Foresman, 1988), 264, 280.
50. Private communication, fall 1987.
51. Alexander, *Reform and Reality*, 8.
52. The "challenge primary" law provides that a candidate who loses at the convention but gets at least 20 percent of the delegates' votes can call for a primary. Candidates rarely do. In 1986, the minority Republicans decided to switch to an open primary for governor in the hope of stimulating more public interest in their party.
53. Private communication, fall 1987.
54. They also approved a competing measure with campaign spending limits and partial public financing of legislative campaigns at the same time. However, because this more restrictive measure won by a narrower margin, state law made it subordinate to the more widely approved measure. See *New York Times*, June 9, 1988. For the earlier discussions that led to the ballot proposals, see California Commission on Campaign Financing, *The New Gold Rush* (Sacramento: California Commission on Campaign Financing, 1985). A portion of this study is reprinted in *California Journal*, December 1985, 511-514.
55. Ronald Elving, "National Drive to Limit Terms Casts Shadow over Congress," *Congressional Quarterly Weekly Report*, October 26, 1991, 3101-3105.
56. See Alan Ehrenhalt, *The United States of Ambition: Politicians, Power, and the Pursuit of Office* (New York: Random House, 1991).
57. Cain, Ferejohn, and Fiorina, *The Personal Vote*, 229.

5 ▬▬▬

Being Governor

Thad L. Beyle

Since the 1960s, state government and politics have been in a state of change. Reform has been most apparent in the governorships of the fifty states. Individually, governors have been strengthened and have become the key political and governmental leaders in their states. As a group, they have worked to solidify their position within the federal system but now find their roles within their states so compelling and difficult, especially with the federal government on retreat from domestic matters, that they have little time to spend on national concerns.

This change in the governorships has had ramifications in other areas of the states' political and governmental policy systems. Conflicts have grown between the governors and certain actors in the executive branches, as well as between the governors and stronger state legislatures. The state supreme courts have become players in the political process, often serving as umpire and as part of the conflict in some states.

Making the governorship stronger and having great challenges to face made the position more attractive. The type of politics used to seek the office, and the kind of person interested in running for it, has changed. Dollar and consultant politics have replaced party leader and factional politics in many states.

With the political changes in the governorship came a change in the presidential recruitment process. In each of the four presidential elections from 1976 to 1988, at least one of the major party candidates served as governor and two became president. Entrants in the 1992 presidential selection process included governors, former governors, and former gubernatorial candidates.

Two basic cycles have a considerable impact on the states in the federal system and on the governors within the states and in the federal system. The first is the cycle of values undergirding the development of American government—representation, neutral competence, and executive leadership. The second is the cycle of leadership, which oscillates between the state and national levels—the shifting locus of activism within the federal system to provide government services.

Tensions between the values of representation, neutral competence, and executive leadership affect governors within their own state governmental systems. Shifting policy activism affects the governors within the federal system as responsibilities for various governmental services are transferred, in subtle and not so subtle ways, from states to the national government and, more recently, back to the states. These two cycles provide the setting in which states and governors function.

Governors as Chief Executive Officers

The office of governor has developed significantly since the establishment of colonial governments in America. After an initial period of imposed executive dominance, the new state constitutions promoted the value of representation. Legislatures reigned supreme, with governors often serving as mere figureheads. By 1800, the situation began to change as the power and prestige of governors gradually increased. However, the direct election of a number of other state administrative officers was an important legacy of the pursuit of representation.

Following the Civil War, and in reaction to the excesses of achieving representation, the value of neutral competence gained in stature. The goal was to remove favoritism and patronage from government, substituting neutrality or the concept of "not who you know, but what you know." This movement fostered the establishment of independent boards and commissions that diluted gubernatorial power. During this period, the drive for a civil service or merit system was launched. Thus, the goal of attaining neutral competence in government was added to the goal of representation. Thousands of state merit service employees were not only insulated from the winds of politics, but also from management by the governor. In the twentieth century, the need for strong executive leadership emerged. New Jersey governor Woodrow Wilson (D, 1911-1913) championed the cause, along with several other strong governors—Charles Evans Hughes (R, 1907-1910) in New York, Robert La Follette (R, 1901-1906) in Wisconsin, Hiram Johnson (R, Prog., 1911-1917) in California, and Frank Lowden (R, 1917-1921) in Illinois.

The stature of governors has increased greatly across the states and in the federal system over the last few decades because of historical reforms, the type of individuals holding office, the actions taken under their direction, and an increased capacity in the office. Governors now are compared with private sector corporate leaders; they are public sector, state-level chief executive officers (CEOs). Expectations for gubernatorial performance have increased, perhaps beyond realistic levels.

Enhanced Capacity

Governors are responsible for running large enterprises that are similar in scope to Fortune 500 companies. For example, when the 1990 general revenues of the states are compared with the sales of the nation's largest companies, eighteen states rank with the top fifty corporations and thirty have revenues equal to or greater than the top one hundred.[1]

The magnitude of the dollar decisions made by California and New York governors and legislators is comparable to those made by executives at Ford Motor Company, IBM, and Mobil Oil, the third, fourth, and fifth largest companies, respectively; those by Texas governmental leaders, to management at Chrysler and Amoco, the eleventh and twelfth largest companies; those by Ohio and Pennsylvania, to Boeing and Shell Oil, the thirteenth and fourteenth largest companies; those by Michigan, Illinois, and Florida, to Procter and Gamble and Occidental Petroleum, the fifteenth and sixteenth largest companies; and those by New Jersey, to United Technologies, the seventeenth largest company. Other states in range of the top fifty corporations were Georgia, Indiana, Maryland, Massachusetts, Minnesota, North Carolina, Virginia, Washington, and Wisconsin.

Do the governors have adequate executive tools to manage such large enterprises? Are they as prepared to be the CEOs of their states as their private sector counterparts are to run businesses? Do the offices of the governors have the necessary capacity to assist the governors in managing their enterprises in state government?[2] Certainly, progress has been made. Since the early 1960s, no shortage of reforms has taken place throughout the states. The agenda for these reforms was drawn from changes at the national level initiated by the president and from a series of reports calling for reform in state governments.[3]

The general goals of government reforms have been to enhance gubernatorial and legislative abilities to lead the states in more progressive directions. In 1967, former North Carolina governor Terry Sanford called upon the states "to make the chief executive of the state the chief executive in fact"; and a decade later political scientist Larry J. Sabato declared that executive branch reforms had made the governors "truly the masters" of state government.[4]

One common reform put in place is longer terms of office. Since 1955, the number of governors eligible for four-year terms instead of two-year terms increased from twenty-nine to forty-seven. This change allows governors to spend more time on policy and administrative concerns and less on reelection campaigns.[5] By 1992, only New Hampshire, Rhode Island, and Vermont still restricted their governors to a two-year term.

Another reform increased opportunities for succession. Since 1955, the number of governors precluded from succeeding themselves after a single term declined from seventeen to two—Kentucky and Virginia. Meanwhile, states allowing a governor to serve two consecutive terms increased from six to twenty-nine. Sixteen states in 1992 had no restrictions on the number of terms a governor could serve, although a movement to impose term limits was spreading throughout the country. Changes in succession ability potentially allow a governor a longer time to spend on policy and administrative concerns—if the voters decide to return the governor to office. Lifting term limitations also allows voters to retain a governor who is doing a good job.[6]

Yet another reform shortens the ballot. In 1956, 709 separately elected state level officials, beside the governor, headed 385 state agencies. In 1990, 481 separately elected officials, other than the governor, headed 277 state agencies.[7] Fewer elective offices, and thus more appointed offices, gives the governor a broader policy and administrative reach and gives the citizens a governor who is more in charge of the executive branch of state government. However, the numbers indicate more modifications are needed to reduce the still large number of separately elected officials.

And the final reform is the veto. Between 1956 and 1988, the number of governors who could veto all legislation rose from forty-seven to forty-nine. Only the governor of North Carolina lacks the veto power, and while continuing attempts have been made to change this, they have been stalled by partisan and separation-of-powers fights. The number of governors with an item veto rose from thirty-nine to forty-three; and ten governors now have the power to cut individual appropriations items. Eighteen other governors have the power to veto the language in appropriations bills.[8]

Governors' offices have expanded rapidly over the past decades. In 1956, political scientist Coleman B. Ransone, Jr., reported governors' offices averaging 11 staff members, with a range from 3 to 43 among the states.[9] In 1976, the National Governors' Association (NGA) found an average of 29 staff members, with a much broader range from 7 to 245.[10] The most recent survey, taken in 1990, indicated slightly more than 50 staff members per governor's office, with a range from 8 in Wyoming to 216 in New York.[11] Thus over this thirty-four-year period, the average number of gubernatorial staff members grew nearly fivefold. More staff means more flexibility and support for the governor in the many roles to be fulfilled. Growth also creates more patronage positions—and a greater chance for confusion.

The configurations of gubernatorial staffs can be classified from the very personal to the very institutional. Their makeup correlates closely with the size of the state. Larger states have larger and more institutionalized offices and processes, with adequate and specialized staff resources to assist the governor. Smaller states have smaller and more personalized offices, often lacking the breadth and depth possessed by the larger offices. In the smaller offices, the governor must rely on the same people to cover the necessary responsibilities—and more. In between are the growing mid-size states, in which the governors may feel the need for an institutionalized office but often have only small, personalized staffing structures and processes.[12]

The budget process, as an expression of gubernatorial authority, is critical. A chief executive must be able to control the development and execution of the state's budget. Only six governors lack the power to develop an executive budget for submission to the legislature; and the governors of South Carolina and Texas must share that responsibility with a joint legislative-administrative committee.[13] Mississippi's governor obtained the right through legislation passed in 1984; North Carolina's governor gained the responsibility via a 1982 state supreme court decision based on the separation-of-powers clause in the state constitution.

Governors consolidated their power over the budget process by placing state budget offices under their direct control. With that, the budgetary process often was changed from an earlier preoccupation "with the custodial functions of auditing and accounting to undertaking new and conceptually rich systems of management decision making." [14] The budget and the budgetary process still are methods of financial control used by the governors. But, as the budget process has been opened to include planning and policy analysis approaches, the management capability of governors has been greatly enhanced, and the budget can more nearly approximate being "the ultimate statement of any government's (and governor's) policy choices." [15]

The policy-planning process also is critical. Initially seen as part of the economic development function of state government and located in those departments, state planning agencies have been migrating closer to the governor. In 1960, only three of the thirty-seven state planning agencies were located in the governor's office and two others were housed in departments of administration and finance. By 1971, all fifty states had state planning agencies. Twenty-nine were in the governor's office and seven were in departments of administration or finance.[16]

Since the 1970s, many of these agencies became policy-planning offices and took on a broader set of activities and responsibilities. By 1988, all but five states had policy-planning offices to assist the governor. In forty states, these offices were located either in the governor's office or with the budget office in the department of administration or finance. The stronger the governorship, the more likely the policy-planning agency is to stand free of the budget agency and process. This suggests that these agencies are closely tied to the governor and the governor's position within the state governmental system.[17]

What do these offices accomplish? A 1985 Council of State Planning Agencies survey indicated they have two major responsibilities that vary in emphasis from state to state—policy development and administration.[18] The goal is to have the policy-planning offices increase the possibility that factors other than protective agency perspectives and purely budgetary or political concerns be brought to bear in the policy process.

But, in the 1990s, the governor's budgetary power has been the engine of gubernatorial policy politics. In almost every state, the impact of the recession, changes in the economy, and a declining federal government presence in domestic affairs caused severe budgetary woes as state revenues fell and need for state governmental actions rose. While hard to quantify, most decisions now being made by state leaders have at their base the realities of state budgetary shortfalls; other issues and perspectives have had to take a back seat to the need to balance the state budgets and keep necessary programs and services going. Raising taxes and cutting back governmental programs are the main agenda items for most of the governors. Sophisticated policy analyses have been put aside because of the continual need to make massive and quick changes in the state budget.

The ability to reorganize government is important to the governor. In the 1960s, many reformers argued that the residue of past trends and decisions left state governments unmanageable and unresponsive to gubernatorial direction. However, since 1965, the executive branches of nearly two dozen state governments underwent comprehensive reorganization, and nearly all states engaged in partial reorganizations. In comprehensive reorganizations, the executive branch is consolidated to various degrees under the control of the governor. Most partial reorganizations bring many programs and agencies working in the same functional area under one departmental roof. Such reforms have been most prevalent in economic development, environmental protection, transportation, and human services.[19]

In 1956, only two governors had the power to initiate state government reorganization by executive order subject to legislative confirmation; by 1990, twenty-two governors had this power.[20] Reorganization enables a governor to reshape the executive branch for a variety of reasons, which include providing a clearer focus on particular problems and delivering governmental services efficiently.

Additional steps can be taken to allow governors to make state governments more focused and responsive. Several states still need comprehensive reorganization, fewer separately elected officials, and governors able to initiate reorganization subject to confirmation by the legislature.

Appointing and Removing Personnel

Chief executive officers, whether in the private or public sector, must be free to chose those who will serve in their administration. The power of appointment is a dual power, for it also includes the power to remove.

Many governors are constrained by the number and types of positions to which they can make appointments, as indicated by the data in Table 5-1. The table excludes one set of positions that governors have little or no appointment powers over—statewide elected boards and commissions. However, it does include between twenty-eight and forty-seven of the major offices in the states classified in *The Book of the States, 1986-1987*. The number of offices among the states varies because some offices fulfill several different functions.

First, governors cannot appoint any of the 204 members of the forty-three separately elected boards and commissions in twenty-eight states. These boards are charged with responsibilities in public education (ten states), public utilities (nine states), higher education (five states), and various regulatory activities.[21]

Second, governors cannot appoint separately elected officials to another office, unless they fill a vacancy created by death or resignation. These officials have their own constitutional base of authority and their own constituency of supporters. On average, six statewide elected officials per state are elected separately, including the governor, or an average of 14 percent of these statewide offices. The range is from only one statewide elected official—the governor in Maine and New Jersey—to ten in North Carolina and North Dakota.[22]

Third, governors cannot appoint officials who by the constitution are to be appointed by some other officer or by the legislature. On average, seventeen such appointments are made per state, or 41 percent of the offices involved. The range is from a low of one in New York to a high of twenty-eight in Oregon.

Some argue that this constraint is less than it seems, as the officials making the appointments are the governor's own appointees. Thus, a two-step appointment process is at work. This may be true in some states, but in Texas, for example, boards and commissions in effect run most of state government. The governor appoints members of Texas's boards and commissions, but, because of the staggered terms of these members, a governor may be well into a second term before gaining some control, and then only indirectly through the newly appointed members.[23] However, Gov. Ann Richards, elected in 1990, was able to get the legislature in 1991 to provide her with more executive power by adding some important appointments to the governorship—education, health and human services, and highways—and by giving the governor control over several others—the departments

Table 5-1   Selection Methods for Selected State Administrative Officials

Classification of state	Separately elected		Appointed by governor		Appointed, not by governor	
	Number	Percentage	Number	Percentage	Number	Percentage
High	11 (North Dakota)	29.7 (North Dakota)	32 (Virginia)	82.1 (New York)	28 (Oregon)	65 (South Carolina)
Low	1 (Maine, New Hampshire, and New Jersey)	2.4 (New Jersey)	5 (South Carolina)	12.5 (South Carolina)	1 (New York)	3.6 (New York)
Average	6	14.5	18.5	44.5	17	41

Source: Washington Research Council, *The Power to Govern: The Reorganization of Washington State Government* (Olympia: Washington Research Council, February 1987), 5; Council of State Governments, *The Book of the States, 1986-1987* (Lexington, Ky.: Council of State Governments, 1986), 51-57.

Note: All fifty states were included in the study.

of commerce and housing and community affairs, and the film and arts commission.[24]

The data presented in Table 5-1 thus indicate that the governors may appoint between eighteen and nineteen state administrative officials on average, or about 45 percent of the offices involved. South Carolina's governor has the fewest with five, Virginia's the most with thirty-two.

Practical, political restrictions on the governors appointment powers also exist:[25]

• The sheer number of appointments governors must make can be so overwhelming that governors fail to focus sufficiently on the key appointments. Replacing too many people angers those being replaced and can draw the governor too deeply into the bureaucracy for any policy or administrative benefits.

• Patronage appointments serve as rewards, but many individuals and groups feel they should be rewarded. Appointments are evaluated with a jealous eye, and jealousy is not a positive basis on which to build a working relationship.

• The governor and those interested in a position often have conflicting expectations that can lead to struggles within the governor's coalition.

The governor's power of appointment did not change dramatically from 1960 to 1986 (see Table 5-2). In 1986, Carol Weissert issued a study based on fifteen offices—those for which data were available from three other studies conducted in 1960, 1968, and 1980.[26] Those offices were administration and finance, agriculture, attorney general, auditor, budget,

Table 5-2 A Comparative Index of Governors' Appointment Power, 1960-1986

Classification of appointment power	1960	1968	1980	1986
Very strong	17	11	19	18
Strong	9	6	6	9
Moderate	7	9	10	9
Weak	6	7	6	6
Very weak	11	17	9	8
Average[a]	45.2	41.8	46.0	46.9

Sources: Data developed from Council of State Governments, *The Book of the States, 1960-1961* (Lexington, Ky.: Council of State Governments, 1960); *The Book of the States, 1968-1969* (1968); *The Book of the States, 1980-1981* (1980); *The Book of the States, 1986-1987* (1986); Joseph A. Schlesinger, "The Politics of the Executive," in *Politics in the American States,* ed. Herbert Jacob and Kenneth N. Vines (Boston: Little, Brown, 1971), 210-237; Thad L. Beyle, "Governors," in *Politics in the American States,* 4th ed., ed. Virginia Gray, Herbert Jacob, and Kenneth N. Vines (Boston: Little, Brown, 1983), 201-203, 458-459; and Thad L. Beyle, "Governors," in *Politics in the American States,* 5th ed., ed. Virginia Gray, Herbert Jacob, and Robert B. Albritton (Glencoe, Ill.: Scott, Foresman, 1990), 220-221, 569.

Note: All fifty states were included in the study. Figures represent the number of states.

[a]Based on scores ranging from 0 to 75.

conservation, education, health, highways, insurance, labor, secretary of state, tax commissioner, treasurer, and welfare. The governors' average power of appointment increased slightly, from 45.2 to 46.9. The number of governors with strong or very strong appointment powers increased from twenty-six to twenty-seven; those with weak or very weak powers decreased from seventeen to fourteen.

Coupled with the power of appointment is the power of removal. Sometimes when positions are filled, officeholders must be removed. If changes in policy are needed, people often must be replaced with those who will carry out the proposed reforms. In most situations, key people will resign their office as the new administration comes in. But conflicts arise when resignations are not forthcoming or a change in priorities with the new administration occurs that elevates previously unimportant positions to importance and creates the need to have new people in them.

Only twenty-three state constitutions provide governors with the power to remove individuals from positions in the state executive branch, and all but six put varying degrees of restrictions on this power. The governor of Indiana has unrestricted power of removal under a state court decision, while the governor of Georgia is greatly restrained by a state court decision. The power of removal is contained in the original constitutions of five states. Eleven of the fourteen states that revised their constitutions after 1945 included this power for the governor. Only the new constitutions of Connecticut (1965), North Carolina (1971), and Georgia (1982) did not. As the original constitutions of the states are being revised, the power of removal is being built in. Other states provide statutory removal powers for their governors.

Governors do experience problems exercising their right to remove personnel. Thus, "even when a governor can remove an official, he is constrained by the wrangle which would result." [27] It is a power, therefore, that tends to be used only as a last resort. Moreover, a series of federal court decisions placed potentially severe restrictions on the removal power. In a 1976 case, *Elrod v. Burns*, the U.S. Supreme Court decided (5 to 4) that a patronage firing violates an individual's political liberties under the First Amendment. The ruling said that "political belief and association constitute the core of those activities protected by the First Amendment of the U.S. Constitution." [28]

This strict standard was relaxed in two subsequent decisions. In a 1980 case, *Branti v. Finkel*, the Supreme Court reaffirmed (6 to 3) its 1976 decision but also ruled that "If the employee's private political beliefs would interfere with the discharge of his public duties, the First Amendment rights may be required to yield to the state's vital interest in maintaining governmental effectiveness and efficiency." The burden of proof would be on the employer.[29] In a 1983 case, *Connick v. Myers*, the Supreme Court decided (5 to 4) to add another restriction on the employee's right by holding "that the First Amendment does not protect from dismissal public employees who complain about their working conditions or their supervisor." [30] In these cases, the Court indicated a balance was needed between an individual's rights and the administration's needs, and the Supreme Court's role was to weigh those conflicts.

Although none of the Supreme Court cases involved them, governors were aware of the problems the decisions could cause and, at the 1982 "New Governors' Seminar," sponsored by the National Governors' Association, the newly elected governors were cautioned:

> Know the *Elrod v. Burns* case, the 1976 five-to-four Supreme Court decision regarding the firing of personnel. You cannot fire for a political reason, and you are personally liable. It even destroys the privacy privilege of counsel.

> The *Elrod v. Burns* decision requires an indemnification statute, and be sure that it covers the unpaid boards and commissions as well as full-time state officials.[31]

In 1990, the Supreme Court handed down a ruling (5 to 4) in *Rutan et al. v. Republican Party of Illinois* that directly affected the removal powers of governors. The decision, which focused on the patronage process of the Illinois governor's office in the James R. Thompson administration (R, 1977-1991), said that state and local governments violate an individual's "First amendment rights when they refuse to hire, promote or transfer ... [an employee] on the basis of their political affiliation or party activity." [32]

The decision on how Thompson handled " 'blue-collar' patronage— the conventional doling out of state jobs to the party faithful"—struck down the "hiring freezes Thompson imposed, more or less continuously throughout his tenure ... [as] merely patronage tools used to ensure that worthy Republicans got available state jobs." Thompson found the decision ironic as he had been chided by Republican party leaders in the state for not being "grateful enough to those who labored in the GOP vineyards." Thompson, at the end of his tenure in office, said "the Supreme Court of the United States certifies what these Republican chairmen refused to believe all along—that I had the best patronage machine in the nation, that it was a Republican machine." [33]

Gubernatorial Powers

Political scientists often have attempted to compare the powers of the fifty state governorships. Research results are presented in a series of comparative indices and analyses, which in turn are followed by critiques of the indices and rejoinders to these critiques. The first such comparative gubernatorial power index was published by Joseph A. Schlesinger in 1965; it has served as the foundation of subsequent academic efforts. [34]

A question persists as to whether these academic pursuits and counter suits have any meaning in the real world of governors. An answer to this question may not exist, but in 1987 the NGA Office of State Services issued a *State Management Note* in which the same questions pertaining to the comparative institutional powers of the governors were addressed.

NGA concluded that "the framework in which a Governor performs his or her job can be an important factor in a successful governorship." NGA noted that the indices were used only as a suggestion of the framework and that some "governors have proven to be vital and strong leaders in many areas despite institutional shortcomings that may hamper their success," while other governors "have failed to provide strong leadership to their states even where formal provisions indicate an authoritative office." [35]

The NGA analysis included six items: the governor's tenure potential, appointment powers, budget-making power, veto power, political strength in the legislature, and the legislature's ability to change gubernatorial budgets. The first three indices primarily concern the governor's power within the executive branch, while the second three concern the governor's power vis-à-vis the legislature. [36] For this presentation, the NGA comparisons have been updated to 1989. [37]

The powers of governors grew from 1965 to 1989 (see Table 5-3).

Table 5-3   The Institutionalized Powers of Governors, 1965-1989

Power	Range of scores possible	1965 average	1989 average	Change in scores	Percentage change in scores
Tenure potential	1-5	3.3	4.2	+.9	27
Appointment	0-7	3.6	4.2	+.6	17
Budget making	0-5	4.3	4.8	+.5	12
Legislative budget-changing authority	1-5	1.3	1.2	−.1	8
Veto	0-5	4.2	4.4	+.2	5
Party control	1-5	3.8	3.1	−.7	18
Summary measure of institutionalized powers	3-32	20.7	21.9	+1.2	9

Sources: Office of State Services, "The Institutionalized Powers of the Governorship: 1965-1985," *State Management Note* (Washington, D.C.: National Governors' Association, 1987); and Thad L. Beyle, "Governors," in *Politics in the American States*, 5th ed., ed. Virginia Gray, Herbert Jacob, and Robert B. Albritton (Glenview, Ill.: Scott, Foresman, 1990), 217-230, 568-574.

Although the overall growth was not great (1.4 points or 7 percent), a considerable differential in the growth of powers occurred. Those powers primarily aimed at gubernatorial performance in the executive branch increased—tenure, appointment, and budget making—and gubernatorial veto powers also grew. However, the other powers aimed at gubernatorial-legislative relations decreased—party control and legislative budget-changing authority.

The findings demonstrate what many have suggested: Reforms have been made on both sides of the separation-of-powers relationship, and while governors may have more institutionalized powers at their disposal, state legislatures have increased powers that often are used at the expense of the executive.

How has the power of governors in individual states fared from 1965 to 1989? To determine this, the scores of each state were totaled and divided into five separate categories: very strong, strong, moderate, weak, and very weak. The range on the scale was from the highest at 29 to the lowest at 14/15. Sixteen states remained in the same power categories between 1965 and 1989,[38] two states moved up three categories,[39] two moved up two categories,[40] and fifteen advanced by one category.[41] Moving downward in power by two categories were four states,[42] while eleven states dropped one category.[43]

Governorships in the Midwest gained the most power (12 percent), followed by those states that had less than 40 percent of their population in metropolitan areas (11.7 percent). The Pacific West states lost the most power (13.6 percent). Other states gaining more than 10 percent above the average were those in which the per capita income was between

$12,000 and $13,500, up 5.7 percent; New England states, up 5.1 percent; and states with a Republican majority, up 5.1 percent.

The only variable that appears to be directly related to changes in institutional power is the percentage of the state's population living in metropolitan areas. The lower the percentage, the greater the change. However, those states with more people living in metropolitan areas already had provided their governors with more institutionalized powers by 1965, which indicates that the more rural states played catch-up and made their governors more powerful.

A major cause of the decline in gubernatorial power indices vis-à-vis the legislature is the increasing number of divided governments in the states. Since World War II, the power of the political parties in the states has declined. Nowhere is this more apparent than in the diminishing number of states having both the governorship and the legislature controlled by the same party.[44] More states have a politically divided government, or "powersplit," in which the governor faces a legislature controlled either totally or in part by the opposition part.[45]

In 1954, nine of the then forty-eight states (19 percent) had a politically divided state government, mainly in states outside the South. By 1966, when these comparative measures of gubernatorial power were first published, only thirteen of the fifty states (26 percent) were divided politically, again mainly outside the South. Since the mid-1980s, about three-fifths of the states had powersplits—thirty states following the 1991 elections. The 1990 election of two independent candidates as governor in Alaska and Connecticut are most extreme examples of this trend.

What the powersplit means is that as the reformers were successfully changing and enhancing institutions at the state level, the growing malaise in the political parties was undermining the ability of certain key state level actors to do what the reformers hoped for and the ability of the political science measures to determine the extent of institutional powers.

Gubernatorial Conflict with Other State Government Actors

Political reforms do not always achieve their intended purposes. Some create unanticipated consequences that then generate additional reforms; others create conflict with previous reforms. And politics may render some reforms unworkable.

Conflicts within the Executive Branch

Governors often face their greatest conflicts within the executive branch. Several governors have had serious problems with the lieutenant governor's power while the governor is out of state. Specific issues have arisen over calling special legislative sessions, appointments to administrative and judicial positions, pardons, the governor's salary, and control of the national guard. Other problems come about when the governor and the lieutenant governor are of different parties or of different factions within the same party; or when the lieutenant governor has constitutional leadership responsibilities in the legislature that provide a separate power base.

Governors also have found themselves at odds with the state's attorney general when legal issues take on a political cast. An attorney general may challenge a gubernatorial action in court on constitutional grounds. Who is to serve as the governor's legal adviser in a legal battle when the attorney general is not on the governor's side? Who is to lead the prosecution of a governor for wrongdoing? The problem arose during Arizona's impeachment of Gov. Evan Mecham (R, 1987-1988).

Finally, governors must face other statewide elected officials who intend to seek the governorship, some even to challenge the incumbent for reelection. In such a milieu, conflict instead of cooperation often is the rule.

Conflicts with Other Branches of Governments

With the concept of "separation of powers" built into most state constitutions and the American constitutional system, conflict between the executive and the legislative branches is inevitable. Conflicts may occur over setting state government policy, raising and spending money, administering policy, appointing officials to executive and judicial positions, controlling the legislative process, and calling special sessions. And when the governor and the legislature are of opposite parties, conflict can take on a divisive partisan tone.

Gubernatorial-legislative tensions are greatest in most states at budget time, when the money and policy decisions must be made. It is the "governor's budget," but the legislature has to pass it; and it must be balanced. Dollar decisions became particularly difficult to make in the harsh economic times of the 1990s. The budget makers faced declining resources coupled with increasing demands for help and services. But, contrary to what many observers might have thought, more cooperation than usual has existed between the two branches in some states in getting a workable budget passed and signed into law.

California governor Pete Wilson (R, 1991-—) received high marks from both the media and the Democratic leadership of the state legislature for his efforts to reconcile the $14 billion deficit the state faced in 1991.[46] Massachusetts governor William F. Weld (R, 1991-—) was likewise commended for his role in dealing with the state's dire fiscal situation.[47] And, despite his need to use the veto to keep the Connecticut legislature "on task" for a state income tax, Gov. Lowell P. Weicker, Jr.,

(I, 1991-—) was able to achieve his goal without any members of his A Connecticut Party in the legislature (not counting the lieutenant governor, who presides over the state senate).[48]

The "execution" of the budget by the governor leads to a second area of potential conflict—the legislature's interest in how its actions are administered. Legislatures have tried several ways to make sure "legislative intent" is followed. Governors often read these efforts as legislative intrusion into executive branch responsibilities. For example, some executive branch positions are appointments that, constitutionally, must be confirmed by the legislature. However, in some states, legislatures have either constitutional or statutory authority to make appointments. In certain cases, they can appoint legislators to boards, commissions, or councils in the executive branch. If these bodies remain in an advisory role, problems may not arise. However, if they exercise management responsibilities, as twenty states allowed in the mid-1980s, charges of "legislative intrusion" may be lodged and challenged in state courts as a violation of separation of powers.[49]

Another area of conflict concerns vetoes, both gubernatorial and legislative. In 1947, governors vetoed about 5 percent of the bills presented to them; the vetoes were overridden by a legislative vote in only 1.8 percent of the cases.[50] In 1977-1978, 5.2 percent of the legislation was vetoed by governors; 8.6 percent of the vetoes were overridden. While the frequency of gubernatorial vetoes remained roughly the same, legislative overrides jumped nearly fivefold.[51] As the ability of governors to use the item and amendatory vetoes grows, conflicts with the legislative branch escalate. A governor can veto special policy provisions in budget bills that have not run the full course of legislative review, thereby forcing the legislature to consider the issues in open debate.[52]

State legislatures have turned to the legislative veto—a procedure permitting them "to review proposed executive regulations or actions and to block or modify those with which they disagree."[53] The legislative veto became increasingly popular in the 1970s and into the 1980s, with forty-one states adopting it by mid-1982. However, both federal and state courts have called it an unconstitutional violation of the separation-of-powers concept.[54] Voters in New Jersey (1985), Alaska and Michigan (1986), and Nevada (1988) rejected giving this power to their legislatures.

Conflicts between the executive and legislative branches of state governments increasingly have involved the state courts. They usually decide in favor of the governor and the executive branch, citing the separation-of-powers clause in the state's constitution.[55] However, they sometimes rule against the executive when separation of powers is not at question, as in policy and civil rights issues.

Governors and judges often are at odds over specific decisions, such as the death penalty or the selection and appointment of judges. In 1986, three states had highly contested, negative, policy-related contests for the chief judgeship of the state's supreme court. In all of these races—in California, North Carolina, and Ohio—the incumbent governors were actively involved in judicial politics.

A new area of contention is brewing between the governors and the legislatures on one side and the courts on the other. As governors propose and legislatures adopt state budgets with severe cuts in appropriations, the courts, like all parts of state government, find themselves unable to fulfill their responsibilities with the reduced amounts of available funds. Can the courts force the other two branches to take the necessary monetary actions, including raising taxes, to ensure that the courts receive enough money to operate? According to experiences in fourteen states, yes, they can. In September 1991, the chief judge of New York's State Court of Appeals, that state's highest appellate court, filed suit charging that the governor and the legislature failed to provide the courts with adequate funds—a violation of the state constitution. A decision in favor of the courts is possible as all the earlier suits consistently favored the judiciary.[56]

As governors seek to carry out their responsibilities conflicts arise— conflicts that are built into the charters of state government and exacerbated by political and policy differences.

A Framework of Gubernatorial Legacies

When a governor leaves office, observers, pundits, editorialists, and others begin to define what impact the administration has had on the state and its citizens; that is, they begin to define the governor's legacy. Some, such as Larry J. Sabato and George Weeks, have highlighted governors whose legacies were significant for their state or, in some cases, for other states and the nation as well.[57] The following offers a slightly different perspective on gubernatorial legacies. It not only brings several different categories into the equation, but also provides room for different types of legacies. The major categories are the state context, the political context, the tenure context, the out-of-state impact, and the negative legacy.

The State Context

In some cases the legacy comes with the state; a governor's legacy is closely tied to which state is being governed and when, and not just to the singular performance of a particular governor. In this category are two distinct components: the so-called "mega-states" (California and New York), and those states with a potential for a sea-change in their economy, government, politics, or public policies.

The 'Mega-States.' California and New York are the two largest states in population, have large percentages of votes in the electoral college, and possess governors who likely are considered presidential material.[58] Each state has a large and complex economy and a state government and budget that could be likened to either a separate nation or a major corporation. No other state has the stature of California or New York, not even Texas or Florida, the third and fourth largest states in population, respectively. However, mega-state governors can fritter away the gains afforded them by the status of their states or they may have no interest in pursuing national acclaim.[59]

The Sea-Change States. Some states are considered disadvantaged in societal, economic, political, or public policy terms. They are poor and have suffered tremendously from a lack of strong gubernatorial leadership, among other things, or from strong governors who led them in the wrong direction. These states are ripe for strong, dynamic leadership that will find ways to overcome their disadvantages. They are ready for a sea-change in their way of life and for someone who will navigate them through the change. The tenure of Arkansas governor Winthrop Rockefeller (R, 1969-1971) is an example of one who "exerted a greater—and more beneficial—influence on a single state than any figure of his generation." [60]

The Political Context

In some cases a gubernatorial legacy comes from politics and how the governor relates the campaign to governing. This category contains at least four separate types: governors who use the campaign and its issues to create a mandate for action; governors who take lessons learned from campaigning for office into the administration and establish issue campaigns; governors who are elected by political accident and use the lack of a mandate to their own and the state's benefit; and governors who are political "firsts."

Mandates for Action. Most political consultants and savvy politicians suggest that candidates for governor focus on only a few issues (three to five at most) during the campaign. The issues selected would become the cornerstone of their administrations should they be elected. An agenda with too many issues leads to a lack of focus in the campaign. The question arises, however, whether the candidates should bring their own agenda to the campaign in an attempt to lead and direct the voters or whether they should follow poll results and focus on what people say they want.

With a limited issue agenda undergirding and focusing a campaign, a newly elected governor can argue convincingly to the state legislature and to the state bureaucracy that the voters have provided a mandate for the actions being proposed. Terry Sanford (D-N.C., 1961-1965) and

Lamar Alexander (R-Tenn., 1979-1987) both made education their main policy agenda focus—as candidates and as governors.[61]

Issue Campaigns.   Recently some governors began taking the political approaches used to get elected and applied them to efforts to win approval or policy initiatives in their administration.[62] The techniques meant "going over the heads" of the legislators and directly to the voters, to mobilize public opinion and build support for a specific issue. Citizens then must assist the governor by pressuring individual legislators to act. Governors create issue campaigns when the legislature is unlikely to endorse an administration proposal without strong public support. Governors were most successful in the area of education, a universal issue that affects many citizens.

Issue campaigns work like a regular political campaign; they contain some of the following elements: a campaign organization, a campaign kickoff, a series of campaign speeches, a campaign tour, and a panoply of campaign slogans, endorsements, advertisements, and materials. The goal is not the office, but an issue. Governors used this approach successfully were Jimmy Carter (D-Ga., 1971-1975), Bill Clinton (D-Ark., 1979-1981, 83-—), and Lamar Alexander.[63]

Political Accidents without a Mandate.   Sometimes a person who never has faced the voters as a candidate for governor assumes office. A lieutenant governor, secretary of state, or president pro tempore of the senate, for example, takes over after the death, resignation, or removal from office of the elected governor. Not having campaigned for the office, the new governor comes with few strings attached. The administration begins with a clean slate, and a legacy waits to be created.

Some political accident governors, without a mandate from voters, adopt a caretaker approach. The tenure of Rose Mofford (D-Ariz., 1988-1991), who succeeded impeached governor Evan Mecham (R-Ariz., 1987-1988), is an example.

In a few cases, how they arrived at the governorship was less important than what they did once assuming office. For example, North Carolina governor Luther Hodges (D, 1954-1961) maintained stability in the state during the trying period after the Supreme Court handed down its decision in *Brown v. Board of Education* in 1954.

The Political 'Firsts.'   Some legacies are created because the person, when elected governor, became the first in some category, either in the state or in the nation. Given that most governors have been white males, this category usually applies to the first nonwhite or nonmale to achieve the office.

In 1989, L. Douglas Wilder (D-Va., 1990-—) became the first black elected governor, and since the early 1980s, a number of women became the first woman elected governor in their states. Since the mid-1960s, a series of Republicans first served in the formerly Democratically dominated southern states,[64] and some states saw their first independent governors.[65]

The first women governors can be categorized in at least three ways: (1) The first time a woman was ever elected governor—in the nation (two were elected in 1924[66]) and in each of the fifty states; (2) The women governors who were elected and served as stand-ins for their no-longer-eligible-to-be-governor husbands[67]; and (3) Women, such as Ella T. Grasso (D-Conn., 1975-1980), who actively sought and won the governorship in pursuit of their own political ambitions. Women gubernatorial candidates, as well as women governors, are becoming more commonplace.[68]

The Tenure Context

Another gubernatorial legacy derives from the governor's tenure in office. This category has three classifications: those who served multiple terms; those who were recognized as having done a "good job" while in office, no matter how long their tenure; and those who faced a major problem and handled it well.

Longevity.   Several governors in recent decades have served multiple terms, suggesting, at a minimum, acceptance of their performance by party leaders, party members, and voters. Their longevity also may imply that few, if any, other major potential leaders were on the scene.

With longer tenures, these governors have more time to learn and grow in the job than do most of their peers. Multiple-term governors provide their state with continuity of leadership and are able to follow through on initiatives, evaluate how they work, and make adjustments or shift directions along the way. Republicans representing midwestern states, the most recent being Illinois's James R. Thompson, tend to fall into this category.[69]

The "Good Job" Governors.   Some governors can point to outstanding achievements made during their administration. Their performance is clearly perceived as being much better than average, and they are recognized as being "good governors" by most observers and by their peers. In some cases, the governors also had served two or three terms. George Weeks nominated several governors to his "Hall of Fame"—including Reubin Askew (D-Fla., 1971-1979) and Daniel Evans (R-Wash., 1965-1977)—on the basis of being a good job governor.[70] Another who fits this description is Scott Matheson (D-Utah, 1977-1985).[71]

A defining moment sometimes occurs when the governor's ability and mettle are severely tested and the way the governor reacts sets the tone for the remainder of the term and determines how the governor will be viewed as a public figure. Some pass the test, some do not. For example, Pennsylvania governor Dick Thornburgh (R, 1979-1987) was praised for his handling of the Three Mile Island crisis, which occurred shortly after he took office. Rhode Island governor Bruce Sundlun (D, 1991-—) was faced with a collapsing state banking system and had to take immediate action; the results are not yet in on his effort.[72] And Gov. Edmund G. "Jerry" Brown, Jr., (D, 1975-1983) of California was hurt by perceived inaction in handling the state's Mediterranean fruit fly infestation.

Out-of-State Impact

The legacy of some governors was made not only by what they did within their state, but also for their impact on other states and on the federal system.

The Federal System Governors.   Several governors made their mark "on the inside"; that is, the legacy they created is better known to those who serve in government than to the public in general. Their achievements do not have great "sex appeal" or public notice but had an important impact on how government at one or several levels functions. Weeks cites Evans and Sanford in this regard.[73]

Presidential Governors.   The governorship and individual governors have been important in the more volatile and observable game of presidential politics. During the twentieth century, sixteen men have served as president, six of whom were governors.[74] From 1901 through 1991, former governors occupied the White House for forty-six years (51 percent of the time). If William Howard Taft, who served as provisional governor of the Philippines, were included, the figure would rise to fifty of the ninety-one years (55 percent). Every presidential election of the twentieth century, except during the 1960-1972 period, had a former or incumbent governor as one of the major party candidates (if Taft is included). The governorship in general can be a steppingstone into presidential politics. And successful candidates find their legacies as governors enhanced as they move on to the presidency. The most recent examples are Jimmy Carter and Ronald Reagan (R-Calif., 1967-1975).

All governors who sought the presidency were not able to win their party's nomination or in the general election. But even in losing, some were impressive in their attempts, which often highlighted their successful gubernatorial careers. If nothing else, their performance as governor is a reason for being taken seriously. And their tenure comes under intense scrutiny by their foes and the media, and their legacy is spelled out, good or bad. Two recent examples are Michael S. Dukakis (D-Mass., 1975-1979, 1983-1991), who ran unsuccessfully as the 1988 Democratic candidate, and Nelson A. Rockefeller (R-N.Y., 1959-1973), who sought his party's nomination several times but never received it.

The Negative Legacy

Gubernatorial legacies are not always positive. A governor may leave office in disgrace, having harmed the stature of the state, having served to impede the state's development, having done considerable harm to the governorship, or having damaged the party's ability to win elections in the future. Sometimes the administration's actions prove to be criminal, and the governor ends up in prison. As the result of a negative legacy, a state may be perceived as untrustworthy and corrupt.

Rejection. The negative legacy is clear of a governor who is forced from office or soundly defeated for reelection. For example, Arizona's Evan Mecham became the only governor in recent times to be impeached and removed from office by the state legislature. Also, law enforcement authorities in Tennessee put Lamar Alexander in office early because of serious problems within the Ray Blanton administration (D-Tenn., 1975-1979) in its closing days. Blanton was accused of "selling" pardons, and law enforcement authorities feared he would pardon James Earl Ray, the assassin of Martin Luther King, Jr. Blanton later was indicted on a range of charges, convicted, and served time in prison.[75]

Several governors served their states well for several terms, then were discredited for doing something illegal or apparently unethical. Long tenures can make governors feel immune to political defeat or cause them to relax their standards of behavior.

Edwin Edwards (D-La., 1972-1980, 1984-1988, 1992-—) has been one of the most flamboyant public figures at the state level over the past few decades. His style of laissez les bon temps rouler ("let the good times roll") was legendary both within and outside Louisiana. He successfully fought off indictments of fraud and racketeering in two separate trials during his 1984-1988 term in office but was crippled by the notoriety and lost his 1987 reelection bid. In Louisiana's unique open primary-general election process, he received only 28 percent of the vote in the primary after winning the office in 1983 with 62 percent of the general election vote.[76] But, in a highly publicized 1991 comeback, Edwards was able to beat back the charges launched against him by his opponent, state senator and ex-Ku Klu Klansman David Duke, and win the election. While many undoubtedly voted for Edwards as the lesser of two evils, he will have the opportunity to overcome his past reputation or add to it.

Arch Moore (R-W.Va., 1969-1977, 1985-1989) recently admitted to taking kickbacks, administering coverups, and committing other crimes while in office.[77] Other elected officials in West Virginia also were guilty of unethical or illegal acts; the state treasurer resigned after being impeached,[78] the attorney general resigned one month later after being accused of perjury,[79] and three legislators resigned for taking money.[80] Two of the attorney general's predecessors had been indicted and convicted of felony charges.[81] Moore did not set a high standard of ethical conduct for public officials in the state, and he served time in prison for his own actions.

Impeding a State's Development.   In contrast with those governors who served several terms and left a mostly positive legacy, one recent long-serving governor had a negative impact on his state's development. By pursuing his own personal agenda, sometimes to the exclusion of other agendas, George C. Wallace (D, 1963-1967, 1971-1979, 1983-1987), who "set the tone of public life in Alabama," kept the state behind others in the region and in the nation.[82]

Wallace's early focus on racial politics and on the advancement of his political career skewed what he was able to do for the state, and "his first and critical term as governor was not only a failure, but a tragedy." [83] Yet he persevered and even had his wife, Lurleen Wallace (D, 1967-1968), run in his stead in 1966, because he was statutorily limited to holding office for two consecutive terms. She served until her death.

After being shot during the 1972 presidential campaign, Wallace faded from national view, and his health gradually declined. However, he continued in gubernatorial politics, even though he became "a sad figure, crippled and unable to hear much" who tried to woo the support of those he earlier had scorned—blacks.[84] Since Wallace left office in 1987, the state's politics at the gubernatorial level have been in a turmoil.

Wounded State Institutions.   Some governors left negative legacies that hurt the office of the governor or their political party. In effect, their service left one of these institutions with a lesser ability to perform as it should.

In Illinois, for example, Otto Kerner (1961-1968) and Daniel Walker (1973-1977) were the last two Democrats elected governor of that state, and both ended up in jail for various crimes committed while in office. The last Democrat to serve as governor of Illinois who did not engage in criminal wrongdoing was Adlai E. Stevenson II (1949-1953), the party's candidate for president against Dwight D. Eisenhower in 1952 and 1956.[85] While the 1990 race was close,[86] the Democratic party has not been able to find a winning candidate since Walker left office.[87]

In Maryland, the back-to-back tenures of Spiro T. Agnew (R, 1967-1969) and Marvin Mandel (D, 1969-1977, 1979) left the governorship in considerable disarray. Voters in 1978 turned to a nonglamorous but strong member of the state's administration to be governor, Harry R. Hughes (D, 1979-1987). Hughes had been Maryland's first secretary of transportation, and, as governor, he was asked restore an ethical standard of behavior to the office.

Agnew resigned as governor to serve as vice president in the Nixon administration. He resigned from the vice presidency in October 1973 as part of an agreement with the U.S. Department of Justice, which was investigating him for taking bribes while serving as Baltimore county executive, governor of Maryland, and vice president of the United States.

Mandel, a strong governor with a long tenure in the state legislature, was elected in 1969 to serve the remainder of Agnew's term. He actively sought an increased role for the states in the federal system and a leadership position for NGA. In 1977, he was convicted on federal charges of mail fraud and racketeering, left office, and spent time in a federal prison. His conviction was overturned on appeal, and he returned to serve the last three days of his term in 1979.

The Lasting Impact of Negative Legacies. Two final observations on the impact of negative gubernatorial legacies are needed. First, creating a negative legacy is quicker and easier than creating a positive one. Many of the governors who left positive legacies did so after much effort and force of personality while in office. While some governors with negative legacies did take some time to create them, what caused the legacies to develop probably took little time at all.

Second, a negative legacy often is not confined to a specific administration. A negative legacy can become part of the tradition of the office, spreading widely. Substantial amounts of time and effort are needed to redress the injuries delivered to the state. Government and politicians are seen as corrupt by the public, the media, and out-of-state observers. Basic levels of trust and confidence are broken and must be rebuilt.

Arguably, the state of Arizona's problems stem from the stormy days of the Mecham administration. Despite the better days associated with Gov. Bruce Babbitt (D, 1978-1987), Arizona state government has not been able to shake off the negative effects of Mecham and a legislative bribery scandal. The current governor, Fife Symington (R, 1991-—), elected to restore confidence, now faces charges of irregularities while serving on the board of a failed savings and loan.[88] Arizona may not be able to overcome its wounds until well into the next governor's administration, or maybe even longer than that.

Assuming office after Blanton, Tennessee's Lamar Alexander served as a caretaker and took a low-key approach to rebuilding confidence during his first term to set the stage for making substantive accomplishments during his second term.[89]

Gubernatorial Legacies of the 1990s

Determining the gubernatorial legacies of the 1990s may not yet be possible, but early signs do exist. The political firsts legacy, for example, persists: the first black became governor, and Kansas and Oregon elected women as governors for the first time.[90] But, more significantly, new legacies are being carved out, legacies that are tied to difficult budgetary, policy, and program decisions that reflect deep-seated changes in the national economy and across regions and states. At least three possible legacies are discernable: kill the messenger, entrepreneurial government advocates, and those who fiddled while the state burned.

Kill the Messenger.[91] Beginning in the 1960s, state governments widened the reach of their programs, increased their administrative size, and took on numerous responsibilities. No problems were caused by these developments because an expanding economy provided more revenues. By the 1980s, however, the situation changed. State revenues fell, fiscal support from the federal government declined, and more demands were pressed on state governments from above (federal government) and below (local governments and citizens).

Some governors were put into the position of having to inform the state government and the citizens that, to maintain state programs and commitments, the tax system had to be revamped; that is, taxes had to be raised. The only alternative was deep cuts in expenditures; that is, reductions of programs and services. In most cases, both steps were taken, which meant citizens got less while paying more.

Often these governors called for tax increases because they could not get agreement on what to cut out of state budgets or where to reduce or remove the state's commitment. Sometimes the governors asked for higher taxes because they believed programs had been cut enough or they did not want to eliminate any more services or renege on any more commitments. Whatever their reasons, governors, especially in the northeast, became victims of a "kill the messenger" mentality. Public opinion polls indicated very low approval ratings for their efforts, which resulted in decisions not to run for reelection or in electoral defeat.

In 1990, three of the six eligible incumbent governors in New England decided not to seek reelection because of their low standing with the public over tax issues; a fourth was defeated in the general election in good part because of poor economic conditions in his state.[92] And the travails of New Jersey governor James J. Florio (D, 1990-—) following his push for tax increases may indicate a similar fate. Two other incumbent governors defeated in 1990 could trace a substantial portion of their political problems to their stances on taxes.[93]

As the demand for governmental programs and services becomes stronger and as governors turn increasing to raising taxes—after trying all other available options, including severe budget cuts—more political deaths are likely, especially if the economy stays weak. The concept of "tax-loss" governors is alive and well. However, the added revenue serves only to keep the government going; it does not enhance the role and impact of government.[94]

For a number of governors elected in 1989 and 1990, recent polls demonstrate how their support has deteriorated as they fought the battles of doing what they were elected to do—govern. As indicated by the data in Table 5-4, most of these governors saw their approval ratings slip below 50 percent before the end of their first year in office. Some have higher negatives than positives.

One explanation for the poll results is that the governors are not very good. But to have so many poor governors elected at virtually the same time is outside statistical probability. Instead, perhaps, the "kill the messenger" phenomenon is at work—these governors are bearing the brunt of the anger created by the steps they have had to take to balance state budgets while trying to provide the necessary services at a reasonable level. Furthermore, low gubernatorial ratings are more likely to be a reflection of citizen anger at government in general than at a specific governor's performance.

Entrepreneurial Government Advocates. Another set of governors may be in the process of fleshing out the meaning of what David Osborne calls "entrepreneurial government," those that "are flexible, adaptable, quick to adjust when conditions change. They are lean, decentralized and innovative." [95]

Osborne defines "entrepreneurial government" as catalytic governments, where "governments act more as catalysts, brokers and facilitators than traditional governments" by "steering rather than rowing"; competitive governments, which inject competition into service delivery; results-oriented governments, which fund the outcomes and not the inputs of programs; mission-driven governments, which "spell out the missions they want programs to achieve" and thereby transform rule-driven and budget-driven bureaucracies; and stakeholder governments, which empower service clients, not just serve them. Entrepreneurial governments, according to Osborne, are neither liberal or conservative—thus defying labeling—and focus on "how government does, not what government does." [96]

A possible advocate of entrepreneurial government is Massachusetts governor William Weld. In his inaugural address, Weld spoke of the need to "reinvent state government" and for creating an "entrepreneurial government," and he used some of Osborne's catch phrases: "steering rather than rowing," "results, not rules," "[fostering] competition," and "customer choice." The other governors of this ilk are Lawton Chiles (D-Fla., 1991-—) and Bill Clinton, for whom Osborne is or has served as an adviser.

How these ideas translate into actions or how they will affect a governor's legacy remains to be determined. But, changes are necessary, and these entrepreneurial leaders could be paving the way for government evolution. Is this "entrepreneurial government" approach just another in a long line of managerial fads that will fade as did Program Planning Budgeting System (PPBS) and Management by Objective (MBO)? Time will tell.

Governors Who Fiddled While the State Burned. Instead of taking

Table 5-4 Gubernatorial Job Performance Ratings, 1991-1992

State	Governor	Party	Year elected	Performance ratings Positive	Performance ratings Negative	Source of ratings	When poll taken	Participants in poll
Arizona	Fife Symington	R	1991	35%	55%	KAET-TV poll, Arizona State University	January 11-12, 1992	511 residents
California	Pete Wilson	R	1990	39	46	*Los Angeles Times*	Early October 1991	1,042 adults
				28	67	Field Institute	January 13-18, 1992	1,028 adults
Connecticut	Lowell P. Weicker, Jr.	I	1990	22	74	*Hartford Courant*	Mid-October 1991	500 adults
Florida	Lawton Chiles	D	1990	23	76	Mason-Dixon Poll	December 1991	813 regular voters
Illinois	Jim Edgar	R	1990	65	23	Marketing Strategies	Early September 1991	800 adults
Maryland	William Donald Schaefer	D	1990	39	60	Mason-Dixon Poll	August 1991	824 regular voters
Massachusetts	William F. Weld	R	1990	41	37	Becker Institute	Early October 1991	400 residents
Michigan	John Engler	R	1990	44	43	Marketing Resources Group poll	Late August 1991	800 regular voters
Nebraska	Ben Nelson	D	1990	59	21	*Omaha World Herald*	Late August 1991	614 adults
New Jersey	James J. Florio	D	1989	26	71	*Star-Ledger*/ Eagleton Institute of Politics poll	January 1992	800 adults
Oklahoma	David Walters	D	1990	35	60	Mason-Dixon Poll	July 1991	800+ regular voters

Rhode Island	Bruce Sundlun	D	1990	42	40	Alpha Research Associates	Mid-November 1991	505 regular voters
Texas	Ann W. Richards	D	1990	49	44	Texas Poll	Mid-October 1991	1,004 adults
Virginia	L. Douglas Wilder	D	1989	22	78	Mason-Dixon Poll	January 1992	803 regular voters

Sources: Political Report 14:19 (September 13, 1991): 7-8, and 14:21 (October 10, 1991): 7; Mason-Dixon Poll; and Thad L. Beyle, ed., *Governors and Hard Times* (Washington, D.C.: CQ Press, 1992).

Note: R = Republican. I = Independent. D = Democrat. The ratings categories of 'excellent,' 'good,' 'fair,' and 'poor' were used for all the polls except the *Los Angeles Times* (California), Marketing Strategies (Illinois), Marketing Resources Group (Michigan), *Omaha World Herald* (Nebraska), and Mason-Dixon (Oklahoma) polls, which gave participants the choice between 'approve' and 'disapprove,' and the Alpha Research Associates (Rhode Island) poll, which had 'excellent,' 'above average,' 'below average,' and 'poor' ratings. The positive rating is either the sum of the 'excellent' and 'good' ratings, the 'approve' rating, or the sum of the 'excellent' and 'above average' ratings. The negative rating is either the sum of the 'fair' and 'poor' ratings, the 'disapproved' rating, or the sum of the 'below average' and 'poor' rating. All governors included in the table were newly elected except Maryland's William Donald Schaefer, who was reelected in 1990.

the big steps of raising taxes to the level needed, cutting services to what can be provided, or redirecting how government works, some governors continue coping with fiscal adversities on a piecemeal basis as they arise. Selective cuts in programs are made, across-the-board budget cuts are instituted, and minor nickel-and-dime tax increases are put in place, all of which leave the states and their governments in a weaker position.

Essentially, the governors' approach is to hope the economy improves so that business as usual can return. In the meantime, government remedies are little more than Band-Aids. This tough managerial approach entails little excitement, much gloom, and a prayer for better times ahead. In the process, the state begins to fall behind in providing services to its citizens.

Summary

Over the past few decades, a host of state government reforms have strengthened governorships. In theory, governors now are better able to achieve their goals. Their terms of office are longer; most are allowed to succeed themselves for another term; their budgetary authority has been consolidated and enhanced; and most state government organization structures have been simplified.

However, some important tools needed by governors remain missing in some states or limited in others. A large number of officials, boards, and commissions still are separately elected, and some governors lack full veto power. Some governors have outdated and unresponsive administrative organizations, lack the ability to reorganize portions of state government by executive order, and must function with antiquated constitutions. Although the analogy between a governor and a private sector chief executive officer is apt, governors have a distance to go before possessing comparable power of appointment and removal. Governors need more flexibility in hiring and firing personnel. Even more important, their ability to remove officials when necessary is greatly constrained, first, by the strong value of neutral competence and, second, by the protection afforded appointees by several U.S. Supreme Court decisions.

Conflicts between governors and legislatures have escalated in recent years. Tensions are exacerbated when the governor's office and the legislature are controlled by different political parties. Legislatures have intruded into traditional gubernatorial prerogatives by appointed legislators to state boards and commissions, by enacting legislative vetoes of administrative rules and regulations, and by exercising oversight of administrative agencies. State courts often side with governors in disputes with legislatures when separation-of-powers issues are involved, but now the courts themselves are becoming part of the combat in the states as advocates, not just judges.

The legacies that governors leave their state depends on a variety of factors, including the type of state, the governors' ability to use politics to their advantage, their tenure as governor, and their relationship to concerns outside the state. However, not all legacies are positive. Governors leave office after being rejected, and their actions as governor impede the development of their state or its institutions. While positive legacies take time to build, negative legacies can be created more quickly and have a greater lasting impact.

The 1990s are providing governors with new challenges.[97] Falling revenues, rising needs, a retreating national government, and desperate local governments offer them and state legislatures the responsibility for making no-win decisions: raising taxes while cutting services. Some governors will fall victim to voter wrath for taking extraordinary steps to handle virtually insolvable problems, others are trying to bring new perspectives to the office and to state government, while others try to cope on a day-to-day basis.

A new era of "go-it-alone" federalism has dawned; each unit of government at each level must cope with their own problems and fashion their own solutions. So far, governors, faced with considerable political roadblocks, failing economies, a changing system of government, and restrictions on their powers, have been rewarded by the public with a critical, if not jaundiced, eye. Governors are not seen as saviors trying to cope with great problems, but as individuals failing at their jobs. Many will find continued electoral success hard to come by.

Notes

1. "The Fortune 500," *Fortune*, April 22, 1991, 286-305; and U.S. Bureau of the Census, U.S. Department of Commerce, *State Government Finances in 1989* (Washington, D.C.: U.S. Government Printing Office, 1990), 5.
2. Regina Brough, "Powers of the Gubernatorial CEOs: Variations among the States," *Journal of State Government* 59 (1986): 58-63.
3. Among these were Advisory Commission on Intergovernmental Relations, various reports; Committee for Economic Development, *Modernizing State Government* (New York: Committee for Economic Development, 1967); Terry Sanford, *Storm over the States* (New York: McGraw-Hill, 1967); National Municipal League, *Model State Constitution*, rev. ed. (New York: National Municipal League, 1968); and Citizens Conference on State Legislatures, various publications between 1967 and 1971.
4. Sanford, *Storm over the States*, 188; and Larry J. Sabato, *Goodbye to Goodtime Charlie: The American Governor Transformed, 1950-1975* (Lexington, Mass.: Lexington Books, 1978), 63.
5. Advisory Commission on Intergovernmental Relations, *The Question of*

State Government Capability (Washington, D.C.: Advisory Commission on Intergovernmental Relations, 1985), 129.

6. Thad L. Beyle, "Term Limits for State Elected Executive Officials" (Paper prepared for a conference on "Term Limits and Political Career Choices in State and Local Elective Office" at the Nelson A. Rockefeller Institute of Government, State University of New York at Albany, October 10-11, 1991).

7. Council of State Governments, *The Book of the States, 1990-1991* (Lexington, Ky.: Council of State Governments, 1990), 83-84.

8. Advisory Commission on Intergovernmental Relations, *The Question of State Government Capability*, 129; Council of State Governments, *The Book of the States, 1990-1991*, 157-158; and Ronald C. Moe, *Prospects for the Item Veto at the Federal Level: Lessons from the States* (Washington, D.C.: National Academy of Public Administration, 1988), 3-50.

9. Coleman B. Ransone, Jr., *The Office of Governor in the United States* (University: University of Alabama Press, 1956), 44.

10. Center for Policy Research, National Governors' Association, unpublished data from a 1976 survey of thirty-eight governors' offices. The adjusted averages exclude the one or two largest states as their size would skew the overall averages.

11. Council of State Governments, *The Book of the States, 1990-1991*, 65-66.

12. Thad L. Beyle, "Governors Views on Being Governor," *State Government* 52 (Summer 1979): 108-110.

13. Council of State Governments, *The Book of the States, 1990-1991*, 67-68.

14. Lynn Muchmore, "Planning and Budgeting Offices: On Their Relevance to Gubernatorial Decisions," in *Being Governor: The View from the Office*, ed. Thad L. Beyle and Lynn Muchmore (Durham, N.C.: Duke University Press, 1983), 174.

15. Carl W. Stenberg, "States under the Spotlight: An Intergovernmental View," *Public Administration Review* 45 (March/April 1985): 321.

16. Thad L. Beyle and Deil S. Wright, "The Governor, Planning, and Governmental Activity," in *The American Governor in Behavioral Perspective*, ed. Thad L. Beyle and J. Oliver Williams (New York: Harper and Row, 1972), 194-195.

17. Thad L. Beyle, "The Governor as Innovator in the Federal System," *Publius* 18 (Summer 1988): 133-154.

18. Under policy development were policy analysis and new initiatives (thirty-four states); briefing the governor on policy concerns (twenty-eight states); assisting on major gubernatorial initiatives (fifteen states); and impact analysis (seven states). Under administrative were coordinating and providing service to the governor's cabinet and subcabinet councils (seventeen states) and to interagency commissions, task forces, and working groups (twenty-four states); and programmatic responsibilities in specific functional areas (sixteen states) and in the regulatory areas of state government (ten states).

19. Council of State Governments, *The Book of the States, 1982-1983* (1982), 145-147; *The Book of the States, 1984-1985* (1984), 44-45; *The Book of the States, 1986-1987* (1986), 45-47; *The Book of the States, 1988-1989* (1988), 47-48; and *The Book of the States, 1990-1991* (1990), 75-78. See also James K. Conant, "In the Shadow of Wilson and Brownlow: Executive Branch

Reorganization in the States, 1965 to 1987," *Public Administration Review* 48:5 (September/October 1988), 892-902.

20. Council of State Governments, *The Book of the States, 1990-1991*, 69-70.
21. Ibid., 83-84.
22. Ibid.
23. Jack Brizius, of Brizius and Foster, Management Consultants, telephone conversation with author, September 11, 1987.
24. Richard Murray and Gregory R. Weiher, "Texas: Ann Richards, Taking on the Challenge," in *Governors and Hard Times*, ed. Thad L. Beyle (Washington, D.C.: CQ Press, 1992), 179-188.
25. Diane Kincaid Blair, "The Gubernatorial Appointment Power: Too Much of a Good Thing?" in *Being Governor: The View from the Office*, 118-121.
26. Joseph A. Schlesinger, "The Politics of the Executive," in *Politics in the American States*, ed. Herbert Jacob and Kenneth N. Vines (Boston: Little, Brown, 1965), 217-232; Joseph A. Schlesinger, "The Politics of the Executive," in *Politics in the American States*, 2d ed., ed. Herbert Jacob and Kenneth N. Vines (Boston: Little, Brown, 1971), 210-237; and Thad L. Beyle, "Governors," in *Politics in the American States* 4th ed., ed. Virginia Gray, Herbert Jacob, and Kenneth N. Vines (Boston: Little, Brown, 1983), 203, 458-459.
27. Schlesinger, "The Politics of the Executive," in *Politics in the American States* (1965), 225.
28. Elder Witt, "Patronage Firings," *Congressional Quarterly Weekly Report*, July 3, 1976, 1726.
29. Elder Witt, "Supreme Court Deals Blow to Public Employee Firings for Solely Political Reasons," *Congressional Quarterly Weekly Report*, April 6, 1980, 889-890.
30. Elder Witt, "Employee Rights," *Congressional Quarterly Weekly Report*, April 6, 1983, 791-792.
31. Thad L. Beyle and Robert Huefner, *Evaluation of the 1982 Seminar for New Governors*, report submitted to the National Governors' Association, February 23, 1983.
32. Cheri Collis, "Cleaning Up the Spoils System," *State Government News* 33:9 (September 1990): 6.
33. Charles N. Wheeler III, "Gov. James R. Thompson, 1977-1991: The Complete Campaigner, the Pragmatic Centrist," *Illinois Issues* 16:12 (December 1990).
34. Schlesinger, "The Politics of the Executive," in *Politics in the American States* (1965); Schlesinger, "The Politics of the Executive," in *Politics in the American States*, 2d ed.; Beyle, "Governors," in *Politics in the American States*, 4th ed., 193-203; and Thad L. Beyle, "Governors," in *Politics in the American States*, 5th ed., ed. Virginia Gray, Herbert Jacob, and Robert B. Albritton (Glenview, Ill.: Scott, Foresman, 1990), 217-230.
35. Office of State Services, *The Institutionalized Powers of the Governorship, 1965-1985* (Washington, D.C.: National Governors' Association, 1987).
36. Some differences exist between the NGA index and the previous ones: (1) The NGA indices were called institutional and not formal, which allowed a broader interpretation of what could be brought into the presentation and

analysis. (2) Added were the legislative budget-changing ability and the governor's political strength in the legislature, which probably reflected a real-world view of the constraints on governors not captured in previous efforts. Including the governor's political strength in the legislature could lead to more varied results as each could change this score, especially as so many states are now experiencing a political party power-split between the governor and the legislature. (3) Only six offices were used to develop the appointment power index—and the range of potential appointment power was greater (up to seven) than for the indicators (up to five) reflecting the importance of this one indicator for governors and where a large effect can be felt. (4) A twenty-year comparison of these indices showed just how far the American governorship has come during the most recent era of state government reform.

37. These findings are based on Beyle, "Governors," in *Politics in the American States*, 5th ed.

38. Alabama, Colorado, Delaware, Hawaii, Illinois, Kansas, Maryland, Missouri, New Mexico, New York, Pennsylvania, Rhode Island, South Carolina, Utah, Vermont, and Wyoming.

39. North Dakota and West Virginia.

40. Indiana and Iowa.

41. Arizona, Arkansas, Connecticut, Florida, Louisiana, Massachusetts, Michigan, Minnesota, Mississippi, Nebraska, New Hampshire, New Jersey, Oklahoma, South Dakota, and Wisconsin.

42. California, Maine, Texas, and Virginia.

43. Alaska, Georgia, Idaho, Kentucky, Montana, Nevada, North Carolina, Ohio, Oregon, Tennessee, and Washington.

44. Morris P. Fiorina, "Divided Government in the States," *PS: Political Science and Politics* 24:4 (December 1991): 646.

45. Sharon Sherman, "Powersplit: When Legislatures and Governors Are of Opposing Parties," *State Legislatures* 10:5 (May/June 1984): 9-12.

46. Richard W. Gable, "California: Pete Wilson, a Centrist in Trouble," in *Governors and Hard Times*, 43-59.

47. Dennis Hale, "Massachusetts: William F. Weld and the End of Business as Usual," in *Governors and Hard Times*, 127-150.

48. Russell D. Murphy, "Connecticut: Lowell P. Weiker, Jr., a Maverick in the 'Land of Steady Habits,'" in *Governors and Hard Times*, 61-75.

49. National Conference of State Legislatures, "Legislators Serving on Boards and Commissions," in *State Legislative Report* (Denver, Colo.: National Conference of State Legislatures, 1983), 4-5; and North Carolina Center for Public Policy Research, *Boards, Commissions, and Councils in the Executive Branch of North Carolina State Government* (Raleigh: North Carolina Center for Public Policy Research, 1984).

50. Charles W. Wiggins, "Executive Vetoes and Legislative Overrides in the American States," *Journal of Politics* 42 (1980): 1112-1113.

51. Council of State Governments, *The Book of the States, 1980-1981*, 110-111.

52. Ran Coble, *Special Provisions in Budget Bills: A Pandora's Box for North Carolina Citizens*, A Special Report (Raleigh: North Carolina Center for Public Policy Research, 1986), 9-12.

53. Walter J. Oleszek, *Congressional Procedures and the Policy Process*, 3d ed. (Washington, D.C.: CQ Press, 1988), 297.
54. The federal case was *Immigration and Naturalization Services v. Jagdish Rai Chada* 462 U.S. 919 (1983).
55. Jody George and Lacy Maddox, "Separation of Powers Provisions in State Constitutions," in North Carolina Center for Public Policy Research, *Boards, Commissions, and Councils in the Executive Branch of North Carolina State Government*, 51.
56. Joseph F. Zimmerman, "New York Updates," *Comparative State Politics* 12:6 (December 1991): 32-34.
57. Sabato, *Goodbye to Good-Time Charlie*, 50-56; and George Weeks, "A Statehouse Hall of Fame," *State Government* 55:3 (1982): 67-73.
58. Some examples from California are Earl Warren (R, 1943-1953), Ronald Reagan (R, 1967-1975), Edmund G. "Jerry" Brown, Jr. (D, 1975-1983), and Pete Wilson (R, 1991-—); and from New York, Thomas E. Dewey (R, 1943-1955), Averell Harriman (D, 1955-1959), Nelson A. Rockefeller (R, 1959-1973), and Mario Cuomo (D, 1983-—).
59. Some examples are George Deukmejian (R-Calif., 1983-1991) and Hugh Carey (D-N.Y., 1975-1983).
60. Diane D. Blair, *Arkansas Politics and Government: Do the People Rule?* (Lincoln: University of Nebraska Press, 1988), 49. Two other examples, both from southern states, are William Winter (D-Miss., 1980-1984) and Charles Robb (D-Va., 1982-1986).
61. For accounts of their administrations see Terry Sanford, *But What about the People?* (New York: Harper and Row, 1966); and Lamar Alexander, *Steps along the Way: A Governor's Scrapbook* (Nashville: Thomas Nelson, 1986).
62. This argument is based on Dan Durning, "Governors' Issue Campaigns: An Exploration" (Paper delivered at the annual meeting of the Southern Political Science Association, Memphis, Tenn., November 8-10, 1989).
63. According to Durning, others who used this tactic successfully were Bill Winter (D-Miss., 1980-1984), Dick Riley (S.C., 1979-1987), and Joe Frank Harris (D-Ga., 1983-1990). Those using the technique unsuccessfully were David Pryor (D-Ark., 1975-1979) and Rudy Perpich (DFL-Minn., 1976-1979, 1983-1991).
64. For example, in Alabama, Guy Hunt (1987-—); Arkansas, Winthrop Rockefeller (1967-1971); Florida, Claude Kirk (1967-1971); Louisiana, David Treen (1980-1984); Mississippi, Kirk Fordice (1992-—); North Carolina, James Holshouser (1973-1977); Oklahoma, Henry Bellmon (1963-1967, 1987-1991); South Carolina, James Edwards (1975-1979); Texas, William Clements (1979-1983, 1987-1991); and Virginia, Linwood Holton (1970-1974).
65. James B. Longley (Maine, 1975-1979), Walter J. Hickel (R, 1966-1969; I, 1991-—), and Lowell P. Weiker, Jr. (Conn, 1991-—). All three previously were registered as Republicans, Hickel having served as a governor in the 1960s and Weiker as a U.S. senator from 1971 to 1989.
66. Miriam "Ma" Ferguson (D-Texas, 1925-1927, 1933-1935) and Nellie Ross Taylor (R-Wyo., 1925-1927). Taylor, who ran to complete her deceased husband's term, was sworn in five days before Ferguson.
67. Two are well known: Miriam "Ma" Ferguson was elected governor of Texas

for several terms (D, 1925-1927, 1933-1935) following the impeachment of her husband, James "Pa" Ferguson (D, 1915-1919); Lurleen Wallace (D-Ala., 1967-1968) ran and served when her husband was no longer constitutionally eligible to serve another term.

68. Currently three governors are women: former state treasurer Joan Finney (D-Kan., 1991-—); former secretary of state Barbara Roberts (D-Ore., 1991-—); and former state treasurer Ann Richards (D-Texas, 1991-—).

69. Others included in this category are Bill Milliken (R-Mich., 1969-1983); Bob Ray (R-Iowa, 1969-1983); and James Rhodes (R-Ohio, 1963-1971, 1975-1983). One midwestern Democrat, Rudy Perpich (Minn., 1976-1979, 1983-1991), also served multiple terms.

70. Weeks, "A Statehouse Hall of Fame," 69-71.

71. For an account of his administration, see Scott Matheson, *Out of Balance* (Salt Lake City: Peregrine Smith, 1986).

72. Elmer E. Cornwell, Jr., "Rhode Island: Bruce Sundlun and the State's Crises," in *Governors and Hard Times*, 163-177.

73. Weeks, "A Statehouse Hall of Fame," 69, 71. Others who have been cited for their work with the federal system and with the National Governors' Association are Lamar Alexander (R-Tenn., 1979-1987) and two Democrats from the solidly Republican state of Utah, Calvin Rampton (1965-1977) and Scott Matheson (1977-1985).

74. Theodore Roosevelt (R-N.Y., 1899-1901) was president from 1901 to 1909; Woodrow Wilson (D-N.J., 1911-1913), president 1913-1921; Calvin Coolidge (R-Mass., 1919-1921), president 1923-1929; Franklin D. Roosevelt (D-N.Y., 1929-1933), president 1933-1945; Jimmy Carter (D-Ga., 1971-1975), president 1977-1981; and Ronald Reagan (R-Calif., 1967-1975), president 1981-1989.

75. Alexander, *Steps along the Way*, 21-26.

76. Michael Barone and Grant Ujifusa, *The Almanac of American Politics 1990* (Washington, D.C.: National Journal, 1989), 488-93.

77. Associated Press, "Former Governor of West Virginia to Plead Guilty," (Raleigh) *News and Observer*, April 13, 1990, 8A.

78. "West Virginia Woes," *State Policy Reports* 7:17 (September 1989): 30.

79. LaDonna Sloan, "In Briefs: West Virginia," *Comparative State Politics Newsletter* 10:6 (December 1989): 37.

80. "West Virginia Setbacks," *State Policy Reports* 7:18 (September 1989): 23-24.

81. Associated Press, "W.Va. Attorney General Acquitted in Campaign-Law Case," (Raleigh) *News and Observer*, November 20, 1986, 2A.

82. Barone and Ujifusa, *The Almanac of American Politics*, 2.

83. Ibid.

84. Ibid., 3.

85. Samuel Shapiro (D-Ill., 1968-1969) succeeded to the governorship as lieutenant governor when Kerner resigned to accept an appointment to the U.S. Circuit Court of Appeals.

86. Republican candidate Jim Edgar defeated Democratic candidate Neil Hartigan 52 percent to 48 percent.

87. Samuel K. Gove, "Illinois: Jim Edgar, the New Governor from the Old Party," in *Governors and Hard Times*, 107-125.

88. Ruth S. Jones and Katheryn A. Lehman, "The CEO Approach of J. Fife Symington III" in *Governors and Hard Times*, 29-42.

89. Michael Fitzgerald, Floydette C. Cory, Stephen J. Rechichar, and Abagail S. Hughes, "The 1982 Gubernatorial Election in Tennessee," in *Reelecting the Governor: 1982 Elections*, ed. Thad L. Beyle (Lanham, Md.: University Press of America, 1986), 299-322.

90. L. Douglas Wilder (D-Va., 1990-—), Joan Finney (D-Kan. 1991-—), and Barbara Roberts (D-Ore., 1991-—).

91. Portions of this section were taken from Thad L. Beyle, "New Governors in Hard Economic and Political Times," in *Governors and Hard Times*, 1-14.

92. Those New England governors declining to seek reelection were Michael S. Dukakis (D-Mass., 1975-1979, 1983-1991), Madeleine M. Kunin (D-Vt., 1985-1991), and William A. O'Neill (D-Conn., 1980-1991). The defeated governor was Edward DiPrete (R-R.I., 1985-1991).

93. Bob Martinez (R-Fla., 1987-1991) and Mike Hayden (R-Kan., 1987-1991).

94. Several political scientists have argued that advocating tax increases is not necessarily a risk for governors. See Gerald M. Pomper, "Governors, Money, and Votes," in *Elections in America*, ed. Gerald M. Pomper (New York: Dodd, Mead, 1968), 126-148; Theodore Eismeier, "Budgets and Ballots: The Political Consequences of Fiscal Choice," in *Public Policy and Public Choice*, ed. D. Rae and Theodore Eismeier (Beverly Hills, Calif.: Sage, 1979), 121-150; and Richard T. Winters, "Governors and Electoral Retribution" (Paper delivered at the annual meeting of the American Political Science Association, Chicago, September 3-6, 1987).

95. David Osborne, "Governing in the '90s," *Boston Sunday Globe*, January 13, 1991, 65.

96. Ibid., 65, 68.

97. The following was adapted from Beyle, "New Governors in Hard Economic and Political Times," in *Governors and Hard Times*, 1-14.

6 ▰▰▰▰

The Legislative Institution—In Transition and at Risk

Alan Rosenthal

Legislatures are probably the principal political institutions in the states—the guts of democracy. They have managed to survive, and on occasion even prosper, over the course of more than a two-hundred-year lifetime. But in contemporary times, their standing with the public rarely has been high. They deserve better. They have made considerable progress in a relatively brief period of time, and today they are performing well. Yet, indications are that the legislature, as an institution, may be in serious jeopardy.

Prior to their revitalization, which began in the mid-1960s, legislatures were unrepresentative, malapportioned, and dominated by rural areas of the states. The legislative process was, in many instances, a sham; power within the institution was narrowly held and not democratically exercised. Major issues were sidestepped, and initiatives for state policy were left to the governor. The legislature's role in the most important business of government, that of allocating funds, was minimal. Whatever the positive outcomes and however well served the people of a state might be, relatively little could be attributed to the performance of the legislature.

The reapportionment revolution, precipitated by the Supreme Court decisions in *Baker v. Carr* (1962) and *Reynolds v. Sims* (1965), was the first stage in the transformation of American state legislatures. A new generation of members—led by a number of outstanding leaders and supported by allies drawn from the ranks of citizens, business, foundations, and universities—went to work to reshape legislative institutions.

Within a decade legislatures had been rebuilt.[1] They increased the time they spent on their tasks; they established or expanded their professional staffs; and they streamlined their procedures, enlarged their facilities, invigorated their processes, attended to their ethics, disclosed their finances, and reduced their conflicts of interest.

Thus, the decade from about 1965 to 1975 can appropriately be termed the period of "the rise of the legislative institution." Traditional assemblies became modern ones; reformed legislatures emerged. They substantially improved their capacity to perform the functions they were expected to perform. Some, such as California's, were ahead of their time, and others, such as Vermont's and Wyoming's, lagged behind. Each legislature adapted differently, depending upon its culture and politics, the people and personalities in office, and the circumstances of the time. Each put its newly developed capacity to work, and each continued to evolve in its own particular way.

As a result, state legislatures are in better shape now than they were twenty-five years ago. Whatever the public assessment of legislative performance, legislatures are meeting their responsibilities; they are representative, they are active participants in the policy process, and they are producing informed debate and legislation.

One of the functions of legislatures is to represent the citizens of their state, with members linked to constituencies and groups. Legislatures are much more representative than before. Periodic reapportionment, the emergence of women and minorities in legislative ranks, and the close relationship forged by members with their districts have changed the composition and behavior of legislative bodies.

Another function of legislatures is to participate in the making of public policy and the allocation of public funds. No longer does the governor propose and the legislature dispose. Although most governors still control the agenda on priority measures, in some states the legislature is almost as likely to initiate major policy as is the governor. Today legislatures are in the thick of the policy fray, and as a consequence they frequently come toe-to-toe with their governors. Legislatures also take on governors when it comes to the state budget. In recent years, thanks largely to the growth of their fiscal staffs, legislatures have flexed their budgetary muscle and expanded their budgetary role. Legislatures even have become involved in administration, by means of sunset processes, the review of administrative rules and regulations, and the conduct of program evaluations and performance audits.[2] Increasingly, legislatures and governors are coming into conflict; and not infrequently the courts are being asked to settle disputes.

Legislatures also have to produce outcomes that respond to public demands and needs, command support, and prove effective in application. Although their record is by no means unblemished, legislatures generally have fashioned policies that are responsive to their various publics. Legislatures now duck fewer issues; instead, they wrestle with the most contentious problems. They have adopted noteworthy measures in the areas of the environment, education, and social welfare. And they have raised taxes when additional revenues were necessary to do the job.

Not every legislative policy succeeds, often because of the gap between policy pronouncement on the one hand and the level of funding and vigor of administration on the other. A substantial room for improvement exists, but some progress is evident even in the area of implementation.

While the current legislative record in representation, participation, and production is a good one, the legislature has an additional function. The legislature must provide a process that is authoritative, deliberative, and open—a process that is capable of resolving conflict and building consensus. In short, the legislature must maintain itself as a political institution and tend to the well being of the process. In this regard, today's legislature may be in trouble.

The institution that underwent reform and modernization in the 1960s and 1970s began a period of transition in the 1980s, which is continuing into the 1990s. Its capacity remains substantial, its power is still impressive, and it continues to produce policies that generally are effective for the states. But the legislature's structure and institutional fabric are changing, attributable to several trends: First, the legislative career has become professionalized; second, legislative behavior and the legislative process are increasingly politicized; third, the legislative institution is more and more fragmented; and fourth, the environment in which the legislature functions has become hostile.

Not every state is being affected by each of these four trends, and not every state is feeling the trends equally. The larger states, with the most developed and modernized legislatures, appear to be most affected. California, Illinois, Massachusetts, Michigan, New York, and Pennsylvania are in that category. Other states, such as Colorado, Connecticut, Florida, Kansas, Minnesota, Missouri, Nebraska, Ohio, Washington, and Wisconsin, also are subject to these trends. Still others, such as Montana, New Hampshire, Utah, and Wyoming, are being touched only lightly, if at all. While these trends do not have universal application, in many states they have had a significant impact and may soon transform the legislature as a political institution.

Careerist Bodies

Along with reform and modernization has come the professionalization of state legislatures. In the most commonly used sense, professionalization refers to the improvement of legislative facilities, with the renovation of capitols and the construction of legislative office buildings, the increase in information available to the legislature, and, above all, the expansion of legislative staffs. Professionalization, however, applies not only to the capacity and conduct of the institution but also to the composition of its core personnel. Most significant in this respect is the growing number of career politicians among the membership of many state legislatures. The careerist orientation of legislators is having an enormous impact on legislative life.[3] It is largely responsible for the increasing political nature of legislatures and partly responsible for their greater fragmentation as well.

Citizens and Professionals

Twenty years ago, almost all members, except a few in California, failed to label themselves as legislators in their biographical sketches for the state directory. Instead, they identified themselves by their occupations outside the legislature—attorney, businessperson, insurance broker, farmer, rancher, or whatever. Not anymore. Now, significant proportions of members, in a number of states, acknowledge their occupation to be that of legislator. Even larger proportions are, in effect, full-time or virtually full-time legislators who have made politics their career. Nowadays "citizens" and "professionals" constitute the two principal breeds within the legislator species. The former, or old breed, generally has another occupation or substantial interests outside the legislature. The latter, or new breed, usually has no other significant occupation and little time or interest for anything other than politics. The new breed is on the rise, the old in decline. Indeed, within individual states new breeders are setting the pace, pressuring the citizen legislators either to keep up or get out. Thus, full-timers are driving part-timers out of circulation.[4]

Not all states have proceeded in the careerist direction, or at the same rate. The largest states primarily have had the greatest proportions of members committed to the legislature and political careers. At least two-thirds of the members in Michigan, Pennsylvania, and Wisconsin are career politicians, although a number of them practice law or have "something on the side" that provides additional income. Half or more of those in Illinois, Massachusetts, and New York are full time or practically so. Slightly fewer in Arizona, Iowa, Missouri, and Ohio are full timers, and about one-quarter in Connecticut, Florida, and Minnesota.[5] Only 15 percent are full time in Maryland.[6] Legislatures also exist at the other end of the spectrum, where nearly all the members, with the exceptions of homemakers and retirees, are part time. Indiana, Kentucky, Nevada, New Hampshire, North Dakota, Vermont, and Wyoming are examples. At present, about one-fifth of the nation's legislatures are mainly in the hands of professional legislators and one-fifth are moving gradually, but almost inexorably, toward the professional model. Another two-fifths may or may not go that way in the years ahead. The remaining fifth are not likely to be taken over for some time; they will remain firmly in the hands of citizen legislators.[7]

What Promotes Careerism

The professionalization of legislative careers is attributable to a number of factors. Among the most potent are the increasing demands on members' time, the greater resources available to members, and the rising levels of compensation.[8]

The amount of time that legislatures are in session and that legislators are required to be at the state capital is two or three times greater today than in earlier years. Most legislatures used to meet biennially; today all but seven meet annually.

Although most states constitutionally set limits on the length of legislative sessions, about one-quarter do not. Thus, in Alaska, California, Illinois, Massachusetts, Michigan, New York, Ohio, Pennsylvania, South Carolina, and Wisconsin, the number of days legislatures spend in session has risen markedly. In California, for example, voters in 1966 approved Proposition 1-A, which eliminated constitutional limits on session length (as well as on legislative pay). This measure allowed members to devote more time to the legislature, and they did. The length of sessions increased from 107 days in 1965 to 143 in 1967. In the 1983-1984 biennium, the California legislature spent 282 days in session, and in the 1985-1986 biennium, 251 days.[9]

Where sessions are open-ended, the demands on legislatures are such that they are meeting most of the year every year. California, Illinois, Massachusetts, Ohio, Pennsylvania, and Wisconsin meet ten months a year; Michigan, nine; and New York, seven. Unlike in earlier years, the legislature in more than half the states today are in session almost constantly.

Even where annual sessions are limited, as in Florida (sixty days) or Maryland (ninety days), the time legislators spend on their jobs has increased dramatically. In addition to regular and special sessions, legislators attend meetings of standing committees and special committees during the interim period when the senate and house are not convened. Not only the legislature as a whole meets for longer periods of time, but also more individual legislators are involved in activity between sessions. In Maryland, for instance, relatively few members used to be named to interim committees; now everyone's time can be occupied between legislative sessions by virtue of membership on standing committees. In North Carolina, some legislators serve on as many as thirteen different commissions and councils during the interim period. Probably the greatest recent increase in time spent by members, however, is devoted to constituency affairs. In many states, legislators now politick through their districts, appear before local groups and organizations, deal with constituents in their legislative district offices, and raise funds year round.

The resources now available to legislators, which enable them to do their jobs and help them get reelected, also are appealing. Staff and facilities encourage service. On average, legislative staffs grew by a quarter between 1979 and 1988, by which time the number of full-time professionals exceeded fifty in all but twelve legislatures. The average number of staff per member was as high as 23.9 in California, 17.0 in New York, 9.9 in Florida, 8.7 in Michigan, 8.1 in Texas, 7.8 in Pennsylvania, 6.5 in New Jersey, and 6.0 in Illinois. (By contrast, in Idaho, New Hampshire, New Mexico, North Dakota, Vermont, and Wyoming, one staffer on average served three, four, or five members.[10]) Of special importance to legislators is that staffers are assigned to them personally, and they work out of the statehouse or district offices. This is the most recent trend in staffing; currently seventeen states provide staff or staff allowances to individual members.

The improvement of legislative facilities, with the renovation of capitol buildings and the construction of legislative office buildings, provided space for rank-and-file members that they formerly lacked. As a result, legislators now had the resources they believed were necessary to do their jobs, and members were attracted to their offices to work, even when the legislature was not in session. They soon came to define their positions as practically full time, seeking further resources to allow them to perform the additional tasks that they laid out for themselves.[11]

Whatever the time demands and the resources available, the professionalization of the legislative career probably would not have been as great without a marked rise in legislative salaries.[12] Higher salaries made it possible for members to derive a substantial portion of their income from legislative service. The case of Wisconsin is instructive. The salary of legislators doubled in the 1970s, reaching $17,800, enough to match teachers' salaries. More educators then began declaring their candidacies for the legislature. Wisconsin now pays its legislators $33,622 (as well as $64 per diem), and legislative compensation probably provides three-quarters of the total income of the average member.

In other states, the salaries are as, or even more, attractive. California pays $52,500, plus $92 per diem; Illinois, $35,661, plus $74 per diem; Michigan, $45,450, plus expenses; New Jersey, $35,000; Ohio, $40,406; and Pennsylvania, $47,000, plus $88 per diem. New York salaries are the highest at $57,500. Beyond the base salary, many legislators receive supplements for holding leadership positions or in lieu of other expenses.

In a number of states, by contrast, salaries lag far behind or are abysmally low. People find it financially difficult to abandon outside occupations and income when legislative compensation is $15,000 or less a year, as it is in about half the states. Some do; they can afford it or are willing to make the sacrifice. Yet, most people could not easily spend a substantial amount of time on the legislature if the salary were $65 per day for forty-five calendar days, as in Utah. And most could not serve for long if the salary were $100 a year, with no per diem, as in New Hampshire.

Holding salaries down has allowed states to preserve their citizen legislatures. In Florida, for instance, the salary had been kept at $12,000 a year since 1969 (when it was raised from $1,200), partly out of fear that more money would attract different types of people and the legislature then would lose its citizen status. In 1985, however, legislators voted themselves a pay raise to $18,000 and provided that their salaries would increase automatically every year by the same percentage that the average salary of state employees rose the preceding year. In view of the improved remuneration, as well as the increased time demands, chances are that in the years ahead the proportion of relatively full-time, professional members will grow in the Florida legislature.

As the Florida experience illustrates, the legislature itself has the choice of whether or not to become a place for careerist politicians. Democratic members are more inclined to professionalization than Republicans, because they are more positively oriented toward the role of government and more activist in pursuit of bringing change through legislation. While Republicans are in the business of protecting business, Democrats are in the business of protecting government, which is one reason the incidence of professionalization has been greatest in legislatures controlled by the Democratic party.

In some places, the citizen-legislature ethos continues to be strongly held, but the spectre of careerism looms large. In Indiana, for example, neither Democrats nor Republicans, on the whole, favor a full-time legislature, but some members are pushing for one. In Kansas, where compensation is about $17,000 and sessions last ninety days each spring, an increasing number of members are full time. According to the senate majority leader, "Kansas is in a free fall toward a full-time legislature." One cannot have a commitment to a family and a regular occupation and still serve in the legislature.[13]

Only the smaller states, where the level of compensation is limited by the constitution or strong tradition, may be immune to the trend toward the full-time, careerist legislature, but no guarantees exist. In Vermont, for instance, legislative leaders are trying to devise responses to increasing pressure short of a full-time, professional legislature. Survival of the current system is doubtful, however. "I'm not optimistic that two decades from now," said one senate leader, "you're going to find a citizen legislature in Vermont."[14]

As members spend more time on the job, the legislature can easily become their full-time preoccupation and their main work. The natural tendency is for legislators "to identify with the position" and become rooted in the legislative way of life.[15]

Yet, with the recent move toward limiting the terms of legislators, a possibility exists that legislative careerism will be thwarted. The recent trend is clear; the future remains uncertain.

A New Breed

The new breed of legislators consists of people who enjoy politics and "prefer it to any other line of work." [16] Moreover, different types of people have been assuming positions and embarking upon careers in state legislatures.

Most notably, a marked increase is evident in the number of women. Four percent of the nation's legislators in 1969, women by 1991 accounted for 18 percent of the total. African-Americans also have made gains, up from 2.2 percent in 1970 to 5.8 percent by 1991. Hispanics, too, have been picking up seats but still have less than 2 percent of the total nationwide (but more than 10 percent in Arizona, Colorado, New Mexico, and Texas and more than 5 percent in California and Florida).

The occupational composition of state legislatures has been changing dramatically. The numbers of businesspersons, farmers, and practitioners of various private professions are diminishing. The decline in practicing attorneys is especially noticeable. Attorneys, and especially those in larger firms, cannot afford to spend the time required, and they refuse to jeopardize their practices by disclosing the names of clients, as required by regulations to reduce conflicts of interests. Nationally, the proportion of attorneys serving as legislators declined from 30 percent in 1960 to 20 percent in 1979 and was down to about 16 percent by 1986.[17] In states such as New York, attorneys still abound, but elsewhere few attorneys with substantial experience and law practices are left.

These old breeders, the mainstays of former legislatures, are being replaced by career politicians who come from the ranks of unseasoned lawyers, teachers, preachers, spouses of professionals, single people who can live on a legislative salary, public organizers, legislative aides, and others of like ilk.[18] The new breed has either more disposable time or few outside pursuits. For example, teachers in elementary and secondary schools can spend the fall semester in the classroom and take leave during the spring to attend the legislative session. In recent years, teachers— frequently sponsored by local education associations—have been the largest growing occupational grouping in the legislature. Their numbers are particularly strong in Alabama, and in other states they account for almost one out of five members. Taking their cue from teachers, groups such as police officers and fire fighters, in a state such as Washington, are getting their members to run for the legislature and represent their interests. The younger, newer members also are those who come out of college, graduate school, or law school and go directly into politics. No other significant occupational experience intervenes. More members have been moving up through the political and governmental ranks, and fewer by dint of having achieved successful careers in private life.

Thus far, only in a few states has recruitment been from the ranks of legislative staff, but staff may be a source of membership in the future. In California, one out of every four or five members previously has served as a personal aide to a member or as a consultant to a committee. A few California lawmakers are third-generation staffers. For example, Democrat assemblyman Charles Calderon served on the staff of Assemblyman Richard Alatorre, who had previously been on the staff of Assemblyman Walter Karabian.[19] In Wisconsin, one out of every six members served as either a congressional or legislative staffer before being elected. In Illinois, too, a number of former staffers now are in the general assembly.

Ambition for Public Office

What distinguishes the full-time, professional politicians from the part-time citizens is not only where they have come from but also where they are going. Fewer of the old timers harbored career ambitions in politics. They intended to serve a while and return to private careers. Many of the new breed, by contrast, would like to spend their careers in government or politics. They find public office appealing and the game of politics exhilarating. They take pleasure in their status, delight in the exercise of power, and have policies they want to advance.

These new breeders are professionals who want to stay in public office for the long haul. A number of them are content to remain in the house or senate for eight, ten, or twelve years. Some are like old breeders; they want to spend their last two or three years on the executive payroll, where a significantly higher salary will boost their overall pensions. A growing number are politically ambitious, interested in higher office. A veteran lobbyist in California described this species: "There is an overriding ambition to become something else." [20] Not only in California, but around the country, "something else" means U.S. representative or senator, state attorney general, secretary of state, lieutenant governor, or governor. It may even mean mayor or county commissioner, or, as in New York, judge. Normally, higher office means an expansion of one's electoral base and of one's salary.

Not many contemporary legislators leave the legislature voluntarily. Some go when their pensions vest; a few become frustrated and decide not to run again. Some are frightened off by an unfavorable redistricting after a decennial reapportionment. Some exit for health reasons; and one or two, depending on the state, do not run again because they have been indicted. A few leave after bitter and extended legislative sessions. A number depart as soon as they have a shot—even a long shot—at higher office. Members of the house often run for the senate, and members of either body run for a congressional seat or for statewide office when and if the opportunity arises. One study, for instance, found that, among those who left the legislature between 1986 and 1988, almost one in five ran for some other office.[21]

The appeal of legislative service is illustrated by the case of Florida, despite the low salary paid legislators. In the Florida house from 1968 through 1990, of 120 members, the number of incumbents running either for reelection or for other office ranged from 103 to 117. The percentages ranged from 86.6 in 1972 to 97.5 in 1986 and has not fallen below 93.3 since 1978. In the Florida senate, the pattern is similar. From 1974 through 1990, the percentages running either for reelection or for other office ranged from 80 to 100.

The same trend is evident elsewhere. One study, drawing on data from twenty-nine states for 1966 to 1976, found a decline in the proportion of voluntary withdrawals from office.[22] Another study, which focused on Indiana from 1958 to 1984, also found a smaller percentage of incumbents retiring voluntarily. During the first six years of this period, 20 percent of the members chose to leave. By 1984, only about 7 percent left of their own accord.[23]

The estimates are roughly the same for other states. California and Illinois have been losing only about 5 percent of their members voluntarily at any single election. In Michigan and Wisconsin, the figure of voluntary retirees is roughly the same, and in Ohio, only somewhat higher. In states such as Connecticut and Maryland, which still have predominantly citizen legislatures, about 10 percent of the members have been choosing to return to private life at the conclusion of their terms. Even Kentucky and Tennessee, with their citizen legislatures, are moving along a similar path. Only 10 percent of Kentucky legislators have been departing voluntarily. In Tennessee, although legislators complain about the inadequacy of their pay ($12,500 a year) and working conditions, growing numbers want to return, and since 1984 more than 80 percent of incumbents have sought renomination.[24]

Exceptions exist; New Hampshire is one. A third of the members voluntarily leaves the legislature at term's end. Whatever the trend elsewhere, New Hampshire does not appear in danger of being taken over by career politicians.

Politicization of the Process

The legislature always has been a political body; it has become increasingly so. Electoral considerations always have been salient, especially to house members who had to run every two years. They have become more so because legislative office has become an appealing place—to ply one's political trade, to use as a springboard to higher office, or both. Members choose to run for reelection as a "result of assessments of the attractiveness of the legislature, the feasibility of getting reelected, and the availability of higher office that are more attractive." [25]

State legislatures are becoming like the U.S. House of Representatives. Most members of the U.S. House view politics as a career and care a great deal about retaining their office. "As politics has become a profession, and service in the House a realistic and attractive career, job security has become as important for the professional representative as for any other professional—but more problematic." [26] As in the case of Congress, state legislative office also is prized; thus, as in Congress, incumbents seek to solidify their hold on it.

The preoccupation with retaining one's job is not surprising. For careerists, who devote nearly all of their time to legislative politics, that is their profession. For some, a defeat means not only a loss of status and equanimity, but also of livelihood. "After all," as two scholars wrote, "for the old breed electoral defeat was a disapportionment; for the new breed it may be the end of a career." [27] To reduce occupational risk, therefore, many legislators today make electoral concerns paramount. "They start running the day they take their oath of office" is how one observer characterized their behavior in New Jersey.[28] "Everything they do is geared toward the election," said another in Illinois. In California, where the stakes are high, campaigns and elections are seemingly constant, and the survival mentality dominates legislative life. Even in New Hampshire, where the stakes are low, members appear to be paying more attention to their reelection.

Campaign Resources

While the reelectoral drive of legislators is intense, their opportunities to run successfully are excellent. Available are new technologies, ample finances, and in more and more places considerable legislative assistance.

The marvels of modern technology enable legislators to publicize their names, convey their images, and disseminate their messages to the electorate with more telling effect than in the past. Today's generation of politicians appreciates what new techniques can do for them. They have a better feel for public relations and a keen sense of how to enhance their prospects for reelection.

Radio is a popular medium for candidates because the rates are reasonable. Television may be expensive, and the costs keep going up, but TV has become a common feature of campaigning, especially in the larger and more competitive districts in the big states. In Illinois, for instance, senate Democrats hired a consultant who trained members in how to present themselves before television cameras. But even in a smaller state such as Kentucky, TV is used by candidates in urban areas and in some rural races as well. Public opinion polling, direct mail, and the targeting of voters are well-developed techniques. Not only is the technology more effective, but the corps of consultants and campaign staff also are more skillful. They are adept at marketing their wares, and legislators are willing to buy.

All legislators need to purchase the new technology are financial resources—the "mother's milk of politics," in the words of Jesse Unruh, former Speaker of the assembly and long-time treasurer of California. The new technology is driving up the costs of politics tremendously, and an abundance of campaign contributions are available. California leads the pack when it comes to levels of spending on legislative campaigns. Competitive races in California commonly cost $500,000 and on occasion exceed $1 million. In a special election for a senate seat in 1987, more than $2 million was spent. By contrast, senators in California whose seats are safe spend about $250,000, still a huge sum in comparison with earlier times or other states.

Elsewhere both the totals and costs of single races are significantly lower than in California, but they still are relatively high. In Ohio, a competitive election may cost $300,000; in Michigan, $250,000; and in Wisconsin, $100,000. Even in New Hampshire a contest for one of the twenty-four seats in the senate runs in the neighborhood of $100,000. In most states, as in Connecticut, competitive districts may go for $50,000, while safer districts cost half that—by no means exorbitant amounts by California standards. The cost of races in Indiana is lower still; with few exceptions, they run several thousand dollars.

The key fact is that everywhere costs have been rising. New Jersey is probably typical of the larger states. In 1983, about $5.5 million was spent on the legislative elections for forty senate and eighty assembly seats. More than $100,000 was spent by each of eleven senate and two assembly candidates. In 1987, spending rose to $11.3 million, with twenty-three senate and six assembly candidates hitting the $100,000 mark. In New Jersey's 1991 legislative elections, candidates spent a total of $15.1 million, a 34 percent increase, in the midst of a recession. Thirty-four candidates spent more than $100,000 on their campaigns. Three senate candidates exceeded $400,000 in expenditures, and a number of others spent more than $300,000.[29]

Unless provisions are made for public financing of legislative election, as in Minnesota and Wisconsin, candidates have little reason to stint on fund raising. The costs of new technologies and consultants require ample warchests. Moreover, even those members who appear to be relatively safe—at least statistically—are not inclined to take chances. They believe that, by raising large sums, serious opponents will be discouraged from making what would seem to be a futile race. In any event, money usually can be stockpiled for a future reelection race or a run for higher office.

In addition to what they can raise on their own, incumbents who wish to return find that the legislature itself provides considerable resources that can be used for reelection. First, and foremost, is staff. In the 1970s, legislatures in competitive states began to staff their leadership, the party caucuses of the two houses, or both. In Illinois, over the last twenty years, the size of partisan staffs has tripled or quadrupled, so that today house Democrats and Republicans each have about eighty, while senate Democrats, in the majority, have sixty and senate Republicans, in the minority, somewhat fewer professionals on the payroll. Most of Michigan's nine hundred professionals are organized along partisan lines.

Connecticut exemplifies one way in which partisan staff can mushroom. Until the early 1970s, the Connecticut general assembly had little professional staffing. Then, its nonpartisan central staff—research, fiscal, bill drafting, and program review—became firmly established. Somewhat later, the party caucuses added their own professionals. However, it was not until the Republicans took control of the legislature in 1984, the Democrats regained their majorities in 1986, and additional space was made available by a new legislative office building that the staffing pattern in Connecticut changed dramatically. In 1987, another one hundred partisan staff positions were created, added to the fewer than three dozen already in existence, and divided up among the four legislative parties for allocation to their members. In the early 1980s, Connecticut's caucus staffs were oriented mainly toward legislation; now their orientation is toward constituencies and campaigns.

In California, the politicization of staff has spread to standing committees. Earlier, committee staff was completely nonpartisan. Then the buildup of partisan staff began, so that today partisan professionals staff all the assembly committees as well as the senate fiscal committees. In the words of a long-time observer of the California scene, "The policy experts have been replaced by political hired guns whose main job is to get their bosses elected." [30] But staff support for California legislators will be less in the future than it has been in the recent past. Proposition 140, the term limits initiative of 1990, also cut the legislature's operating budget by 38 percent. Layoffs of staff began soon after, and California's staff has been cut substantially.

The campaign activities of legislative staff have been challenged in several states. In 1987, the Manhattan district attorney brought an indictment for grand larceny and conspiracy against the New York senate minority leader and one of his colleagues. Public funds were being used for campaigns, with eight Democratic candidates, of whom six were challengers, receiving the services of workers on the senate minority's payroll. The minority leader was finally acquitted, but only after a period of painful publicity. A few years later, New Jersey endured its own campaigning scandal. Called into question were the incidental campaign activities of partisan staff on legislative time and the use of public resources, such as office computers and telephones, for campaign purposes. The state attorney general launched an investigation. Although a grand jury returned no indictments, it issued a presentment that was critical of legislative practices.

Officially, partisan staff does not get involved in campaigns. Unofficially, one of their jobs is to maintain their party's majority, help their party achieve a majority, or simply add to their numbers. As one professional, from a large partisan staff, described the task:

> We don't do anything on a campaign, but everything we do is for the campaign. The first year, we set them [members] up legislatively; the second year, we work their constituencies.

The legislative and constituency aspects of reelection intertwine. Legislative accomplishments often are designed and nearly always are packaged for constituency consumption, which is why the computerization of legislatures is such a boon to members who are seeking reelection. The primary interest legislators have in computers is not for lawmaking or simulation (those applications can be left to staff), but in compiling lists and targeting mail to folks back home. Disentangling the legislative and political purposes of mailings is difficult, but the volume of mail sent by legislative offices rises in election years. Some states, such as Connecticut, have a cutoff date for mailings as the election approaches. Others try to specify what is more or less permissible. But, for the most part, anything that casts a member in a positive light accomplishes a political purpose.

The situation may take on an amusing cast, as when assembly Democrats, including the minority leader, in New Jersey filed suit in federal court charging six Republicans, including the Speaker, with improper use of taxpayers' money to send mail with political, and not informational, messages. According to the Democrats, among Republican transgressions was the mailing of the Republican Speaker's speech, which was "blatantly political and partisan, touting accomplishments of the Assembly under Republican control and attacking what used to happen in the Assembly when the Democrats were the majority party." The Democrats also charged that two Republicans sent a report to constituents about a bill to provide funds for the district, a mailing "clearly designed to enhance their political support by emphasizing their role in passage of the bill." As one might predict, the Speaker responded that the object of the mailings was to "inform the public of actions taken in their state assembly." [31] Both sides had a point.

Probably of greatest help to members, as far as reelection is concerned, are the services they perform for constituents. Members of

Congress recognized some time ago that constituency service is an important means to earn electoral support. State legislators also are aware of the benefits they derive from serving their constituents. Although this realization is not completely new, state legislators now are acquiring resources to engage in such endeavors. And as resources increase, so does the amount of constituency service performed.[32] In states where legislators have neither offices in their districts nor personal staff, they are helped by caucus, committee, and central staffs.

Constituency service by U.S. representatives and senators has been shown to help incumbents in their quest for reelection.[33] Although the precise electoral benefits at the state legislative level are not known, legislators—most of whom feel insecure electorally—believe that constituency service pays off. In any event, service is a fact of contemporary political life. In the smaller as well as larger states, the feeling is that if a legislator does not attend to the needs of constituents, then constituents will find someone else who will.

Advantages of Incumbency

Incumbency, or rather the resources that incumbents bring to bear to win reelection, conveys advantage. The success rate in recent elections of incumbents in the U.S. House is well over 90 percent. A number of state legislatures approach the congressional figure. In the professionalized legislature of the large states—California, Illinois, Michigan, New York, and Pennsylvania—nine out of ten incumbents have been returned. The same proportions are successful in Wisconsin, a somewhat smaller state with a professionalized legislature, and in Indiana, Maryland, Minnesota, and Ohio, where career professionalization has not gone as far. The advantages of incumbency can be seen in Florida. The success rate for incumbents running for the house from 1968 through 1990 ranged from 82 percent to 97 percent, and for the senate from 1974 through 1990 it ranged from 71 percent to 95 percent.

Even in legislatures such as those of Connecticut and Tennessee, which are still largely composed of amateur politicians, reelection rates have been high. Tennessee's rate has been about 96 percent for the senate and 87 percent for the house since 1984. Of those incumbents defeated for renomination or reelection, most suffered as a result of national tides.[34] The same pattern holds for Connecticut, where nine out of ten incumbents normally are returned to office. The elections of 1984 and 1986 were aberrations: President Ronald Reagan's coattails pulled in Republicans in the earlier year while Gov. William A. O'Neill's coattails pulled in Democrats the later year. Even so, almost eight of ten incumbents won in these two elections. Nowadays, however, coattails are shorter just about everywhere. A recent study of state elections found that coattails were losing their pull, as state legislative elections were becoming insulated from outside influences and resources available to incumbents more formidable.[35]

Most districts not only have been relatively safe for incumbents, but also for one party or the other. Natural demographic patterns is the main reason. In addition, decennial reapportionments tend to result in district lines that leave most incumbents reasonably secure. And as the proportion of competitive districts in a state declines, the likelihood of incumbents seeking and winning another term increases. Over time, the demography of districts may change and the partisan composition may shift. Thus, an incumbent's partisan advantage within specific districts may diminish. But one or the other party still is likely to maintain partisan advantage even a decade after redistricting, and, in any case, the incumbent has had time to use the available resources to secure an overwhelming advantage.

Because the overall resources of incumbents are greater than those of potential challengers and because redistricting works in the incumbents' favor, three to four out of every five districts are safe—by any objective standard. Yet, subjective standards are what count, for no such thing as a safe district exists for the professional legislator. Perceptions of electoral insecurity are found among careerist members as well as members who serve in part-time legislatures and who face little competition. A study in Alabama, for instance, reported that despite ample evidence of the safety of their districts, 93 percent of the members said their districts were electorally competitive.[36] Legislators everywhere realize that, however safe their district may appear, lightning can strike. Incumbents can be taken out by a national tide, a peculiar issue, or a scandal, especially if an opponent has a large enough warchest to exploit the situation. Because safe candidates have lost, incumbents take no chances.

The advantages of incumbents are not entirely new. A study comparing the period 1968-1976 with 1978-1986 showed that no great change occurred in the percentages winning reelection.[37] Nor were they invariable. In the current climate, the earlier advantages of incumbency appear to have diminished, and the prospects ahead suggest that incumbents will be running at greater risk.

One reason for this is temporary, but periodic. After redistricting, which takes place following the decennial U.S. census, constituencies are reshaped. Not every district undergoes significant change, but several do, with some incumbents losing a good number of their partisan supporters. Other districts undergo some change, with some incumbents losing past supporters while picking up unknowns. Legislative turnover is higher in the election after redistricting, with more members than usual voluntarily retiring instead of risking defeat and others losing in general elections.

Another reason for the cloudier prospects of incumbents relates to the economic condition of the nation. The 1990-1992 recession created significant budgetary problems for more than half the states, requiring governors and legislatures to cut state employees, reduce state services, or raise taxes. Actions taken by public officials have been highly unpopular, and governors across the country have seen their performance ratings decline.[38] Legislators also are likely to incur blame for hard times in the states. This was the case in New Jersey's legislative elections of 1991, when a $2.8 billion tax package proposed by Gov. James J. Florio and passed by the Democrats in the legislature led to an overwhelming defeat for the party in power. About one out of four incumbents lost, all Democrats save for a single Republican. If a state's economy is stagnant, while public needs continue to grow, lawmakers will suffer the consequences at the voting booth.

A final reason for the increasing difficulties faced by incumbents is the highly critical attitude many Americans have toward government and politics and an overall anti-incumbency mood. This contemporary climate derives partly from economic woes and fears, but it also is a manifestation of a longer-term orientation of voters.

Leadership Roles

The impact of politics and elections on the legislative process extends beyond the activities of individual members. As a result, campaign management has become one of the essential tasks of legislative leaders, absorbing much of their attention and energy.

Having been inaugurated by Jesse Unruh in California in the 1960s, the practice of leaders raising campaign funds for members has spread widely in the last few years. Leaders in more than half the states are raising funds and allocating money and other forms of support to members of their legislative parties. As the minority leader in the New York assembly commented, "Among the many things I do, I go out and raise money for my members, and that's heavy lifting." Seeing a Speaker of the house or a president of the senate collaring a lobbyist in a capitol corridor and inquiring, "How is it that I don't have your check for tickets to my fundraiser yet?" or "Did you realize that you contributed $500 to the senate president's (or the house Speaker's) fund and only $250 to mine?" is not unusual.

Willie Brown, Speaker of the California assembly, set the pace by raising millions for Democratic candidates and intervening in primary races. Both Brown and David Roberti, the president pro tempore of the senate, were elected to their leadership positions on a platform that said they would raise money and protect the seats of their members. California's legislative leadership political action committees customarily were responsible for more than one-fifth of all the funds raised in legislative elections.³⁹ Recently, raising money has become more difficult for California's leaders. In 1988, voters passed Proposition 73, which prohibited leaders from transferring funds they raised to candidate accounts. Although leadership PACs no longer serve such purposes, leaders continue to be involved in fund raising for members, and members continue to expect it.

Leaders elsewhere also are heavily involved in fund raising. Tom Loftus, when he served as Speaker of the Wisconsin assembly, acknowledged his role as "campaign manager." He chaired the Assembly Democratic Campaign Committee, helped recruit candidates, furnished them with schooling in campaign techniques, provided personnel and logistical support, issued position papers on their behalf, and did fund raising.⁴⁰ In New Hampshire, leadership also takes part in the election of members. The Granite Committee, for instance, is the organization of house Republicans. Chaired by the majority leader, it raises and doles out money to candidates in close races. The committee is a relative newcomer to the scene, having been started only in 1988, but it is becoming an important part of the electoral environment.

Legislative leaders and party committees want their resources to be used as effectively as possible, so they are targeted close races, given to challengers as well as incumbents. In those states where political parties compete vigorously in legislative elections, one of the chief jobs of the leader is to win or maintain the majority of seats in the chamber. This is the situation in Connecticut, Illinois, Michigan, Minnesota, New Jersey, New York, Ohio, Pennsylvania, and Washington. For example, look at the experience of Chuck Hardwick, who had been minority leader in the New Jersey assembly. For a full year he spent part of every day working for the Republican's 1985 campaign, holding the hand of each candidate with a chance of winning. His efforts (and Gov. Thomas H. Kean's coattails) paid off; the Republicans won control, and Hardwick became Speaker. In an address on his new role, enumerating twelve different tasks of the Speaker, Hardwick put "preparing for the next campaign" first. The ordering was no accident, for if he neglected maintaining his majority, he would not have to concern himself with most of the other tasks. The Republicans in 1987 kept control of the assembly, although by a smaller margin.

The primary focus of the legislative party and legislative party leadership used to be governing. Now, legislative parties are displacing party organizations at state and local levels, taking over the electoral function as well. Thus, a major shift in political power is occurring, at least in a number of states. Newly acquired power, however, can absorb much of the time of legislative leaders and distract them from their other responsibilities. Leaders generally see the benefits of the new system but acknowledge that it may go too far. According to Tom Loftus:

It's when it's overdone that I think it's of some concern. What happens is that the leaders then become expected to raise money for candidates, the system gets out of control, it isn't a unifying force. . . . And it may not bring a caucus together, it may not strengthen leadership, it may indeed give leadership an additional job and be a distraction.[41]

Furthermore, the electoral activities of leaders—and particularly their fund-raising efforts—raise questions regarding the ethics of the legislature. The controversy surrounding the issue of campaigning within the legislative context was highlighted most dramatically in New York by the indictment of the senate minority leader. "I don't know which side of the line those guys were on," the assembly minority leader commented, "because I'm not sure where the line is." [42]

Leadership takes care of the electoral needs of its party's incumbents in strictly legislative ways, too. Freshmen members from tough districts are helped by every means practicable. They may be given a vice chairmanship of a committee that can benefit them in their district or with a key group. They may be counseled on how to vote as safely as they can on a variety of issues, given the nature of their constituencies. If they can be spared, they can vote as they please on controversial party votes. While targeted members in competitive districts naturally receive special treatment, all legislative party members are favored in ways that will benefit them and the party electorally.

Electoral Competition and Partisanship

Electoral concerns cannot fail to affect the legislative process. Members facing strong electoral challenges behave differently from how they would otherwise, because they are under severe stress. For example, the statewide candidacies of a number of legislators were especially disruptive of the legislative process in Florida during the 1986 session. Three candidates, including the president of the senate, were running for governor. A former representative also was running for governor. Another representative was in the race for lieutenant governor, two senators and a representative were seeking the office of attorney general, and two representatives and one senator were vying for commissioner of education. Another senator was running for an open congressional seat, and two house members were competing to be major of Jacksonville. A number of house members were running for the senate. And the Democratic governor was seeking to unseat the Republican U.S. senator.

Electoral considerations were pervasive throughout the legislative session. Photographers trailed candidates in the corridors; television crews wired candidates for sound and filmed them on the floor of the chamber; and several members left Tallahassee for campaign appearances around the state, even though important business was under way at the capitol.

One candidate for attorney general attacked his opponent in radio and television advertisements, on the senate floor, and in committee. A contingent of house Republicans supported one of their own for governor; a contingent of house Democrats supported their former colleague (who ultimately won the Democratic nomination, but lost the general election) for governor; and a contingent of senate Democrats favored the president of their chamber. Tension always exists between the Florida house and senate, but that year it was sharper than usual.

Issues in the 1986 session of the Florida legislature also were influenced by electoral politics. Bills on drunken driving were introduced, not by chance but after polling and with the impending election in mind. The senate's reluctance to raise taxes for educational funding was in part a function of the president's candidacy and the tough reelection races facing several Democratic incumbents.

Electoral competition among individual members, as in Florida, weighs heavily upon the legislature. Competition between the parties weighs upon it even more. In the early 1960s, only a dozen or so states had competitive parties. Now more than half the states have substantial competition at the legislative as well as the gubernatorial level, and in most of the rest competition has been increasing since the early 1980s. Partisanship, which is associated with party competition, is growing at the state level.

Some legislatures, however, are not partisan, such as in states where few Republicans hold seats. In Maryland, for example, only 9 members of the 47-member senate and 25 of the 141-member house in 1991 were Republicans. Few policy issues in Annapolis see a division by party. The minority gives little thought to trying to embarrass the majority; nor does much sniping take place. In terms of partisanship, life in the Maryland general assembly is calm. When conflict occurs, it tends to pit legislators from the rural, western part of the state allied with those of the Eastern Shore against legislators from Baltimore and its suburbs. Still, Republicans have been gaining recently, even in Maryland.

Overall, partisanship has grown, particularly in states where the effects have been greatest, such as California, Michigan, New Jersey, and Wisconsin. It also has been on the rise in states where it meant relatively little—in Florida, for instance. The number of Floridians who identify with the Republican party has been increasing, as has Republican registration. By 1991, GOP strength measured 43 percent in the senate and 38 percent in the house. Texas has been moving in the same direction, with Republicans holding 38 percent of the seats in the house.

What stimulates partisanship is the strong concern of both leaders and rank and file with the maintenance (or acquisition) of party majorities and leadership positions. A governor and legislature controlled by different parties also can be a stimulant. California is a case in point.

Over the years partisanship has been intensifying (especially in the senate, which once had been a comradely institution—much more of a club). Willie Brown gained his assembly Speakership with Republican support. Two years later, when he had consolidated his position within the Democratic caucus, he no longer needed support from Republicans. His treatment of them became less beneficent, which exacerbated partisan feelings in the assembly. The sides hardened further because of the ideology and practice of the Republican governor. In California, partisanship has become nasty and is undoubtedly fueled by the Republican challenge to eighteen years of Democratic control of the legislature. Whereas legislators used to fight one day and come together again the next, now they hold grudges.

When Democrats and Republicans are ideologically at opposite poles on major issues, partisanship will be more intense. Along with other factors, patterns of policy difference can sharply divide the parties. A study of legislative voting in California showed that both the house and senate are polarized, with liberals and conservatives falling almost completely in opposite partisan camps. In the assembly, for example, not one Republican was more liberal than the most conservative Democrat, and in the senate only one Republican was more liberal than the most conservative Democratic.[43]

Whatever the ideological split, issues also are raised and used for electoral purposes, as vehicles in the quest for power. Nothing new exists in the legislative parties taking into account the potential effects that their position on legislation will have on their electoral prospects. As the story goes, a legislative staffer cautioned a party leader in Ohio, "If you pass this bill, you're going to screw up the state for the next thirty years." "We can't worry about the next thirty years," the leader replied. "We have to worry about the next election."

Beyond merely taking into account the electoral effects of legislative positions, the parties in the senate and house go further today. They raise and exploit issues, more than previously, to gain partisan advantage rather than to enact legislation to their liking. One way that a legislative party attempts to secure an edge electorally is by "making a record" that will help it, embarrass the opposition, or both. Floor amendments, requiring record votes, is the conventional device used. As one observer noted, "Clearly, efforts are made to establish records on which to run or on which to try to maneuver your opponents into an undesirable position." Typically, Democrats will try to get Republicans on record against teachers or environmental interests, while Republicans will try to get Democrats on record against economic development.

Partisan positioning has become routine in states such as California, Connecticut, Illinois, Iowa, Michigan, and Wisconsin. In some legislatures, a large part of the floor session seemingly is managed at least partly with the next election in mind. In Michigan, for example, the custom has been to forego record votes so that colleagues would not be embarrassed. Now, both sides call for roll calls to put the opposition on record. In addition, in the past, Michigan legislators quickly forgot the votes cast against them by their colleagues.

Perhaps nowhere has partisanship been sharper than in New Jersey. After the Republicans, campaigning in the 1991 election against the Democratic tax increases, won control of both houses of the legislature, the Democrats quickly retaliated for their defeat. In the lame-duck session, the outgoing senate Democratic majority voted to sunset the entire $2.8 billion tax package to force the incoming Republican majorities to vote to restore part of it. The assembly Democrats, however, fell short of the forty-one votes needed for passage. The Democratic intent had been to exercise revenge, compel the Republicans to raise taxes, and then use their votes against them during the next election.

In many races—and particularly the larger, competitive, professionalized ones—winning power is becoming more important to legislators than exercising it. After all, if power cannot be won, it cannot be exercised. Thus, legislators can justify the efforts they devote to their reelection. No one else will do it for them, and they have everything to lose. But the impact of their activities is great. As one critic of the California legislature argued:

> [The system] has been politicized and corrupted by the pervasive influence of money in politics and government, politics as a career orientation, the need for legislators to reassure their reelection, and the lack of time to consider policy because time must be spent raising money.[44]

Other states may lag behind California and New Jersey, but the politicization sweeping a growing number of legislatures is leaving its mark on the process and the institution.

Fragmentation

In any American state legislature, power is highly decentralized. Some legislators have somewhat more power and others somewhat less, but essentially each elected representative has a vote and a say. Power is divided, not only among individuals but also between houses and parties and among committees, delegations, and other groupings. Reaching agreement in the legislature on a controversial issue is not easy.

The natural state of a legislature is fragmentation. But in a number of respects, the legislature is even more fragmented today than twenty years ago. Earlier, leaders were truly in command, and power was tightly held. Partly as a consequence of modernization and reform, legislatures have been democratized.[45] Resources are more broadly distributed, and the gap between leaders and other legislators is narrower.

Committee systems have been strengthened significantly. Now, standing committees are agencies of specialization, and the legislative workload is parceled out among them. Each committee rules over its own turf and possesses substantial power. The chairpersons set their own agendas, shape their committee's decisions, and negotiate issues with one another. They are figures with whom lobbyists, executive officials, legislators, and legislative leaders must reckon. Ten or twenty standing committees, each in its own domain doing its own thing, constitute a formidable centrifugal force in a legislative body.

Legislative staff is far more dispersed than it used to be. Years ago, the dominant staff was the office of legislative council or an equivalent service agency. It provided information and research for the two chambers, both parties, every committee, and the entire roster of members. Recently, however, staffing patterns changed. First, partisan staffing for the legislative parties in each house was established in a dozen or so states, challenging the dominance of the nonpartisan centralized staffs. Second, in a number of places—most recently Louisiana and Oklahoma—agencies that worked for both the senate and house split up, so that each chamber wound up with its own base of support. Third, standing committees, in states such as California and New York, acquired their own professionals whose primary loyalty was to the committee, to the chair, and to a specific policy domain. Fourth, a growing number of legislators are being staffed as individuals at the capitol or in their districts, in response to their demands for help or as a reward for the backing they give their leaders. Whatever the pattern, practically everywhere current staffs are larger and more accessible to members. If the knowledge provided by staff constitutes power, then power within the legislature is shared among more members today.

Another fragmenting tendency results from the many groups and lobbyists promoting their particular interests. Their overall influence may or may not be greater than formerly, but their numbers and activities have grown substantially. Years ago relatively few interests were represented at the state level; now many are. This is because of the heightened political awareness and mobilization of previously uninvolved segments of the population; the substantial development of multistate business enterprises; the upsurge in ideological politics and single-issue groups; and the reduction of the federal government's role in various policy arenas coupled with the increase in action at the state level. With the federal government leaving a power vacuum for the states to fill and the state governments moving into new fields, such as consumer affairs, the environment, the workplace, and other areas dealing with social issues, interest groups have targeted state capitals. Each interest has a specific agenda that it presses upon the legislature.

New interests have formed and traditional interests have fragmented, but each has provided for its own representation. The result is that most states have witnessed an explosion of lobbyists as well as a growth in the number of groups. An Associated Press survey found that in 1990 more than 42,500 lobbyists registered in the fifty states, an increase of about 20 percent in four years. The contemporary lobbyist has an array of approaches to legislative issues and legislators: coalition building; grass roots mobilization, media, and public relations efforts; contributions to and involvement in legislator campaigns; entertainment and socializing; and various techniques of direct lobbying. As they seek to satisfy their concerns, lobbyists and their clients pull legislators in a myriad of directions.[46]

Probably the greatest impetus toward institutional fragmentation is the constituency basis of legislative representation. Legislators owe their first and foremost allegiance to their constituents. They introduce local bills to benefit their districts; they endeavor to get more than a fair share for their districts from state aid formulas, particularly school aid; they seek to have funds for statewide programs spent in their districts; they try to get as much pork for their districts as possible; and, with or without personal staff and local offices, they manage to deliver more mail and more services to the folks back home. Added to all the mix is that the trend over the years has been away from multimember districts—where more than one representative is elected by the same voters—and toward single-member ones, thus encouraging greater parochialism on the parts of members. As a recent study of members of Congress observed, "Single-member district systems do not provide elected representatives with compelling personal incentives to pursue common interests." [47] Or, from a state legislative perspective, the closer legislators are tied to their district, the more difficult they may find considering statewide interests.[48]

These fragmenting tendencies buttress the individualism of members. Because of the candidate-centered nature of political campaigns, the opportunities offered by television and other media, and the legislative resources at their disposal, the individualism of legislators has increased markedly. The media exert a special appeal by paying attention to members who are different—independents, mavericks, rebels. If members aspire to higher office and seek statewide name identification, individualism offers a most promising route.

In the face of such fragmentation, legislative leadership may be the only glue that holds the institution together. The power of leadership, however, is on the decline. Although the length of leadership tenure gradually has increased over the years and rotational systems have been fading,[49] most leaders today live precariously. A number have been challenged, and several have been overthrown, by their colleagues in the party caucus or by bipartisan coalitions. Individual leaders have been ousted recently in Connecticut, Kentucky, Mississippi, North Carolina, and Oklahoma. Moreover, assaults have been made on the institutional powers of leadership to manage legislative personnel and the legislative process. Notable limitations have been instituted in California, Colorado, Kansas, Mississippi, North Carolina, and Rhode Island.[50] One observer has concluded that

> [Power] may be dispersed so broadly that it might well have disappeared into thin air. And leadership, which ultimately depends upon the existence of power, may disappear along with it.[51]

An Unfriendly Environment

One of the nation's most powerful legislative leaders is John Martin, the veteran Speaker of the Maine house. Martin recently served as president of the National Conference of State Legislatures. In an address to that organization's 1991 annual meeting, he lamented on the current state of state legislatures:

> We have been battered by fiscal crises. We have been victimized by the unabated federal government storm of mandate and preemption. We have felt the alienation and distrust of voters. We have been saddened by sting operations and other ethics investigations.

Expectations and Demands

Despite their increased power, the states and their legislatures bear responsibilities that are extraordinarily difficult to fulfill. During the Nixon, Carter, and Reagan administrations, Washington, D.C., devolved itself of a measure of power that had been accruing since the New Deal. State governments thereby found themselves with greater power to make policy and regulate economic activity. But they were left with larger bills to pay, because the federal government also reduced its financial aid commitments to the states.

Citizens expect their state governments to deliver programs and services. Their expectations have been fed by government itself, which has been dealing with more issues and mandating more programs, and by political candidates, who in addressing the issues continue to hold out solutions and promise results.

Whatever they expect to receive, citizens are insistent that their governments hold the lid on taxes. Increased services for expanding populations can be provided without raising taxes, but greater productivity and a growing economy, which has not been the case, would be required. In the late 1980s and into the 1990s, revenues have lagged and budgets in more than half the states have been hard pressed. In California, Connecticut, Maine, New York, and Pennsylvania, especially, budget problems have been so severe that governors and legislatures both have emerged battered and bloody. Few have emerged victorious of late. Even with a brighter outlook for the economy in mid-1992, economic and budgetary problems will persist in many places.

Campaigns and Ethics

For many Americans, therefore, governments at all levels have failed to meet the demands made upon them. Furthermore, political institutions—and particularly representative assemblies—are inspiring neither confidence nor trust among the electorate. Congress is no doubt the principal target for public disdain, but state legislatures also are under attack. While part of the explanation of the waning of public support for representative institutions relates to the gap between expectations and results, legislative behavior and ethics and public perceptions of them also are to blame.

The costs of political campaigns and the efforts legislators devote to raising funds accounts for much of the problem. Most unfortunate is the impact that the emphasis on money and some of the attendant solicitation methods are having on the political atmosphere. Occasionally a fund-raiser is held just before a vote on a controversial bill or while an appropriations bill is in its final stages. Usually a fund-raiser is held during the legislative session (although in some states, such as Kentucky, none is permitted until the session is over). The message that is communicated, critics maintain, is blatant: "Contribute, or else." For lobbyists, interest groups, and political action committees, no end to giving is apparent; they feel that they are being shaken down. The requests from legislators have doubled or tripled in the last few years. If lobbyists used to prey on legislators, the tables have turned; now, legislators seem to be preying on lobbyists.

Some question exists as to whether campaign contributions have the impact that is attributed to them. Nevertheless, citizens believe that campaign finance has a corrupting influence on members of the legislature. For example, an Associated Press/Media General poll (September 1989) found that four out of five people believed legislators were overly influenced by campaign contributions, and a *Los Angeles Times* poll (December 1989) revealed that two out of three Californians agreed that most of their state legislators were up for sale to their largest campaign contributors.

The way in which campaign money must be raised is not the only disturbing factor associated with elections. The way in which campaigns are conducted also has consequences that are unhealthy for legislatures and the political system. Negative campaigning and attack ads, in the opinions of candidates and consultants, are necessary to win races. So, negatives have become staples of many campaigns, particularly close ones. With each side attacking the record, motivations, and even ethics of the other, the suspicion and cynicism of the electorate gets further feeding.

Beyond campaigns practices per se, a sufficient number of cases of corruption and abuse by legislators add to popular distrust. Recently, a sting operation in Arizona resulted in the indictment of seven members. Similar investigations have taken place in California, South Carolina, Tennessee, and West Virginia, with a number of legislators being convicted. A *Los Angeles Times* poll (December 1989), for example, reported that 53 percent of Californians believe that "taking bribes is a relatively" common practice among legislators. Even where bribery or extortion are not at issue, the life of a legislator arouses the press and the public. The perquisites of office, which are few and far between, tend to be exaggerated. And relationships between legislators and lobbyists—especially the gifts, entertainment, and trips that the latter bestow on the former—give rise to further criticism of legislative ethics.

The press compounds the problem. The legislature is far more open than it used to be, and both the print and electronic media coverage of legislatures have increased since the early 1970s.[52] But the press tends to report the worst possible cases, not the best. People naturally generalize from what they read or see—corruption, special interests, excess, wastefulness, partisan game playing, policy stalemate. While the positive feelings that people have for their own legislator do not rub off on the legislature as a whole, "any hint of scandal attached to one legislator tars the entire institution." [53] Because of the very nature of the media, the case against the legislature is grossly distorted. Whatever the sins of state legislatures, they are by no means commensurate with the bad press legislatures receive and the low esteem in which they are held.[54]

The integrity of the legislative institution and legislative process is under siege. Recent polling data on the performance of a number of legislatures are indicative. Positive evaluations (excellent or good) of 24 percent for Alabama; 22 percent, California; 20 percent, Illinois; 44 percent, Kentucky; and 36 percent, Mississippi were received for 1990 and 34 percent, Illinois, and 32 percent, New Jersey, for 1991.[55] Another recent study, employing focus groups in various regions of the nation, found that Americans believed the present political system was run by a political class, not by the people, and controlled by money, not by votes. In their view, the political system was impervious to public direction. They blamed officeholders, interest groups, and lobbyists, and they were angry.[56]

The Assault on the Legislature

The current drive to limit the terms of state legislators (as well as members of Congress) probably is the most serious assault on the legislature in years. Earlier challenges to legislatures, however, mainly in states that permit voters to initiate measures changing the constitution and the law have taken place. In recent years, initiatives have been introduced to reduce the size of the legislature, shorten the session, convert to a unicameral body, reduce compensation to members, provide for a part-time institution, or otherwise modify legislative procedures or limit legislative power. California, Colorado, Florida, Illinois, Michigan, Nevada, Ohio, Oklahoma, Oregon, and South Dakota have all witnessed one or several drives from the outside.[57] Colorado's GAVEL (Give a Vote to Every Legislator) initiative went further than most others in trying to restrict party caucuses and limit the authority of leaders to control the agenda of their chamber.

The term limits idea caught fire in 1990, when California, Colorado, and Oklahoma initiated constitutional changes that will impact the way their legislatures work.[58] In California, Proposition 140 passed with 52 percent of the vote. It subsequently was challenged by the legislature but was upheld by the state supreme court. The measure limited members of the assembly to three two-year terms and senators to two four-year terms, allowing them to run for other office after their terms expired. The Colorado initiative (which also applied to congressional terms) passed by 71 percent, and the Oklahoma initiative, 67 percent. In November 1991, however, Washington voters rejected Initiative 553, which provided for term limits, by 54 to 46 percent, mainly because the measure was such an extreme one.[59] In 1991, term limits legislation was introduced in forty-five states, while at least ten states were to have initiatives on their ballots in 1992.

The term limits movement is endorsed for different reasons by different backers. Many adherents want to get rid of professional legislators, who they claim serve too long. Some of these people are nostalgic for the days of citizen legislators; many are populists; and a good number are political activists. While state legislative turnover has been on the decline, a substantial turnover does occur. Taking the period from 1979 to 1989, for example, turnover averaged 72 percent in state senates and 75 percent in statehouses. Fresh blood, therefore, does make its way to the legislature. After the 1990 elections, 16 percent of senate members and almost 20 percent of house members were new to their office. However, turnover is less in the larger states with more professionalized legislatures, running at about 10 percent a biennium in California, Illinois, Michigan, New York, and Ohio.

Some people favor term limits because they want to curtail government. They tend to regard government as the adversary, something to be controlled. They are not displeased by inexperienced leadership or by deadlock in the legislature.[60] Those who led the fight for Proposition 140 in California, for example, tended to come from the militant right; they were opposed by liberal interest groups, such as teachers and state employees.[61] Republicans appear to be among the key proponents. President George Bush publicly favors term limits, and Americans to Limit Congressional Terms is run out of a Republican consultant's office.

Public support for term limits derives largely from economic fear and negative attitudes toward politics. In California, Colorado, and Oklahoma, state electorates, in voting to limit legislators' terms, were expressing their anger at political institutions. They could do so, moreover, without directly punishing their own legislator. That is what happened in California, where 92 percent of all state legislative incumbents won reelection in 1990, even as voters were passing the term limits initiative. Whatever the underlying motivations, national and state polls show growing and overwhelming public backing for the idea. A *Newsweek* poll (October 1990) generally put support for term limits at 73 percent; in a *New York Times*/CBS poll (October 1991), 68 percent favored term limits for members of Congress. Depending on the particular wording of the question, majorities of 63 to 81 percent in Arizona, Florida, Georgia, Louisiana, Montana, North Dakota, and Wisconsin also backed limits.[62]

Predicting what will happen to those legislatures where term limits are imposed is difficult.[63] The impact will be less on part-time, low-salaried legislatures, which already have high turnover. Still, the few senior members in these institutions will have to depart. The impact will be greater in states with more full-time legislatures, such as California. But, generally, term limits will cut short the legislative careers of some talented legislators (as well as some less talented ones) and of many who retain the confidence of their constituents. The expertise available to the institution probably will decrease and much of its memory will be abolished. Limiting terms, moreover, will redistribute power. Legislators will wind up with somewhat less, while legislative staff, lobbyists, the executive bureaucracy, and the governor will wind up with somewhat more.

Institutional Challenges

It may be ironic that the public's regard for legislatures declined not long after legislatures modernized, developed the capacity to govern, and expanded their role. But contemporary trends—including the professionalization of careers, politicization and preoccupation with elections, and fragmentation—have something to do with heightened public cynicism.

Today legislators run their own campaigns, promote the interests of the districts they represent, and pursue their political ambitions. With the disintegration of political parties, legislators have personalized their appeals and become individual entrepreneurs. The capital community of legislators, lobbyists, and other participants is more diffuse. Few values are shared, and legislative norms are weaker than they used to be. Trust is still important, but as a bond it links fewer members together than formerly.

The process remains a remarkably open one but is less deliberative than it should be. Given the goals of members, the demands of groups, and the heavy workload, deliberation gives way to expediency. Members frequently are unwilling to say no to their colleagues, lest their colleagues say no to them. They also are adverse to saying no to constituents, lest their constituents withdraw support. The process has become porous; much seeps through that probably should not. Standing committees do not screen the wheat from the chaff as diligently as they might.

In view of the individualism of members and the fragmentation of the institution, the legislature probably will continue to enact policies that respond to constituents and interest groups. But will the legislature be able to sustain its capacity to make policies that benefit the states' entire citizenry? One observer has expressed doubt: "[Americans] have elected and empowered a generation of political professionals whose independence and refusal to defer makes concerted action, even when necessary, quite difficult." [64] If the U.S. Congress is any indication, then state legislatures may be at risk of losing much of their ability to fashion consensus, not on narrowly focused matters, but on major statewide policies.

One of the responsibilities of legislators, and of leaders especially, is to protect their institution and maintain its integrity. A declining number, however, have much institutional commitment. And those that do are so embattled that they have neither time nor energy left for tending to institutional matters. Rules and procedures, the organization and performance of staff, the job being done by committees and on the floor, and the public's understanding and perception of the legislature are not immediate problems. Thus, they get short shrift.

The legislative process has been suffering neglect for a while now, and the fabric of the legislative institution has been wearing thin. Members need to pay more attention to their institution, and the press and public need to develop some appreciation of legislatures and the legislative process. That will not come without effort. As David S. Broder, the nationally syndicated columnist, recently wrote: "It's all too easy in stressful times, for everyone to forget how valuable—and how fragile— these representative institutions are." [65] People may not have forgotten; few may ever have really known.

Notes

1. For an account of the legislative reform movement, see Alan Rosenthal, "Reform in State Legislatures," in *Encyclopedia of the American Legislative System* (New York: Scribner's, forthcoming).

2. Alan Rosenthal, *Governors and Legislatures: Contending Powers* (Washington, D.C.: CQ Press, 1989).

3. On this subject, see Alan Ehrenhalt, *The United States of Ambition: Politicians, Power, and the Pursuit of Office* (New York: Random House, 1991); Burdett A. Loomis, "Political Careers and American State Legislatures" (Paper delivered at the "Symposium on the Legislature in the Twenty-First Century" held by the Eagleton Institute of Politics, Rutgers University, Williamsburg, Va., April 27-29, 1990); and Alan Rosenthal, "The Changing Character of State Legislators—Or: Requiem for a Vanishing Breed," *Public Affairs Review* (1985): 80-93.

4. Ehrenhalt, *The United States of Ambition*, 14.

5. In Minnesota, although 28 percent of the members surveyed admitted to being full time, 88 percent believed the legislature should not be full time and 90 percent believed legislators should have another occupation. Charles H. Backstrom, "The Legislature as a Place to Work: How Minnesota Legislators View Their Jobs" (Paper prepared for the Hubert H. Humphrey Institute of Public Affairs, University of Minnesota, December 1986), 5.

6. The percentages of full-time members reported here are estimates furnished by in-state sources. Those who identify their occupations as "legislator," as reported in state blue books and directories, tend to be somewhat lower. See National Conference of State Legislatures, *State Legislators' Occupations: A Decade of Change* (Denver, Colo.: National Conference of State Legislatures, March 25, 1987); and Peverill Squire, "Career Opportunities and Membership Stability in Legislatures," *Legislative Studies Quarterly* 13 (February 1988): 75, 78.

7. Other categorizations differ somewhat. One based on session length, staffing, compensation, and membership turnover groups states into three broad categories. In the first category are eight states with the more professionalized legislatures, and in the third category are seventeen with the less professionalized legislatures. In the second are twenty-five states. Karl T. Kurtz, "The Changing State Legislatures," in *Leveraging State Government Relations*, ed. Wesley Pedersen (Washington, D.C.: Public Affairs Council, 1990), 23-32.

8. Also see Squire, "Career Opportunities and Membership Stability in Legislatures," 69.

9. Charles G. Bell and Charles M. Price, "Twenty Years of a Full-Time Legislature," *California Journal* (January 1987): 36-40.

10. Brian Weberg, "Changes in Legislative Staff," *Journal of State Government* 61 (November/December 1988): 190-197.

11. Loomis, "Political Careers and American State Legislatures," 10.

12. Jerry Calvert, "Revolving Doors—Volunteerism in State Legislatures," *State Government* 52 (Autumn 1979): 179. See also Squire, "Career Opportunities and Membership Stability in Legislatures."

13. Quoted in Rich Jones, "The Legislature 2010: Which Direction?" *State Legislatures*, July 1990, 24.
14. *New York Times*, January 17, 1988.
15. John Brandl, "Reflections on Leaving the Minnesota Legislature," *Humphrey Institute News*, June 1990, 14-15.
16. Ehrenhalt, *The United States of Ambition*, 20.
17. See National Conference of State Legislatures, *State Legislators' Occupations*, 9.
18. As characterized by a member of the new breed, former Speaker Tom Loftus, in "New Breed Legislator/Legislative Leader: Sun Spot Number One," unpublished paper, Institute of Politics, John F. Kennedy School of Government, Harvard University, October 3, 1984.
19. Bell and Price, "Twenty Years of a Full-Time Legislature," 38.
20. Quoted in the *Los Angeles Times*, January 29, 1984.
21. Karl T. Kurtz, "Life after the Legislature," *State Legislatures*, July 1989, 47.
22. Calvert, "Revolving Doors—Volunteerism in State Legislatures," 175.
23. Gary L. Crawley, "Electoral Competition, 1958-1984: Impact on State Legislative Turnover in the Indiana House," *American Politics Quarterly* 14 (January-April 1986): 114. See also Lucinda Simon, "The Mighty Incumbent," *State Legislatures* (July 1986): 31-32; and Wayne L. Francis and John R. Baker, "Why Do U.S. State Legislators Vacate Their Seats?" *Legislative Studies Quarterly* 11 (February 1986): 119-126.
24. Steven D. Williams, "Incumbency in the Tennessee General Assembly," *Comparative State Politics Newsletter* 8 (June 1987): 22; and Steven D. Williams, "Legislative Term Limitation and the Tennessee Republican Party," *Comparative State Politics* 12 (December 1991): 1.
25. Crawley, "Electoral Competition, 1958-1984," 107-108. See also Squire, "Career Opportunities and Membership Stability in Legislatures."
26. Bruce Cain, John Ferejohn, and Morris Fiorina, *The Personal Vote* (Cambridge, Mass.: Harvard University Press, 1987), 7. See also Lawrence C. Dodd, "A Theory of Congressional Cycles: Solving the Puzzle of Change," in *Congress and Policy Change*, ed. Gerald C. Wright, Jr., Leroy N. Rieselbach, and Lawrence C. Dodd (New York: Apathon Press, 1986), 3-44.
27. Joel A. Thompson and Gary Moncrief, "Changing State Legislative Career Patterns: Institutional Change and Legislative Careers," in *Changing Patterns in State Legislative Careers*, ed. Gary Moncrief and Joel A. Thompson (Ann Arbor: University of Michigan Press, forthcoming).
28. Unless otherwise noted, quotations are from interviews conducted by the author.
29. Although Democrats outspent Republicans, $9.3 million to $5.7 million, in 1991 they suffered their worst defeat in two decades. Of the twenty highest spending candidates, thirteen—all but one a Democrat—were losers. *Star-Ledger*, December 18, 1991.
30. Sherry Bebitch Jeffe, "For Legislative Staff, Policy Takes a Back Seat to Politics," *California Journal* (January 1987): 42.
31. Vincent R. Zarate, "Assembly Dems Sue Six Republicans over Mailings," *Star-Ledger*, August 7, 1987.
32. See Malcolm Jewell, *Representation in State Legislatures* (Lexington: Uni-

versity of Kentucky Press, 1982): 9-10.

33. Richard F. Fenno, Jr., *Home Style: House Members in Their Districts* (Boston: Little, Brown, 1978), 109. See also Robert S. Erickson, "The Advantage of Incumbency in Congressional Elections," *Polity* 3 (Spring 1971): 395-405; and Cain, Ferejohn, and Fiorina, *The Personal Vote*, 135-194.

34. Williams, "Incumbency in the Tennessee General Assembly," 22. See also Williams, "Legislative Term Limitation and the Tennessee Republican Party," 1.

35. John E. Chubb, "Institutions, the Economy, and the Dynamics of State Elections," *American Political Science Review* 88 (March 1988): 133-154. See also Crawley, "Electoral Competition, 1958-1984," 110.

36. Jeffrey E. Cohen, "Perceptions of Electoral Insecurity among Members Holding Safe Seats in a U.S. State Legislature," *Legislative Studies Quarterly* 9 (May 1984): 366-367.

37. David Breaux and Malcolm Jewell, "Winning Big: The Incumbency Advantage in State Legislative Races," in *Changing Patterns in State Legislative Careers*.

38. See Thad Beyle, ed., *Governors and Hard Times* (Washington, D.C.: CQ Press, 1992).

39. See Anthony Gierzynski and Malcolm Jewell, "Legislative Caucus and Leadership Campaign Committees," in *Changing Patterns in State Legislative Careers*.

40. Tom Loftus, "The New 'Political Parties' in State Legislatures" (Address made at the annual meeting of the Council of State Governments, 1984).

41. Alan Rosenthal, ed., *The Governor and the Legislature* (New Brunswick, N.J.: Eagleton Institute of Politics, Rutgers University, December 1987).

42. As quoted in Frank Lupin, "Case against State Senators Linked to a Shift in Political Campaign Power," *New York Times*, September 17, 1987.

43. Elaine Guidoux, "Who's Conservative? Who's Liberal?" *California Journal* (June 1988): 242-245. See also Andrea Margolis and Richard Zeiger, "Bleeding Hearts, Stone Hearts," *California Journal* (January 1987): 30-32.

44. Jeffe, "For Legislative Staff, Policy Takes a Back Seat to Politics," 42-43.

45. Fragmentation in the U.S. House is more attributable to careerism than to reform. See Dodd, "A Theory of Congressional Cycles," 12-18.

46. Charles G. Bell, "Legislatures, Interest Groups, and Lobbyists: The Link beyond the District," *Journal of State Government* 59 (Spring 1986): 14-15. See also Alan Rosenthal, *The Third House: Lobbyists and Lobbying in the States* (Washington, D.C.: CQ Press, forthcoming).

47. Cain, Ferejohn, and Fiorina, *The Personal Vote*, 209.

48. See Alan Rosenthal, "The Consequences of Constituency Service," *Journal of State Government* 59 (Spring 1986): 25-30.

49. Peverill Squire, "Changing State Legislative Leadership Careers," in *Changing Patterns in State Legislative Careers*.

50. See Alan Rosenthal, "A Vanishing Breed," *State Legislatures*, November/December 1989, 30-34.

51. Ehrenhalt, *The United States of Ambition*, 37-38.

52. Karl T. Kurtz, "The Public Standing of the Legislature" (Paper delivered at

the "Symposium on the Legislature in the Twenty-First Century" held by the Eagleton Institute of Politics, Rutgers University, Williamsburg, Va., April 27-29, 1990), 5.

53. Ibid., 14.
54. Martin Linsky, "Legislatures and the Press: The Problems of Image and Attitude," *Journal of State Government* 59 (Spring 1986): 41.
55. Reported in Kurtz, "The Public Standing of the Legislature," 2.
56. Harwood Group, *Citizens and Politics* (Dayton, Ohio: Kettering Foundation, 1991).
57. David B. Magleby, "Legislatures and the Initiative: The Politics of Direct Democracy," *Journal of State Government* 59 (Spring 1986): 35-36.
58. See Gerald Benjamin, "The Term Limits Movement in American Politics" (Paper delivered at the "Term Limits Conference" held by the Rockefeller Institute, Albany, N.Y., October 11-12, 1991).
59. It almost immediately would have curtailed Tom Foley's career in Congress and as Speaker of the House of Representatives. Foley's personal involvement in the campaign and the argument that Washington would lose influence to California worked against the proposition.
60. Gary W. Copeland, "Term Limitations and Political Careers: Up, Down, In, or Out" (Paper delivered at the "Term Limits Conference" held by the Rockefeller Institute, Albany, N.Y., October 11-12, 1991). See also Stuart Rothenberg, "How Term Limits Became a National Phenomenon," *State Legislatures*, January 1992, 35-39.
61. Charles M. Price, "Term Limits Politics in California" (Paper delivered at the "Term Limits Conference" held at the Rockefeller Institute, Albany, N.Y., October 11-12, 1991).
62. *Polling Report* 7 (October 28, 1991).
63. For a brief discussion of possibilities, see Karl T. Kurtz, "Limiting Terms— What's in Store?" *State Legislatures*, January 1992, 32-34.
64. Ehrenhalt, *The United States of Ambition*, 40. See also Alan Ehrenhalt, "An Embattled Institution," *Governing*, January 1992, 28-33.
65. David S. Broder, "Legislatures under Siege," reprinted in *State Legislatures*, July 1991, 21.

7 ▬▬▬

Making Judicial Policies in the Political Arena

Lawrence Baum

State supreme courts are policy makers of considerable and wide-ranging importance. Supreme courts[1] help allocate the power to govern corporations and public schools. Their decisions define the responsibilities employers have toward employees, drivers toward pedestrians. They adjudicate disputes over the apportionment of legislatures and the veto powers of governors.

Observers of state politics increasingly recognize the significance of state supreme courts. But they tend to see the courts as separate from the main arenas of government and politics. And they sometimes view the courts as insulated from politics and policy making.

The reality of state courts does not match those perceptions. A considerable overlap exists between policy making by the courts and by the other branches of state government. And, far from being insulated, state supreme courts influence and are influenced by the whole array of institutions in their states, as well as the federal government and the courts of other states.

In the past few decades, perhaps the most important trend in state supreme courts has been a movement toward ideologically liberal policies. That trend has been shaped by other political groups and institutions, which in turn aroused reactions from these groups and institutions. By focusing on these recent developments, the links between state supreme courts and the system of governmental and political institutions in which they work can be examined.

State Supreme Courts in the Policy Process

Areas of Activity

The activity of state supreme courts as policy makers covers a vast range. Legally, that activity takes three general forms. The first is interpretation of state statutes in such fields as criminal law, labor relations, and environmental protection. Through its interpretations of a statute over time, a supreme court inevitably shapes the meaning of the statute and thus its impact in practice. And single statutory decisions can make a considerable difference. Examples from the past few years include a 1987 Massachusetts decision that required a massive increase in spending for public welfare and a 1989 Maine decision that severely restricted public access to beaches.[2]

Second is development and interpretation of what is called the "common law." In certain areas of the law, the basic legal rules were established almost entirely by state courts instead of through statutes. Even though legislatures held power to make the rules themselves, they exercised this power only to a limited degree and otherwise deferred to the courts. The most important common law areas are property law, rules governing ownership and transfer of property; contract law, rules for the enforcement of contracts; and tort law, a broad area that centers on liability for wrongful acts causing property damage, personal injuries, or death.

Legislatures now play a more active role in the common law fields, but courts remain the primary decision makers. Indiana's chief justice noted in 1991 that the Indiana statutes had "grown to more than 12,000 pages," but "subjects like torts, contracts, landlord/tenant, and employment are still governed substantially by common law."[3]

Finally, state supreme courts interpret the federal and state constitutions. Their interpretations of the federal Constitution are subject to review by the U.S. Supreme Court, and such review is common. In contrast, state supreme courts are the ultimate interpreters of their state constitutions. Federal courts must accept the meaning of state constitutional provisions and of state statutes, as determined by a state's highest court. This role gives supreme courts opportunities to address such issues as the division of legal power between governors and legislatures, the balance between free speech and other values that conflict with it, and the obligation of state taxpayers to fund the public schools.

Variable Roles

As policy makers, state supreme courts change a good deal over time and differ considerably from each other. The most important dimensions of variation concern the extent of a court's activism and the content of its policies.

Activism is a complex and multifaceted concept.[4] As used here, the term refers to significant policy-making activities, particularly those that make substantial changes in existing policy or that challenge directly the policies of other institutions. The most prominent type of activism involves rulings that state statutes are unconstitutional. The frequency of such rulings has varied a good deal among the states and over time.[5]

The level of activism aside, courts can differ in the positions that they take on legal issues. To a great extent, these differences can be summarized in terms of the liberal-conservative spectrum. A liberal court generally could be expected to favor the interests of "economic underdogs" and of those who seek legal protection for civil liberties, while a conservative court would be less sympathetic to those interests. On this dimension, too, considerable variation has been evident among the state supreme courts.

Relationships with Other Policy Makers

State supreme courts are part of a larger policy-making system, and they are connected to other policy makers along several lines. Like other state institutions, supreme courts operate in the context of federalism, both "vertical" (the federal-state relationship) and "horizontal" (relationships among states).[6] Their primary vertical relationship is with the U.S. Supreme Court. Because the Supreme Court is the ultimate interpreter of the U.S. Constitution and federal statutes, state judges are obliged to follow those interpretations whenever they are relevant to a case. In this way, the Supreme Court influences the content of the decisions that state supreme courts make. More broadly, the Supreme Court and state supreme courts help to shape each other's agendas with their decisions and their policy choices.

Horizontally, a state supreme court is parallel to supreme courts in other states, courts that often face similar legal and policy issues. Not surprisingly, state supreme courts serve as important sources of policy cues to each other. While no court is obliged to adopt the legal interpretations of courts in other states, judges often choose to follow policy initiatives of other supreme courts and trends in state courts across the nation.

Within its own state, a supreme court operates alongside the legislature and executive branch. The other branches hold considerable legal power over state courts, on matters ranging from jurisdiction to budgets, and this power helps them to influence judicial action. The other branches also provide alternative forums for those who seek favorable government policies. People who fail to secure what they want from the governor or legislature may bring their demands to the courts. Similarly, those who are unhappy with court decisions may "appeal" to the legislature or the executive branch. The federal government also serves as an alternative forum on some issues. For example, people can seek relief from unfavorable state court policies in Congress or the federal courts.

The electorate is another institution that affects state supreme courts.

Voters hold the power to accept or reject proposed constitutional amendments, and in twenty-three states they can adopt amendments on their own through the initiative process. Such amendments sometimes are directed at judicial policies. Voters in most states also have power to retain judges in office or remove them when their terms expire.

Interest groups play an important part in forging links between state supreme courts and other institutions. They help to inform supreme court justices of developments in other courts. More fundamentally, organized groups primarily "appeal" to state courts for redress from the policies of other institutions, or to the legislature, the electorate, or the federal government as a result of unfavorable court decisions.

The relationships between state supreme courts and other institutions help determine the ultimate impact of court policies. Those relationships also help account for change in court policies. Supreme courts respond to new situations created by legislatures, by the U.S. Supreme Court, or by courts in other states. By examining a period of change in state supreme courts, the complex relationships between supreme courts and other institutions are revealed.

The Liberal Trend

Change in State Supreme Court Policies

Generalizing about the ideological positions of the state supreme courts as a group for any given period of time is difficult. For most of the nation's history, however, supreme court policies tended in a conservative direction. In economic policy, conservatism meant support for business interests over the interests of competing groups such as employees and consumers. In civil liberties, conservatism meant narrow interpretation of legal protections for individual liberties. A great many individual decisions, however, did diverge from this overall conservative stance. But these decisions were exceptions to the general pattern.[7]

Despite the historical tendencies of the courts, during the past half century a substantial movement has taken place in a liberal direction. That shift has been most evident in two areas: tort law and civil liberties.[8]

Tort Law.   In tort law, most supreme courts in the nineteenth century adopted basic rules that limited legal liability for property damage, injuries, and death.[9] For instance, employees were limited in their ability to sue employers for injuries on the job by the fellow servant rule, under which employers had no responsibility for injuries caused by the conduct of fellow employees. Under the contributory negligence rule, an injured party who bore any share of the fault for the injury could not recover damages from someone who was primarily at fault.

Beginning in the first half of the twentieth century, and accelerating in the 1950s, this thrust was largely reversed.[10] On issue after issue, supreme courts eliminated traditional doctrines that limited tort liability, replacing them with doctrines that favored plaintiffs (those seeking compensation for losses) over defendants (those allegedly responsible for damage or injuries). Although the states differed in the speed and extent of this shift in tort law, every state participated in it, and most took major steps to change their traditional doctrines.

The range of issues involved in this reversal of traditional doctrines is impressive. And in undertaking these changes, courts frequently had to make sharp breaks with well-established legal principles. When the South Carolina Supreme Court in 1985 decided to abolish the immunity of state and local governments from lawsuits, it overruled at least 118 of its past decisions, handed down from 1820 through 1984.[11]

This liberal trend has slowed considerably in the past few years. Supreme courts have shown an increasing reluctance to adopt new doctrines that expand the legal rights of tort plaintiffs, and some drawing back from pro-plaintiff doctrines adopted in the past has occurred. In part, this change reflects reactions outside the courts to the liberal trend.

Civil Liberties. During the 1950s and 1960s, the U.S. Supreme Court gave unprecedented support to civil liberties. It broadened the scope of legal protection for freedom of expression, expanded the civil rights of racial minority groups, and established a series of new protections for criminal defendants. In this period, some state supreme courts opposed the decisional trend at the federal level. While state courts could not legally reject the U.S. Supreme Court's interpretations of the federal Constitution, they could—and some did—weaken the impact of the Court's decisions through narrow interpretations and sometimes outright evasion of the Court's commands. Such opposition was particularly strong on issues of racial equality, where some southern supreme courts worked to maintain the status quo of segregation.[12]

As the Burger and Rehnquist Courts became more conservative in interpreting federal protections of civil liberties, some state supreme courts responded by adopting expansive interpretations of their own constitutions—holding that state constitutions protect rights to a greater degree than the federal constitution. State courts always were free to do so, provided that the rights they established did not contradict federal rights. But such action first became common during the Burger Court, and the number of decisions establishing independent state rights grew enormously from the early 1970s on.[13]

By no means have all supreme courts participated actively in this development. Many courts continue to rely on the U.S. Constitution and federal rulings in their decisions on civil liberties. Others have turned their attention to state constitutions but usually interpret their constitutions to provide only those protections guaranteed by the federal Constitution.[14] Those supreme courts that make frequent use of their constitutions to protect liberties are a distinct minority, concentrated most heavily in the West and Northeast.[15] Thus, the state supreme courts as a whole have not been unequivocally more favorable to civil liberties in recent years than has the U.S. Supreme Court.[16] But the use of state constitutions to expand protections of civil liberties has been sufficiently widespread to constitute a major movement.

The issues involved also range widely. Supreme courts have been most active in criminal procedure. They also have taken significant action in freedom of expression, with some courts limiting legal regulation of obscenity or establishing rights of free speech in private shopping malls. And, primarily in states whose constitutions contain equal rights amendments, some supreme courts have taken a vigorous role in striking down discriminatory government practices.

Sources of the Liberal Trend

What accounts for the liberal trend in state supreme courts, this departure from the historical pattern? Several interrelated conditions seem to have played a part in creating and sustaining this trend.

One condition is change in the social and political attitudes of the judiciary. In tort law, state supreme court policies reflect changes in societal views about accidents and injuries; during the twentieth century, support grew for the premise that people who suffer serious losses should be compensated. In turn, this feeling led to greater sympathy for individuals who seek compensation through the courts, a sympathy reinforced by the general availability of insurance to pay court judgments against defendants.[17] The result has been what one commentator described as "a change in the ideology that courts bring to tort cases." [18]

In civil liberties, the Warren Court did much to reshape the thinking of lawyers by showing that protection of civil liberties could be an appropriate role for the courts. As judges who received their legal training in the 1960s join the state supreme courts, many bring with them an expectation that the courts should play such a role. As Justice Christine Durham of Utah has said,

> most of us who sit on state supreme courts, and most of the lawyers who appear before us, were educated during a generation of expansivist, creative, and enormously "generative" thinking on the subject of the federal constitution and in the context of civil liberties. We saw in the Warren Court era an enormous and impressive reshaping of our attitudes and our assumptions about what the purposes of constitutional law could include.[19]

The social composition of state supreme courts also has changed,[20] and some of the changes have helped to foster a different set of collective attitudes. The proportion of justices with law school training grew considerably in the twentieth century. Supreme courts are dominated far less by white Protestant males than was the case even thirty years ago, and the proportion of justices who came from families with high economic status likely has declined. Each of these changes probably has had an impact, bringing to supreme courts more people who diverge from the social and legal perspectives that traditionally dominated these courts. One specific change with considerable relevance to civil liberties is the declining presence of criminal prosecutors: In the 1960s, about half of all justices had served as prosecutors, while in 1980 only one-fifth had that experience.[21]

A second condition is changes in legal services and interest group activity, particularly in civil liberties. People with civil liberties claims frequently had difficulty bringing those claims to and through the court system. But the increasing availability of lawyers to people with low incomes has facilitated litigation involving claims of individual rights on both the civil and criminal sides of the law. And the growth of interest groups that undertake litigation on civil liberties issues has increased the feasibility of cases involving these issues reaching appellate courts.

Finally, and of particular interest, trends within the judiciary have helped to guide developments in state supreme courts. In tort law, state supreme courts have influenced each other. Even more than other state policy makers, judges take cues from their counterparts in other states.[22] In this cue-taking process, a certain momentum may develop: If a doctrine has been adopted in a number of states, judges may come to view it as the accepted approach to a particular issue, and its widespread acceptance will influence additional courts to adopt it.

Since World War II, liberal innovations in tort law have benefited from this kind of momentum. Improvements in communication have increased judges' awareness of developments in other supreme courts, and their opinions often reveal a desire to follow a seemingly dominant trend in tort doctrines. Thus, the general movement of state courts toward support for tort plaintiffs has exerted considerable influence on judges who did not want to be left behind.

In civil liberties, state supreme courts have been influenced by trends at the federal level. The growing conservatism of the U.S. Supreme Court created an opportunity for state judges to assert an independent role by establishing civil liberties protections based on state constitutions. In a widely noticed 1977 article, Justice William J. Brennan, Jr., of the U.S. Supreme Court sought to alert state judges to this opportunity.[23] For those judges who favored strong protections of liberties, the opportunity was highly attractive. And civil liberties groups such as the American Civil

Liberties Union have begun to transfer their litigation activity to the state level, thereby providing a better base for decisions expanding liberties at that level.

Political scientist Richard P. Nathan noted a cyclical pattern in American history, a tendency for state governments to play their most active and innovative roles during periods of conservatism in the national government.[24] More specifically, Nathan and Martha Derthick have argued that "the Burger Court was to the judicial system what the Reagan Administration has been to the Presidency: a conservatizing force that deflected liberal effort to the state level." [25] It was not just that pro-civil liberties groups redirected their litigation campaigns to the state level; more important, pro-civil liberties judges asserted independent roles for their states. State supreme court justices who participated in the broadening of rights wrote with evident pride about their courts' filling the vacuum left by the U.S. Supreme Court and giving more life to state courts and state constitutions.[26]

The strength of this force should not be exaggerated, especially when many supreme courts have chosen not to join the movement to expand state protections of civil liberties. But one spur to the development of civil liberties activism at the state level is a reaction to contrary developments in the U.S. Supreme Court, and the growing conservatism of the Rehnquist Court will continue to feed that reaction.

Responses to the Liberal Trend

Like other developments in state supreme courts, the liberal trend in fields such as torts and civil liberties has evoked responses in other state institutions as well as the federal government. And, as has been true in general, interest groups have played an important part in spurring those responses.

Because of their power to overturn common law decisions with new statutes, state legislatures are attractive targets for groups representing tort defendants. Legislatures had done much to reinforce the pro-plaintiff trend in state courts, because the same changes in social thinking that influenced judges affected legislators. But in recent years the general sympathy of state legislators for business interests and the capacity of interest groups to raise fears about the social and economic costs of pro-plaintiff doctrines have worked in favor of defendant groups. These groups have won some important legislative victories, particularly in medical malpractice. But their successes have been limited by the increasingly strong lobbying of groups representing plaintiffs.

As a result, those who seek to reverse the judicial trend in tort law have given attention to other forums. The most important are Congress, which can preempt state tort rules, and voters, who can override judicial doctrines directly and who can influence doctrine indirectly by replacing liberal judges with conservatives. Defendant groups thus far have had little success with Congress but some success with the voters.

By and large, judicial action to expand civil liberties is unpopular among state legislators. But the legislature's legal position is weaker in civil liberties than in torts. Decisions that find new rights in state constitutions generally cannot be overturned except through the cumbersome process of amending constitutions. As a result, legislative action has been limited to a few proposals for constitutional amendments. But legislators do have powers over courts as institutions and over their judges. The New Jersey legislature has used those powers twice, limiting the state courts' jurisdiction in one area of conflict and confirming the chief justice of its supreme court for a new term only after it subjected him to considerable criticism for his court's activism.

As in tort law, those who oppose the liberal policies of some supreme courts on civil liberties have turned to the federal government and to the voters. The U.S. Supreme Court has created some procedural difficulties for state courts that attempt to establish independent rights under state constitutions, but it has not—and could not—eliminate their power to do so. Voters have shown some willingness to override unpopular civil liberties decisions by adopting initiatives and referendums and to defeat judges who are identified with those decisions, but both forms of reaction have been relatively uncommon.

Like supreme court decisions themselves, reactions to those decisions by other institutions may not settle the issues in question. In some areas, a long and complex interaction has taken place between supreme courts and other policy makers over matters on which they disagree. Such interactions underline the interdependence of state supreme courts and other participants in the policy making process.

Specific Areas in Civil Liberties and Torts

Generalizing about fields as broad and as varied as civil liberties and torts is difficult As a result, looking closely at some specific areas within those fields can be useful. The areas examined—product liability, criminal procedure, school finance, and abortion—illustrate some important patterns in the work of state supreme courts and in their interactions with other policy makers.

Product Liability

Among the most important areas of tort law is the set of rules governing liability for damage caused by defective products. As the twentieth century began, two doctrines severely restricted consumers in their ability to sue manufacturers for allegedly defective products. One doctrine was the privity rule, which prohibited suits against any party except the business that had sold the product directly to the consumer; the other was the negligence rule, which required the consumer to prove negligence in the manufacture of a defective product.

From 1913 on, state supreme courts began to establish exceptions to these rules for food and drink and for inherently dangerous products. After World War II, more courts adopted these exceptions. Then they began to overthrow the rules themselves. The first major steps were taken by the supreme courts of Michigan in 1958 and New Jersey in 1960.[27] In a 1963 decision, the California Supreme Court went even further in eliminating the privity and negligence requirements. The court held that a manufacturer was strictly liable, whether or not proved negligent, for damages caused by defective products.[28]

The strict liability rule was a radical departure from traditional tort rules; in effect, it replaced one legal framework with another. Yet other states quickly jumped on the bandwagon. Within four years, courts in a dozen other states had followed California's lead; by 1976, thirty-seven states had established strict liability by judicial decision. By 1992, all but a few states operated under the strict liability rule. The speedy and overwhelming acceptance of this rule underlines the strength of the liberal wave in tort law.

The pro-plaintiff trend in product liability did not end with the adoption of strict liability.[29] A variety of other doctrines favoring injured parties gained acceptance in state supreme courts. In the 1970s and early 1980s, for instance, state courts greatly expanded the liability of manufacturers for defective product designs.

Initially, this trend received little attention outside the legal community. For example, the landmark California decision on strict liability was not reported in the leading San Francisco newspaper. By the 1980s, interest was growing in product liability law and other areas of torts. Primarily responsible was a concerted campaign by tort defendant groups, including manufacturers and other business interests, the medical community, and insurance companies.

The heart of this campaign has been an effort to convince people, especially policy makers, that pro-plaintiff trends in tort law have had damaging consequences. Through widespread advertising and other vehicles, defendant groups have sought to connect judicial doctrines favoring plaintiffs with what they depict as a burgeoning of lawsuits. In turn, they argue, such lawsuits have a variety of negative results, ranging from decisions by manufacturers not to produce desirable products to a general weakening of American economic competitiveness.

In conjunction with this effort to shape attitudes about product liability, defendant groups have taken more direct action to change policy. They have worked to overturn unfavorable judicial doctrines through state legislation, and their efforts have produced considerable success. Since 1985, according to one count, forty-one states have adopted some of the product liability rules sought by manufacturers.[30] Many legislatures, for instance, have provided additional legal defenses in suits for product liability. One example is provisions holding that a manufacturer would not be liable if the product in question met the "state of the art" at the time it was made. Another common action has been to establish direct or indirect limits on the damages that plaintiffs can win under particular circumstances. The level of success for defendant groups would have been even greater except for increasingly strong counter-pressure from groups that favor plaintiffs' interests, including the segment of the bar that represents tort plaintiffs, labor unions, and consumer groups.

Since 1976, the same forces have contended over federal product liability legislation. Business groups seek national rules that limit liability for defective products, and the Reagan and Bush administrations have supported their effort. In 1991, Vice President Dan Quayle took a prominent role as advocate for federal product liability rules favoring defendant interests, as part of a broader campaign for action to limit litigation. But Congress has not yet acted. Its inaction reflects the difficulty of achieving the support needed for significant federal action in a traditional field of state law—particularly in the face of strong interest-group opposition.

The effort to reverse the pro-plaintiff trend in state supreme courts has extended even to the election of judges. In Texas, where the supreme court hears only civil cases, tort issues have become the centerpieces of supreme court elections, both as a matter of public debate and as a source of massive funding of candidates by both sides.[31] Tort issues have entered into judicial campaigns in a few other states, but more often they motivate the funding of candidates. In the 1986 contest for Ohio chief justice, for instance, the Republican candidate's campaign was dominated by charges about the Democratic incumbent's conduct, but that campaign was financed heavily by insurance companies, manufacturers, and the medical community.[32]

These electoral efforts have had an impact. In 1986, financial contributions by defendant groups helped to defeat liberal justices in California and Ohio, and those supreme courts then adopted more conservative positions in tort law. But this shift in policy has not been limited to states where liberal justices have been replaced by conservatives. Since the early 1980s, a broader change has taken place in state supreme court policies on product liability. This new trend is summarized well by legal scholars James A. Henderson, Jr., and Theodore Eisenberg:

Courts once favorably inclined to break new ground and to discard doctrine blocking recoveries [of compensation for injuries] now are inclined to reflect more cautiously on the implications of their decisions. Courts continue to break new ground and discard doctrine in ways that favor plaintiffs. But they are increasingly apt to change the law to preclude liability rather than to promote it.[33]

Perhaps a slowing of the long pro-plaintiff trend was inevitable. That it occurred in the 1980s, however, seems to reflect the efforts of defendant groups to turn the tide. To a degree, judges may have reassessed their positions in light of the legislative reaction and the activity of pro-defendant groups in judicial elections. More important, however, is the apparent effectiveness of the campaign to connect pro-plaintiff doctrines with a "liability crisis" and economic harm. Working in court systems that must cope with growing caseloads, judges may be particularly receptive to arguments that litigation has become too common, that doctrines favoring injured parties have gone too far. In a new climate of opinion, many supreme courts seem to have adopted a new perspective on product liability.

Criminal Procedure

Active use of state constitutions to protect civil liberties began with issues of criminal procedure, and this area has remained the primary one for expansion of rights by state courts. One reason is that the Burger Court narrowed rights most quickly and most decisively in criminal procedure, providing state courts with a large void to fill if they wished. Perhaps equally important, the steady flow of criminal cases to state supreme courts provided frequent opportunities to act, whereas state litigation in other civil liberties fields has been relatively limited.

During the Warren Court era, the distaste of many state supreme court justices for expansions of defendants' rights was highly evident.[34] That distaste did not disappear when the Burger Court began to narrow those rights, and today most supreme courts seem to share the Rehnquist Court's conservative views on criminal procedure issues. But a number of supreme courts have more liberal collective views on these issues, and they have been able to use their constitutions to resist the conservative trend at the national level. Because judges' views about defendants' rights typically have strong ideological roots, a court's membership largely determines its stance on issues in this area. In New Jersey, for instance, new appointments shifted the supreme court from a body that resisted the Warren Court's expansions of defendants' rights to one that used the state constitution to thwart the Burger Court's narrowing of those rights.[35]

A study by Barry Latzer showed both the strength and the limits of the movement to broaden defendants' rights under state constitutions.[36]

Latzer identified 232 decisions between the late 1960s and 1989 in which a state supreme court had rejected U.S. Supreme Court doctrines by finding broader protections of rights under their own constitutions. Those 232 decisions, made by forty-four state supreme courts, constitute a great deal of rights expansion. But twice as many decisions were handed down in which supreme courts interpreted their constitutions to provide no broader protections. And most supreme courts tended either to adopt such narrowing interpretations of their constitutions or not to look for rights in their constitutions at all.

Where state courts have adopted expansive interpretations of their constitutions, these decisions have affected a number of rights for criminal defendants.[37] The supreme courts of California, Colorado, Massachusetts, and Oregon struck down the death penalty. In search and seizure, where the Supreme Court has narrowed rights to the greatest extent, state courts have overridden several of the Court's rulings through their state constitutions. Perhaps the most important is the Court's 1984 decision establishing a "good faith" exception to the rule that excludes introduction of evidence seized on the basis of a faulty search warrant.[38] Five supreme courts have rejected the good faith exception in interpreting their own constitutions. Some supreme courts have held, in contrast with a Supreme Court ruling, that under the prohibition of double jeopardy a defendant whose conviction was overturned could not be given a heavier sentence on retrial; this example is interesting because the Supreme Court decision was issued by the liberal Warren Court.[39] But it should be noted that on each issue described here, the courts that expanded defendants' rights instead of adopting the Supreme Court's position were in the minority.

In an era of limited sympathy for criminal defendants, rulings that do favor defendants tend to produce negative reactions. Officials in the other branches frequently criticize liberal court decisions and initiate efforts to overturn them. But such overturnings generally require constitutional amendments, so that voters are the critical policy makers—deciding whether to ratify amendments proposed by the legislature or, in states that allow initiative measures, deciding whether to adopt amendments proposed by petition.

Occasionally, voters have taken such action. Massachusetts voters reestablished the death penalty in 1982. Florida in 1982 and Pennsylvania in 1984 overturned state supreme court decisions to broaden the range of evidence that could be used against defendants.[40] The Florida Supreme Court was much less willing to broaden rights under its state constitution after the 1982 measure was adopted.[41]

Voters also can react against judges who participate in the expansion of defendants' rights. Incumbent judges typically have little difficulty in winning reelection, and contests for judicial office seldom feature policy issues—in part because rules of legal ethics virtually preclude discussion of such issues by candidates. But in recent years the conservative views of most voters on criminal justice issues have tempted a good many judicial candidates to use such issues explicitly or implicitly in their campaigns, especially to criticize incumbents who can be labeled as unduly sympathetic to defendants.

Several such campaigns have occurred at the supreme court level, in states such as Louisiana, North Carolina, Oklahoma, and Wisconsin. Most often, these campaigns focus on capital punishment, with allegations that the justice under attack has voted too often to overturn death sentences. Whether or not these attacks on incumbents are successful, they potentially influence the policy choices of other judges. As a former member of the California Supreme Court said,

> there's no way a judge is going to be able to ignore the political consequences of certain decisions, especially if he or she has to make them near election time. That would be like ignoring a crocodile in your bathtub.[42]

That this justice served in California is not surprising because in that state the public has reacted most negatively to expansions of defendants' rights. The supreme court in California was the court that most frequently found independent protections for defendants in its state constitution, and this stance aroused considerable public wrath. The court's 1972 decision striking down the death penalty was overturned by a public vote later the same year, and in 1982 and 1990 the voters approved initiative measures that cut back on a variety of defendants' rights under the state constitution. (The supreme court struck down the most far-reaching provision in the 1990 measure, one that could have eliminated the court's power to establish independent protections of rights for criminal defendants under the state constitution.[43])

After the California death penalty was restored, for many years the supreme court reversed specific death sentences in the great majority of cases. Public opposition to the court's liberal justices grew, and in 1986 capital punishment was the centerpiece of a heavily financed and well publicized electoral campaign against Chief Justice Rose Bird and two of her colleagues. (In California, the public votes "yes" or "no" on retention of appellate judges in office.) Ultimately, all three justices were defeated—the first three appellate judges in California who failed to win the majority necessary for retention on the bench.

In defeating the three justices, the majority of voters achieved the impact that they wanted. Appointments by a Republican governor made the court considerably more conservative, and it changed direction on criminal procedure issues. Most notably, it affirmed the preponderance of death sentences that it reviewed. One newspaper editorial, citing what its writer regarded as highly questionable affirmances, accused the court of "pandering to public opinion." [44] Whether or not that accusation was justified, it underlines the potential influence of the public—and of the environment in general—on a supreme court's policies.

School Finance

Traditionally, public schools in the United States have been financed primarily by local property taxes. One result is to produce differences in funding levels among school districts with differing property values. A district with limited wealth may tax its citizens at a high rate but produce considerably less funding per student than a wealthier district that has lower tax rates. State funding of public education grew over the years, and this funding typically reduced financial disparities among school districts. But major disparities remained, and state action to reduce them more substantially was politically impossible.

In 1968, citizens of a low-income district in San Antonio brought a lawsuit challenging the school funding disparities in Texas on the ground that they violated the equal protection clause of the Fourteenth Amendment. The lawsuit did not reach the Supreme Court until 1973, when four appointments of justices by President Richard Nixon had made the Court more conservative. The result was a 5-4 decision holding that the Texas funding system did not violate the Fourteenth Amendment. [45]

That decision foreclosed the possibility of relief for low-income districts in federal court. But state supreme courts provided another possible route. Even before the 1973 Supreme Court decision, citizens and school boards had begun to attack education funding systems for violating provisions of state constitutions—specifically, guarantees of due process or equal protection and clauses dealing with the provision of education to state residents. [46]

In the first three cases that they resolved, supreme courts held that the school funding systems in their states violated state constitutions: California in 1971, Michigan in 1972, and New Jersey in 1973. These decisions helped to encourage lawsuits in other states. By 1989, twenty-two supreme courts had decided school funding cases. Twelve funding systems were upheld, while ten were struck down.

While supreme courts have been closely divided on this issue, it is striking that ten supreme courts have acted to require fundamental changes in systems for educational finance. The pattern of decisions suggests some of the reasons for their willingness to take this action. Among the states in which supreme courts have decided funding cases, on the whole those in which states systems were struck down have had larger funding disparities, more serious education problems, and more liberal supreme courts. [47] The importance of the courts' ideological positions was underlined in 1973, when the Michigan Supreme Court reversed its 1972 decision and upheld the state funding system after a change in the court's membership.[48]

Decisions striking down property tax-based financing of schools require legislative implementation; state legislatures must adopt new systems to overcome the inequalities produced by differences in local wealth. Legislators from property-rich areas seldom welcome such action, which often requires the infusion of substantial state funding in states that are financially strapped.

Nonetheless, some state governments have acted readily to comply with the requirements of supreme court decisions. One striking example is Kentucky, where the legislature responded to a 1989 supreme court decision by providing major new funding for education. Kentucky legislators may have welcomed the decision as an impetus for improvement of the state's education system.[49]

Frequently, however, legislatures have balked at carrying out a supreme court's mandate. Perhaps the most striking example is New Jersey. The legislature provided the funding to carry out a 1973 decision only after three years and a supreme court order that closed the state's schools until the legislature acted.[50] Advocates for low-income districts argued that the legislative action still left the state short of full compliance with the supreme court's mandate, and in 1990 the court required a massive transfer of funds to low-income districts. With Gov. James J. Florio taking the lead, the legislature acted to carry out the decision, but low-income districts returned to court in 1991 with a claim that the legislative action was highly inadequate.[51]

Such renewed lawsuits are common, and they are likely to become even more common in the future. A burgeoning number of challenges to state funding systems has been made in the late 1980s and early 1990s. Where courts strike down such systems, most states will find it difficult to raise the money needed to establish new systems that comply with judicial requirements and that are politically feasible. The result is likely to be a growth in the number of states with explicit or implicit conflicts between the supreme court and the other branches.

Abortion

Prior to 1973, state courts adjudicated some challenges to restrictive state laws on abortion. The Supreme Court's decision in *Roe v. Wade* (1973)[52] essentially removed the issue from state courts. State supreme courts could hardly have expanded abortion rights beyond the very broad limits established by *Roe v. Wade*. And when state legislatures adopted new restrictive laws after 1973, challenges to those laws almost invariably went to federal court.

The Supreme Court's decisions on government funding of abortion in 1977 and 1980 opened up a possible role for state courts. The Court held that the federal and state governments were not required to pay for abortions in the Medicaid program for people with low incomes, even if the abortions were medically necessary.[53] These decisions precluded further challenges to federal restrictions on abortion funding, but they left open the possibility of challenges to state restrictions under state constitutions.

Most state legislatures had established substantial limits on state Medicaid funding of abortions, and legal challenges to these limits were brought in a number of states. In four states, supreme courts ruled that restrictions on funding of abortions violated state constitutional provisions altogether or in part. On abortion, unlike school finance, legislative resistance to supreme court decisions was ineffective. The California Supreme Court in 1981 held that the legislature could not exclude abortion from its Medicaid program.[54] Each year thereafter, the state legislature inserted such an exclusion in its budget for Medicaid; state judges then held the legislative action invalid and funding was maintained.

In 1989, in *Webster v. Reproductive Health Services*,[55] the Supreme Court expanded the scope of allowable state regulation of abortion, and four justices indicated that they were inclined to overturn *Roe v. Wade*. After *Webster*, President George Bush selected David H. Souter and Clarence Thomas to replace the Court's two most liberal members, who were retiring. Those appointments made it virtually certain that the states would be given more power to regulate and limit abortion, and *Roe v. Wade* likely would be overturned.

Thus, the focus began to shift to the states. A new wave of efforts to secure strong anti-abortion laws began in 1989. These efforts resulted in many laws restricting abortion to some degree and a few that largely prohibited abortion. The most sweeping new laws were challenged in federal court, but a full or partial reversal of *Roe v. Wade* would channel such challenges to state courts. The Florida Supreme Court already has acted, holding in a 1989 case that the protection of privacy in the Florida constitution encompassed abortion.[56] Inevitably, that decision was controversial, and in 1990 anti-abortion groups sought to defeat the chief justice who had written the court's opinion in a retention election. The chief justice won retention, but the campaign against him underlined the extent of the conflict in which supreme courts will become involved if abortion litigation becomes concentrated on the state level.[57]

Conclusion

The roles of state supreme courts within a larger policy-making system illustrate the impact of fragmented governmental power in the

United States. Both the federal system and the overlapping powers of the three branches of government create multiple points of access for interest groups that seek to influence policy. They also create a potential for conflict among institutions over policy issues on which they share power. Tort and civil liberties policy involve several different institutions in state government as well as the federal government. In these two areas, government policy is a complex and often contradictory aggregation of rules adopted by an array of policy makers.

As part of this system, state supreme courts do not—and cannot—work in isolation from their environments. The policy choices that they make inevitably are influenced by the activities of interest groups and the policies of other institutions in state and federal government. In turn, their policies inevitably generate reactions from those groups and institutions. As a result, court decisions—and the supreme courts themselves—are caught up in a political process that extends well beyond the judicial branch.

Future directions of state supreme court policy are impossible to predict. But the supreme courts certainly will continue to play important roles as policy makers. And, as in the past, the policies of supreme courts will shape and be shaped by the political environments in which the courts operate.

Notes

1. Throughout this chapter, the term "supreme court" will be used to refer to the highest court of each state. Most of these courts are known formally as supreme courts, but exceptions exist. For instance, in New York, the court called the supreme court is a lower court and the highest court is the court of appeals. The supreme courts of Texas and Oklahoma hear only civil cases; each state has a court of criminal appeals that is in effect its supreme court for criminal cases. Where "Supreme Court" is capitalized, without any state designation, the reference is to the Supreme Court of the United States.
2. *Massachusetts Coalition for the Homeless v. Secretary of Human Services*, 511 N.E.2d 603 (Massachusetts 1987); and *Bell v. Town of Wells*, 557 A.2d 168 (Maine 1989).
3. Randall T. Shepard, "Indiana Law, the Supreme Court, and a New Decade," *Indiana Law Review* 24 (1991): 502.
4. Bradley C. Canon, "A Framework for the Analysis of Judicial Activism," in *Supreme Court Activism and Restraint*, ed. Stephen C. Halpern and Charles M. Lamb (Lexington, Mass.: Lexington Press, 1982), 385-419.
5. Oliver Peter Field, *Judicial Review of Legislation in Ten Selected States* (Bloomington: Bureau of Government Research, Indiana University, 1943); and Craig Emmert, "Judicial Review in State Supreme Courts: Opportunity

and Activism" (Paper delivered at the annual meeting of the Midwest Political Science Association, Chicago, April 8-10, 1988).

6. G. Alan Tarr and Mary Cornelia Aldis Porter, *State Supreme Courts in State and Nation* (New Haven: Yale University Press, 1988), 2.

7. See Stanton Wheeler, Bliss Cartwright, Robert A. Kagan, and Lawrence M. Friedman, "Do the 'Haves' Come Out Ahead? Winning and Losing in State Supreme Courts, 1870-1970," *Law and Society Review* 21 (1987): 403-445; and Lawrence M. Friedman, *A History of American Law*, rev. ed (New York: Simon and Schuster, 1985).

8. State supreme courts have taken a liberal direction on some issues outside these areas as well. One important example is a widespread weakening of the traditional rule that employers could fire employees for any reason they chose. See Fred Strasser, "Employment-at-Will: The Death of a Doctrine?" *National Law Journal*, January 20, 1986, 1, 6-7.

9. Lawrence M. Friedman, *Total Justice* (New York: Russell Sage, 1985), 53-60.

10. See Lawrence Baum and Bradley C. Canon, "State Supreme Courts as Activists: New Doctrines in the Law of Torts," in *State Supreme Courts: Policymakers in the Federal System*, ed. Mary Cornelia Porter and G. Alan Tarr (Westport, Conn.: Greenwood Press, 1982), 83-108.

11. *McCall v. Batson*, 329 S.E.2d 741 (South Carolina 1985).

12. Tarr and Porter, *State Supreme Courts in State and Nation*, 74-82.

13. Ronald K. L. Collins, Peter J. Galie, and John Kincaid, "State High Courts, State Constitutions, and Individual Rights Litigation since 1980: A Judicial Survey," *Publius* 16 (Summer 1986): 141-161.

14. One clear example is New Hampshire. See Barbara A. Ucasz, "The Recent Development of State Constitutional Law in Vermont and New Hampshire," senior honors thesis, Dartmouth College, 1991.

15. Collins, Galie, and Kincaid, "State High Courts, State Constitutions, and Individual Rights Litigation since 1980."

16. See Harold J. Spaeth, "Burger Court Review of State Court Civil Liberties Decisions," *Judicature* 68 (February/March 1985): 285-291.

17. Evidence for such a change in attitudes is suggested by the increasing success of tort plaintiffs in jury decisions, though jury sympathy for plaintiffs has been exaggerated by many commentators. See Deborah R. Hensler, "Trends in Tort Litigation: Findings from the Institute for Civil Justice's Research," *Ohio State Law Journal* 48 (1987): 479-498; and Mark A. Peterson, *Civil Juries in the 1980s: Trends in Jury Trials and Verdicts in California and Cook County, Illinois* (Santa Monica, Calif.: Rand Corporation, 1987).

18. Peter H. Schuck, "The New Judicial Ideology of Tort Law," in *New Directions in Liability Law*, ed. Walter Olson (New York: Academy of Political Science, 1988), 6.

19. Lawrence Baum and David Frohnmayer, eds., *The Courts: Sharing and Separating Powers* (New Brunswick, N.J.: Eagleton Institute of Politics, Rutgers University, 1989), 17.

20. See Robert A. Kagan, Bobby D. Infelise, and Robert R. Detlefsen, "American State Supreme Court Justices, 1900-1970," *American Bar Foundation Research Journal* (Spring 1984): 371-408; and Henry R. Glick and Craig F. Emmert, "Stability and Change: Characteristics of State Supreme Court

Judges," *Judicature* 70 (August/September 1986): 107-112.

21. Glick and Emmert, "Stability and Change," 108.
22. On legislatures, see Jack L. Walker, "The Diffusion of Innovations among the American States," *American Political Science Review* 63 (September 1969): 880-899; and on courts, see Martin Shapiro, "Decentralized Decision-Making in the Law of Torts," in *Political Decision-Making*, ed. S. Sidney Ulmer (New York: Van Nostrand Reinhold, 1970), 44-75.
23. William J. Brennan, "State Constitutions and the Protection of Individual Rights," *Harvard Law Review* 90 (1977): 489-504.
24. Richard P. Nathan, "Federalism—The Great 'Composition,'" in *The New American Political System*, 2d ed., ed. Anthony King (Washington, D.C.: American Enterprise Institute for Public Policy Research), 1990), 231-261.
25. Richard P. Nathan and Martha Derthick, "Reagan's Legacy: A New Liberalism among the States," *New York Times*, December 18, 1987, A39.
26. See, for instance, Robert F. Utter, "Freedom and Diversity in a Federal System: Perspectives on State Constitutions and the Washington Declaration of Rights," *University of Puget Sound Law Review* 7 (1984): 491-525.
27. *Spence v. Three Rivers Building and Masonry Supply Inc.*, 90 N.W.2d 873 (Michigan 1958); and *Henningsen v. Bloomfield Motors*, 161 A.2d 69 (New Jersey 1960). These decisions held that manufacturers make an implied warranty of their products' safety to the ultimate consumers of the products.
28. *Greenman v. Yuba Power Products*, 377 P.2d 897 (California 1963).
29. James A. Henderson, Jr., and Theodore Eisenberg, "The Quiet Revolution in Products Liability: An Empirical Study of Legal Change," *UCLA Law Review* 37 (February 1990): 483-488.
30. Linda Lipsen, "The Evolution of Products Liability as a Federal Policy Issue," in *Tort Law and the Public Interest*, ed. Peter H. Schuck (New York: W. W. Norton, 1991), 248.
31. See Anthony Champagne, "Judicial Reform in Texas," *Judicature* 72 (October/November 1988): 148-149; and Donald W. Jackson and James W. Riddlesperger, Jr., "Money and Politics in Judicial Elections: The 1988 Election of the Chief Justice of the Texas Supreme Court," *Judicature* 74 (December/January 1991): 184-189.
32. Mary Grace Poldomani, "Insurance Lobby Dug Deep for Moyer," *Akron Beacon Journal*, June 14, 1987, A1, A8.
33. Henderson and Eisenberg, "The Quiet Revolution in Products Liability," 498.
34. Bradley C. Canon, "Organizational Contumacy in the Transmission of Judicial Politices: The Mapp, Escobedo, Miranda, and Gault Cases," *Villanova Law Review* 20 (November 1974): 50-79.
35. Tarr and Porter, *State Supreme Courts in State and Nation*, 197-209.
36. Barry Latzer, "The Hidden Conservatism of the State Court 'Revolution,'" *Judicature* 74 (December/January 1991): 190-197.
37. This discussion is based largely on Daniel C. Kramer, "Reactions of State Courts to Pro-Prosecution Burger Court Decisions," in *Human Rights in the States: New Directions in Constitutional Policymaking*, ed. Stanley H. Friedelbaum (Westport, Conn.: Greenwood Press, 1988), 121-144.
38. *United States v. Leon*, 468 U.S. 897 (1984). The Court held that, if an officer

who seizes evidence on the basis of a faulty search warrant reasonably believed that the warrant was valid, the evidence could be admitted in court.
39. The Supreme Court decision was *North Carolina v. Pearce*, 395 U.S. 711 (1969). The Court held that a judge could impose a heavier sentence on a defendant who was convicted again, so long as the judge was not acting vindictively.
40. Janice C. May, "Constitutional Amendment and Revision Revisited," *Publius* 17 (Winter 1987): 175-176.
41. Latzer, "Hidden Conservatism of the State Court 'Revolution,'" 192-193.
42. Paul Reidinger, "The Politics of Judging," *American Bar Association Journal* 73 (April 1, 1987): 58.
43. *Raven v. Deukmejian*, 52 Cal. 3d 336 (1990). The court held in essence that this provision would create such a sweeping change in the state constitution that it constituted a "revision" and thus, under the constitution, could not be adopted through an initiative.
44. "Death without Deliberation," *San Francisco Examiner*, February 17, 1991, A16.
45. *San Antonio Independent School District v. Rodriguez*, 411 U.S. 1 (1973).
46. This discussion of state cases is based in part on Bill Swinford, "A Predictive Model of Decision Making in State Supreme Courts: The School Financing Cases," *American Politics Quarterly* 19 (July 1991): 336-352.
47. Ibid., 346.
48. *Milliken v. Green*, 203 N.W.2d 457 (Michigan 1972), 212 N.W.2d 711 (Michigan 1973).
49. William Celis III, "Kentucky Begins Drive to Revitalize Its Schools," *New York Times*, September 26, 1990, B6.
50. Richard Lehne, *The Quest for Justice: The Politics of School Finance Reform* (New York: Longman, 1978). The decision was *Robinson v. Cahill*, 303 A.2d 273 (New Jersey 1973).
51. Rorie Sherman, "Tackling Education Financing," *National Law Journal*, July 22, 1991, 22.
52. 410 U.S. 113.
53. *Maher v. Roe*, 432 U.S. 464 (1977); and *Harris v. McRae*, 448 U.S. 297 (1980). *Harris*, the more important of the two decisions, held that a denial of Medicaid funding for abortions that were medically necessary but not required to save the pregnant woman's life did not violate the equal protection clause of the Fourteenth Amendment or the equal protection component of the Fifth Amendment.
54. *Committee to Defend Reproductive Rights v. Myers*, 625 P.2d 779 (California 1981). The basis for the decision was the state constitutional clause protecting the right to privacy, which the court interpreted to encompass abortion.
55. 492 U.S. 490. The Court upheld provisions of Missouri law that prohibited almost entirely the involvement of public employees or public funds in abortions and in "encouraging or counseling" women to have abortions and that upheld, with a narrow interpretation, a requirement that a physician test a fetus for viability before performing a late-pregnancy abortion. In his opinion, Justice Antonin Scalia said that he would have preferred that the

Court overturn *Roe v. Wade* in that case, while in another opinion Chief Justice William H. Rehnquist and Justices Byron R. White and Anthony M. Kennedy seemed to imply that they would vote to overturn *Roe* in an appropriate future case.

56. *In re T. W.*, 551 So. 2d 1186 (Florida 1989). The decision established a state-level protection of the right to abortion that was similar to the rules of *Roe v. Wade.*

57. See "State's Chief Justice Keeps His Seat," *Miami Herald*, November 7, 1990, A17.

8 ━━━━━

Accountability Battles in State Administration

William T. Gormley, Jr.

State bureaucracies have paid a price for their growing importance, and that price is a loss of discretion. In recent years, state bureaucracies have become more permeable, more vulnerable, and more manipulable. They are subject to a growing number of controls, as governors, state legislators, state judges, presidents, members of Congress, federal bureaucrats, interest groups, and citizens all attempt to shape administrative rule making, rate making and adjudication at the state level. Of equal significance, they are subject to tougher, more restrictive, and more coercive controls.

In other words, state bureaucracies have become more accountable for their actions. In a sense, this is both understandable and desirable. Even state bureaucrats concede the virtues of accountability, at least in theory. Yet accountability is a multidimensional concept. Increasingly, the question is not whether state bureaucracies shall be accountable but to whom. A related question is how accountability can best be structured to avoid damage to other important values, such as creativity and flexibility.

A variety of controls that limit the discretion of state bureaucracies recently has proliferated, primarily in the areas of legislative oversight, executive management, due process, and regulatory federalism. For example, "coercive controls" rely on coercion for bureaucratic performance, while "catalytic controls" may yield comparable progress with fewer adverse side-effects. The emergence of accountability battles pit competing claimants against one another, in bitter struggles over authority, with state bureaucracies as the ultimate prize. Courts increasingly are being asked to resolve these disputes, but the courts are not disinterested claimants. Often they wish to shape the behavior of state bureaucracies. Thus, judges have emerged as key arbiters and managers, deciding accountability battles in some instances, triggering them in others.

The Proliferation of Controls

During the 1970s and the 1980s, as state bureaucracies grew larger and more important, politicians, judges, and citizens strengthened their leverage over state bureaucracies by institutionalizing a wide variety of control techniques. Some of these techniques, such as sunset laws and ombudsmen, were new. Others, such as executive orders and conditions of aid, were old but not much utilized. Control techniques also differed in their directness, formality, durability, and coerciveness. However, they all shared a common purpose—to make state bureaucracies more accountable to other public officials or to the people.

Legislative Oversight

During the 1970s, state legislatures discovered oversight as a form of bureaucratic control. Legislative committees took an active interest in bureaucratic implementation or nonimplementation of state statutes and conducted hearings aimed at identifying and resolving problems. This became easier as the legislator's job became a full-time profession in most states and as legislative staffs became larger and more professional. More than their congressional counterparts, state legislators decided not to leave oversight to chance. Perhaps oversight needed an extra push at the state level. In any event, state legislatures established regular mechanisms for legislative review.

Following the lead of Colorado, approximately two-thirds of the state legislatures adopted sunset laws, which provide for the automatic expiration of agencies unless the state legislature acts affirmatively to renew them. Although the threat of extinction is far-fetched in the case of large agencies, the threat of review must be taken seriously by all agencies. The sunset review process is especially important for obscure agencies that might otherwise escape scrutiny by legislative committees.

In addition to sunset laws, many state legislatures substantially upgraded the quality of their legislative audit bureaus. Gradually, these organizations came to place greater emphasis on program evaluation and policy analysis, less emphasis on auditing and accounting. To ensure careful, well-crafted evaluations, state legislatures augmented the staffs assigned to these organizations.

Finally, the overwhelming majority of state legislatures provided for legislative review of administrative rules and regulations. In sixteen states, legislative vetoes enable the legislature to invalidate an administrative rule or regulation. Through the legislative veto process, state legislatures have exercised closer scrutiny of administrative rule making. The U.S. Supreme Court declared the legislative veto unconstitutional at the federal level,[1] and state courts have invalidated legislative vetoes in eight states.[2] Nevertheless, the legislative veto continues to be an important mechanism for legislative control in one-third of the states.

In thinking about legislative controls, a useful distinction can be made between inward-looking and outward-looking legislative changes. As political scientist Alan Rosenthal has observed, state legislatures have become more fragmented, more decentralized, and less cohesive in recent years. In some sense, this might be characterized as legislative decline. However, a fragmented legislature is not necessarily weaker in its dealings with other units of government, such as state bureaucracies. A highly fragmented legislature may provide more occasions for legislative oversight and more incentives for individual legislators to engage in oversight. Thus, as legislatures become weaker internally, they may become stronger externally. This is especially true of those forms of legislative control that do not require a legislative majority.

Executive Management

For years, governors have complained about the fragmented character of the executive branch. Many executive branch officials are elected or appointed to office for fixed terms that do not coincide with the governor's term. The number of state agencies, boards, and commissions can be overwhelming and disconcerting. Also, agencies have their own traditions and habits and may be reluctant to follow the priorities of a new governor. All of these factors have inhibited executive integration, coordination, and leadership.

During the 1970s and the 1980s, many governors took steps to deal with these problems. Most governors spearheaded major reorganizations of the executive branch, striving for greater rationality and for a reduction in the number of boards and commissions. Minor reorganizations also were commonplace. In Minnesota, for example, five governors issued a total of 155 reorganization orders between 1970 and 1988.[3]

Governors also institutionalized cabinet meetings, subcabinet meetings, or both to secure greater coordination and integration. During the 1970s, approximately fourteen governors established a cabinet for the first time and approximately twenty-five governors established subcabinets to advise and coordinate in broad policy domains.[4] The hope was that these meetings would ensure that key executive branch officials marched to the same drumbeat.

In addition, governors relied on new budget techniques, such as zero-based budgeting, to increase their control over agency budget submissions and, ultimately, agency budgets themselves. Under zero-based budgeting, the previous year's budget base is not taken for granted, although it may be incorporated into alternative budget submissions. During the 1970s, approximately twenty-five states adopted a modified form of zero-based budgeting.[5]

At the same time, governors fought successfully for shorter ballots to bring more top state officials under gubernatorial control. Between 1962 and 1978, the number of elected state executives declined by 10 percent.[6] As a result of these reforms, governors today are more likely to deal with state agencies headed more often by gubernatorial appointees in whom they can have confidence.

Finally, executive orders have become more popular in recent years. In Wisconsin, Gov. Lee Sherman Dreyfus issued more executive orders in 1979 than his predecessors had issued during the 1960s and 1970s.[7] Dreyfus's successor, Anthony S. Earl, issued even more executive orders than Dreyfus.[8] Similarly, in Massachusetts, the number of executive orders issued between 1965 and 1980 rose 206 percent over the preceding fifteen years.[9] Many of these executive orders were aimed at controlling state bureaucracies.

Interest Representation

Unable or unwilling to control state agencies directly in every instance, politicians relied on surrogates to ensure better representation for favored points of view, such as consumers, environmentalists, and the elderly. Political scientists Matthew McCubbins and Thomas Schwartz referred to this phenomenon as "fire-alarm oversight" because politicians in effect depend on citizens or other public officials to spot fires in the bureaucracy and help stamp them out.[10] During the 1970s and the 1980s, states took a number of steps to improve representation for broad, diffuse interests or other underrepresented interests, especially before state regulatory agencies—a "representation revolution" occurred.[11]

For example, many established "proxy advocacy" offices to represent consumer interests in state public utility commission proceedings, such as rate cases. In some instances, attorneys general served this function; in other instances, separate consumer advocacy offices were established. Wisconsin, meanwhile, established a Citizens Utilities Board, funded by citizens through voluntary contributions but authorized by the state legislature to include membership solicitations in utility bills.[12] State legislatures in Illinois, Oregon, and New York subsequently established similar organizations, though without provisions for inserts.[13]

Disappointed in the performance of occupational licensing boards, state legislatures mandated lay representation on the boards in the hope that fewer anti-competitive practices would result. Wisconsin law specifies that at least one public member shall serve on each of the state's occupational licensing boards. California goes even further. Since 1976, California has required that all occupational licensing boards have a majority of public members, except for ten "healing arts" boards and the Board of Accountancy.[14]

Many state legislatures require public hearings in various environmental policy decisions. Pursuant to the California Coastal Act of 1972, a coastal zoning commission must call for a public hearing whenever a developer submits a construction permit request for a project that might have an "adverse environmental impact" on coastal resources.

Some interest representation reforms that occurred on the state level were mandated by or encouraged by the federal government. For example, Congress required states to cooperate with the Environmental Protection Agency (EPA) in providing for public participation under the Federal Water Pollution Control Act; the Resource Conservation and Recovery Act; the Comprehensive Environmental Response, Compensation, and Liability Act; and other statutes. Through the Older Americans Act, Congress required states to establish long-term care ombudsman programs to investigate complaints by nursing home residents and to monitor the development and implementation of pertinent laws and regulations.

Regulatory Federalism

The dynamics of regulatory federalism differ significantly from those of interest representation reforms. In both cases, politicians exercise indirect control over state bureaucracies, relying on surrogates to articulate their concerns. However, regulatory federalism is much more intrusive. If a consumer advocacy group recommends a new rule or regulation, a state agency may consider and reject it. If a federal agency instructs a state agency to adopt a rule or face a sharp cutback in federal funds, the state agency does not have much of a choice.

Regulatory federalism is a process whereby the federal government imposes conditions on state governments that accept federal funding.[15] Regulatory federalism arose as an adjunct to the new social regulations of the 1970s and as an antidote to the laissez faire of general revenue sharing. Regulatory federalism includes a variety of techniques, such as direct orders (unequivocal mandates), crossover sanctions (threats in one program area if actions are not taken in another program), crosscutting requirements (obligations applicable to a wide range of programs), and partial preemptions (the establishment of minimal federal standards if states wish to run their own programs).[16] Some of these techniques apply to state legislatures; some apply to state agencies; many apply to both.

The number of federal statutes imposing significant new regulatory requirements increased dramatically during the 1970s. Given the Reagan administration's public support for federalism and deregulation, many observers expected regulatory federalism to decline during the 1980s.

However, as political scientist Timothy Conlan has shown, the number of federal statutes with significant intergovernmental controls directed at the states increased even further.[17] Moreover, a disproportionate increase came about in the most coercive regulatory control techniques—namely, direct orders and crossover sanctions. In Conlan's words, "the 1980s rivaled the previous decade as a period of unparalleled intergovernmental regulatory activity." [18]

In some cases, Congress imposed new regulatory requirements on the states despite Reagan's philosophical reservations. This was especially true in environmental policy. In other cases, however, the Reagan administration fully supported tougher controls on the states. For example, in transportation policy, it endorsed a variety of crossover sanctions,[19] and in welfare policy, it advocated limits on eligibility to receive public subsidies.[20]

Several regulatory federalism initiatives of recent years have been challenged in court. However, the courts have routinely upheld the federal government's right to impose constraints on state governments accepting federal funds.[21] The courts also have upheld partial preemptions,[22] crossover sanctions,[23] and direct orders.[24]

Due Process ·

In addition to serving as arbiters in intergovernmental disputes, federal judges have been active participants in efforts to control state bureaucracies. They have intervened vigorously in pursuit of such constitutional rights as "due process of law" and freedom from "cruel and unusual punishment." Dissatisfied with progress at the state level, they have gone so far as to seize, for example, state prisons and homes for the mentally ill or the mentally retarded, substituting their managerial judgment for that of state public administrators.

Wyatt v. Stickney[25] was the first in a long line of institutional reform cases in which federal judges decided to play a strong managerial role. Alabama's homes for the mentally ill and the mentally retarded were overcrowded, understaffed, dangerous, and unsanitary. In response to a class action suit, Judge Frank Johnson held that mental patients have a right to adequate and effective treatment in the least restrictive environment practicable. To secure that right, he issued extremely specific treatment standards and ordered rapid deinstitutionalization.

Shortly after the *Wyatt* decision, Judge Johnson found himself embroiled in an equally bitter controversy over Alabama's prisons. By most accounts, conditions in the state's prisons were deplorable. Rapes and stabbings were widespread; food was unwholesome; and physical facilities were dilapidated. In response to inmate complaints, Judge Johnson issued a decree calling for adequate medical care, regular fire inspections, and regular physical examinations.²⁶ When conditions barely improved, he issued detailed standards, including cell-space requirements, hiring requirements, and a mandatory classification system.²⁷

The Alabama cases set the stage for a large number of similar cases throughout the country. In state after state, federal judges mandated massive changes in physical facilities, staffing ratios, health services, and amenities. They specified the size of prison cells, the credentials of new employees, and plumbing and hygiene standards. They shut down facilities and prohibited new admissions, even where alternative facilities were not available.

The U.S. Supreme Court finally applied the brakes on mental health orders in *Youngberg v. Romeo.*²⁸ In that decision, the Court ruled that mentally retarded clients are constitutionally entitled to minimally adequate treatment and habilitation but that professionals, including state administrators, should be free to decide what constitutes minimally adequate training for staff. Thus, the decision was viewed as a partial victory for state administrators.

The Supreme Court has yet to focus on prison reform cases, which continue to drag on in many states. In Texas, for example, Judge William Justice has been locked in a bitter battle with the Texas Department of Corrections since he called for sweeping reforms in *Ruiz v. Estelle.*²⁹ By 1992, thirty-seven states were under some kind of court order for their prisons. In nine states, the entire state prison system was under court order.³⁰

As Republican presidents have appointed more conservative judges to the federal bench, court takeovers of prisons and other public institutions would be expected to decrease. However, as political scientist Robert Bradley has noted, judges appointed by Republican presidents are no more likely than judges appointed by Democratic presidents to issue structural reform decrees in state prison cases.³¹ Additional reasons exist to doubt that this phenomenon will diminish. As John DiIulio, Jr., has observed, "Demographic and sentencing trends make it likely that institutional overcrowding will worsen over the next decade. If that happens, and if prison and jail officials prove unable to maintain any semblance of safe and humane conditions behind bars, then sweeping judicial intervention into prisons and jails may be more of a growing prospect than a fading memory." ³²

Types of Controls

Useful in thinking about recent efforts to control state bureaucracies is to imagine a spectrum ranging from catalytic controls, at one end, to coercive controls, at the other end, with hortatory controls falling in between. Catalytic controls stimulate change but preserve a great deal of bureaucratic discretion. Coercive controls require change and severely limit bureaucratic discretion. Hortatory controls involve more pressure than catalytic controls but more restraint than coercive controls.[33]

Moreover, different types of controls have different types of effects. In their public policy implications, catalytic controls have been surprisingly effective and coercive controls have been notably counterproductive.

Catalytic Controls

Catalytic controls require state bureaucracies to respond to a petition or plea but do not predetermine the nature of their response. As a result, such controls are action-forcing but not solution-forcing. They alter bureaucratic behavior, but they permit the bureaucracy a good deal of discretion and flexibility. Examples of catalytic controls include public hearings, ombudsmen, proxy advocacy, and lay representation.

Public hearings have enabled environmentalists to win important victories in their dealings with state bureaucracies. For example, citizens have used public hearings on state water quality planning in North Carolina to secure important modifications of state plans concerning waste water disposal, construction, and mining.[34] Similarly, citizens used public hearings before the California Coastal Commission to block permits for development projects that would have an "adverse environmental impact" on coastal resources.[35]

Ombudsmen have been active in several areas but especially on nursing home issues. According to one report,[36] nursing home ombudsmen have been effective in resolving complaints on a wide variety of subjects, including Medicaid problems, guardianship, the power of attorney, inadequate hygiene, family problems, and the theft of personal possessions. Another study[37] found that nursing home ombudsmen provide useful information to legislators and planners.

Proxy advocates have effectively represented consumers in rate cases and other proceedings held by state public utility commissions. As a result of the interventions, utility companies have received rate hikes substantially lower than those originally requested. Proxy advocates also have been instrumental in securing policies on utility disconnections and payment penalties that help consumers who are struggling to pay their bills.[38] Even in complex telecommunications cases, proxy advocates have successfully promoted competition on behalf of consumers.[39]

Catalytic controls may be too weak in some instances. In several Southern states, for example, public hearing requirements in utility regulatory proceedings have been pointless because consumer groups and environmental groups have not materialized to take advantage of such hearings.[40] Lay representation on occupational licensing boards also has been a disappointment. Lacking expertise, lay representatives typically have deferred to professionals on these boards.[41]

Overall, though, catalytic controls have been remarkably successful in making state bureaucracies more responsive to a vast array of formerly underrepresented interests. In effect, they have institutionalized what political scientist James Q. Wilson refers to as "entrepreneurial politics" [42] or the pursuit of policies that offer widely distributed benefits through widely distributed costs. Moreover, catalytic controls have achieved results without engendering bureaucratic hostility and resentment. Studies show that state administrators welcome citizen participation[43] and interest group interventions.[44] At their best, catalytic controls provide state bureaucrats with ammunition to justify policies that promote the public interest.

Hortatory Controls

Hortatory controls involve political pressure or "jawboning," usually by someone in a position of authority. They strike a balance between bureaucratic discretion and bureaucratic accountability. Some, such as sunset laws and administrative reorganizations, are relatively mild; others, such as partial preemptions and crossover sanctions, are relatively strong.

The strength of hortatory controls depends primarily on two factors: their specificity (are the goals of the controllers clear?) and the credibility of the threat (how likely is it that penalties will be invoked?). Thus, sunset laws are relatively weak because the threat of termination is remote, except in the case of extremely small agencies.

To argue that some hortatory controls are mild is not to say that they are ineffective. A study of legislative audit bureau reports reveals that they do lead to changes in legislation, administrative practice, or both. Research by legislative audit bureaus is more likely to be utilized by state legislators than other types of research.[45] The literature on administrative reorganizations reveals that they do not reduce government spending but that they can promote coordination and integration if they are well-crafted and well-executed.[46] The key seems to be to put agencies with interrelated missions under the same roof.

Research on sunset laws roughly parallels the findings on administrative reorganizations. As a cost-containment device, sunset legislation has been a failure. However, as a mechanism for focusing legislative attention on agencies and issues low in visibility, sunset legislation has been a success. In a number of states, such as Connecticut and Florida, sunset laws have resulted in significant changes in statutes and agency rules.[47]

Stronger hortatory controls have been even more effective, though they also have been dysfunctional in some respects. In response to quality control systems in welfare, "errors of liberality" have declined, but "errors of stringency" have increased.[48] In effect, states have sacrificed accuracy for cost-containment. States also have enforced federal regulations that they know to be unreasonable, in response to partial preemptions in environmental policy. For example, the Minnesota Pollution Control Agency enforced a rigid EPA definition of hazardous waste, even though it meant that a lime sludge pile could not be removed from a highway site, could not be used for waste-water treatment, and could not be used to clean an electric utility company's smokestack emissions.[49]

Strong hortatory controls place a premium on uniform standards and universal compliance with such standards. In some instances, such as civil rights, no practical alternative exists to strong controls, because local prejudices are too deeply ingrained to permit cooperation. In others, however, strong hortatory controls may impose premature closure, discouraging innovation and experimentation and proving difficult for the states to serve as "laboratories" for the nation and for other states.

Despite the new federalism, strong hortatory controls have been particularly prominent in intergovernmental relations. Although federal aid to state and local governments has declined, no commensurate decrease has taken place in federal regulations. Political scientist Richard P. Nathan cites state reforms in health, education, and welfare as evidence of a growing state role in a conservative era.[50] Yet state administrators cite precisely these issue areas, along with environmental policy, as ones where federal influence is relatively strong.[51] States can be both innovating and responding. Or perhaps the state legislatures are innovating, while the state agencies are responding. In any event, regulatory federalism has not abated in recent years, even if the goals and purposes of federal overseers have changed during the Reagan and Bush administrations.

Coercive Controls

Coercive controls rob state bureaucracies of their discretion. They compel a specific response, often within a specific time frame. Neither the solution nor the deadline may be reasonable, but the state bureaucracy does not have the luxury of responding reasonably. Immediate compliance becomes more important than rationality, and short-term "outputs" become more important than long-term "outcomes."

Coercive controls often trigger bureaucratic circumvention or resistance. In the former case, bureaucrats comply with the letter, but not the spirit, of a tough requirement. In the latter case, the bureaucracy goes to court. In both cases, an adversarial relationship develops that precludes cooperation, bargaining, and persuasion.

As a response to legislative vetoes, some state agencies have issued emergency rules, which are not subject to the usual legislative review process. In Wisconsin, for example, state agencies issued a total of fifty-four emergency rules during the 1985-1986 legislative session—a sharp increase over earlier years.[52] Reliance on emergency rules is especially unfortunate, because they do not involve public hearings. Thus, to escape highly threatening legislative vetoes, agencies have escaped less-threatening public hearings as well.

Court orders have triggered some of the more dysfunctional bureaucratic responses. When Judge Frank Johnson required state prisons to reduce their overcrowding, Alabama prison officials simply released large numbers of prisoners, forcing county jails to take up the slack. Unfortunately, county jails were poorly equipped for the task; they lacked adequate space and personnel. Consequently, many prisoners, shipped to county jails, were forced to endure conditions even worse than those they experienced in the state prisons.[53] Yet the state agency was technically in compliance with the court decree.

A key problem with coercive controls is that they place far too much emphasis on formal authority. Many state agencies depend considerably on a series of informal understandings. This is especially true of prisons, where quick-thinking guards and cooperative inmates help to maintain a delicate balance between order and chaos. When that balance is disrupted, tragedy may result. This is precisely what happened in Texas, where Judge Justice's court orders dissolved the informal networks that enabled the prisons to function on a daily basis. As guards became more timid, direct challenges to authority rose sharply. Disciplinary reports reveal abrupt and dramatic increases in incidents where a guard was threatened or assaulted.[54] Inmates also turned on themselves, with their fists or with makeshift weapons. By generating rising expectations and undermining bureaucratic morale, Judge Justice created a temporary power vacuum that prison gangs quickly filled. The tragic result was a series of riots and violent episodes that left fifty-two inmates dead within two years.[55]

Accountability Battles

Accountability battles have become more prominent in state politics for three principal reasons: (1) the proliferation of controls; (2) the intensification of controls; and (3) the judicialization of controls. As controls multiply, some are likely to be contradictory. Competing claimants emerge. As controls intensify, contradictory controls generate more friction. Competing claimants press their claims. As controls spill over into the courts, disputes are resolved according to legal criteria. Moreover, the courts themselves become active participants in these battles. Frustrated with both state politicians and state bureaucrats, judges have decided that they can do a better job and that they are entitled to do so under the U.S. Constitution, the state constitution, or both.

State Legislatures versus Governors

Accountability battles between state legislatures and governors have erupted in recent years. Although such disputes are not new, they seem to focus increasingly on directives to administrative agencies and on questions of legal authority instead of political preference. As a result, state judges have found themselves playing a key role in arbitrating disputes between governors and state legislatures.

Legislative vetoes have aroused considerable conflict between state legislatures and governors, even when the same party controls both branches of government. In New Jersey, for example, the Democratic state legislature and Democratic governor Brendan T. Byrne clashed in court over a generic legislative veto and a more specific veto, whereby certain building authority proposals must be approved by both houses or the presiding offices of the legislature, depending on the nature of the proposal.[56] The New Jersey state supreme court upheld the specific legislative veto[57] but ruled the generic veto unconstitutional, citing violations of separation of powers and the presentment clauses of the state constitution.[58]

Executive orders also have triggered conflict between state legislatures and governors. In Pennsylvania, for example, Republican governor Dick Thornburgh issued an executive order "privatizing" the state's liquor control store system. The Democratic state legislature, which had just rejected such a plan, promptly took the governor to court. A Commonwealth Court judge ruled in favor of the legislature, noting that the governor's privatization plan was "without authority and contravenes the Sunset Act." He also accused both sides of playing an unseemly game of political football at the public's expense.[59]

Money, the "mother's milk of politics," has fueled many disputes between state legislatures and governors. In Wisconsin, Republican governor Tommy Thompson refused to accept a decision by the Democratic state legislature to maintain welfare benefits at existing levels. Stretching the outer limits of his line-item veto authority, Thompson vetoed two digits and a decimal point from the state legislature's benefit formula, thereby effecting a 6 percent reduction in welfare benefits. The legislature promptly took the governor to court, but the Wisconsin supreme court upheld a generous interpretation of the governor's line-item power.[60]

The most striking aspect of accountability battles between state legislatures and governors is that they often have a partisan edge, pitting a

Republican governor against a Democratic state legislature or vice versa. As divided government has become more common at the state level, state agencies find determining whether they are in Democratic or Republican hands increasing difficult. Thus, the voters' ambivalence has triggered important legal battles with high stakes.

Federal Politicians versus State Politicians

State bureaucracies increasingly are being asked to implement federal statutes, such as environmental protection statutes. Often these federal statutes contradict state statutes or the policy preferences of the state's governor. Under such circumstances, a showdown is likely, with the federal government citing the "commerce clause" or the "take care clause" of the U.S. Constitution, while the state government cites the Tenth Amendment.

The U.S. Supreme Court and other federal courts have routinely sided with the federal government in accountability battles where the allocation of federal funds is at issue. If states accept federal funding, they also must accept the conditions the federal government attaches to those funds. However, many intergovernmental disputes do not involve federal funding but a federal effort to preempt state activity in a particular policy domain. Here, also, the U.S. Supreme Court has sided with the federal government, though with occasional exceptions.

In *National League of Cities v. Usery*,[61] the Supreme Court surprised many observers by rejecting the federal government's attempt to extend minimum wage and maximum hour provisions to municipal employees. In doing so, the Court said that the Tenth Amendment prohibited any federal action that impaired "the State's freedom to structure integral operations in areas of traditional governmental functions." Thus a key provision of the 1974 Fair Labor Standards Act Amendments was ruled unconstitutional. The decision was an important victory for both state and local governments.

In subsequent cases, the Supreme Court wrestled gamely with the "traditional governmental functions" criterion and offered further clarification. For example, in *Hodel v. Virginia Surface Mining and Reclamation Association*,[62] the Court articulated a three-fold test for determining when Tenth Amendment claims shall prevail. Specifically, the Court extended protection to the states if federal regulations: (1) regulate the states as states; (2) address matters that are indisputably attributes of state sovereignty; and (3) impair the states' ability to structure integral operations in areas of traditional function. In *Hodel*—a strip mining case involving a partial preemption statute—the Court concluded that Congress had acted properly and with restraint. Similarly, in *FERC v. Mississippi*,[63] the Court applauded Congress for imposing modest constraints on state public utility commissions, when it could have preempted the field entirely.

Finally, after years of painful efforts to distinguish between "traditional government functions" and other functions, the Supreme Court abandoned that doctrine outright in *Garcia v. San Antonio Metropolitan Transit Authority.*[64] Writing for the majority, Justice Harry A. Blackmun concluded that "State sovereign interests . . . are more properly protected by procedural safeguards inherent in the structure of the federal system than by judicially created limitations on federal power." [65] In effect, the states would have to protect themselves through vigorous lobbying on Capitol Hill. The Supreme Court no longer would invoke a rule that was "unsound in principle and unworkable in practice." [66]

Although most accountability battles between federal and state politicians have focused on the commerce clause, one celebrated dispute involved the constitutional provision (in Article I) that the states shall have the authority to train state militia. A number of governors, opposed to the Reagan administration's Central America policies, objected to White House orders, backed by Congress, to use the National Guard for training exercises in Honduras. The governors feared that their troops would directly or indirectly support the contras' efforts to overthrow the Sandinista government in Nicaragua. Gov. Rudy Perpich of Minnesota and ten other governors sued the federal government to protest the deployment of National Guard troops without gubernatorial consent. The governors did not dispute the president's authority to federalize the Guard to deal with a national emergency, but they noted pointedly that no state of emergency existed.

On August 5, 1987, a federal district court upheld the federal government's right to deploy National Guard units while the Guard is on active duty. In the words of Judge Donald Alsop, "All authority to provide for the national defense resides in the Congress, and state governors have never had, and never could have, jurisdiction in this area." [67] That decision was subsequently affirmed by the U.S. Court of Appeals and by the U.S. Supreme Court.[68] Here, as in other disputes between federal and state politicians, the federal government has been successful in establishing its preeminence.

Federal Judges versus State Politicians

In accountability battles between federal politicians and state politicians, federal judges have served as arbiters. In other disputes, however, federal judges have served as both arbiters and combatants. In numerous institutional reform cases, federal district court judges have ordered sweeping changes that are attainable only if state legislatures allocate more money than they wish to spend in a particular policy domain. These decisions have had tangible effects on state budgets.[69] The decisions also have raised important questions concerning both federalism and the power of the purse.

Confronted by shocking conditions in Alabama's prisons, Judge Frank Johnson ordered the entire prison system overhauled. He required immediate action to provide adequate food, clothing, shelter, sanitation, medical attention, and personal safety for inmates. He ordered individual cells, with each cell being at least 60 square feet. He required educational and rehabilitative services. And to ensure swift implementation, he established human rights committees.

Other federal judges have acted with equal vigor. Judge William Justice, appalled by conditions in Texas prisons, ordered an end to quadruple cells, triple cells, and double cells. He restricted the use of force by prison guards and ordered an end to the state's "building tender" system, in which inmates in effect guarded other inmates. In addition, he ordered sharp improvements in health care, fire and safety standards. He also insisted on prompt punishments for violations of constitutional rights.

In other institutional reform cases, federal judges have ordered sweeping changes in state treatment of the mentally ill and the mentally retarded. In New York, Judges Orrin Judd and John Bartels demanded more ward attendants, eighty-five more nurses, thirty physical therapists, and fifteen more physicians at the Willowbrook Developmental Center on Staten Island. They prohibited seclusion of patients and called for the immediate repair of broken toilets. They also ordered a sharp decrease in the Willowbrook population, stressing the advantages of deinstitutionalization. To implement these reforms, they appointed and preserved a Willowbrook Review Panel, which developed into a powerful agent of change.

In Pennsylvania, Judge Raymond Broderick went ever further, after learning of unsanitary, inhumane, and dangerous conditions at the Pennhurst State School and Hospital for the mentally retarded. In a strongly worded opinion, Broderick ordered the eventual closing down of the Pennhurst facilities, with residents being relocated in community facilities. In the meantime, he insisted on clean, odorless, and insect-free buildings, no new admissions, and less reliance on forcible restraint and unnecessary medication. To achieve these results, he appointed a special master and set deadlines for compliance.

More often than not, accountability battles between federal judges and state politicians have been won by federal judges. In reviewing lower court decisions, appeals court judges and the U.S. Supreme Court have agreed that "cruel and unusual punishment" is intolerable in state prisons and that the mentally ill have a constitutional right to "treatment" if admitted to a state facility. However, appeals courts also have raised questions about the extraordinarily detailed and specific remedies mandated by federal district court judges.

In *Newman v. Alabama*,[70] the U.S. Court of Appeals for the Fifth Circuit ruled that Judge Johnson went too far in specifying the size of new prison cells, in appointing human rights committees, and in insisting on rehabilitation opportunities for all prisoners. In the words of the court: "The Constitution does not require that prisoners, as individuals or as a group, be provided with any and every amenity which some person may think is needed to avoid mental, physical and emotional deterioration." In *Ruiz v. Estelle*,[71] the U.S. Court of Appeals for the Fifth Circuit ruled that Judge Justice went too far in outlawing double cells in Texas prisons (but supported his ban on triple and quadruple cells). In *New York State Association for Retarded Children v. Carey*,[72] the U.S. Court of Appeals for the Second Circuit concluded that Gov. Hugh Carey could not be held in contempt of court for failing to provide funding for the Willowbrook Review Panel. In *Pennhurst State School and Hospital v. Halderman*,[73] the U.S. Supreme Court ruled that a right to treatment exists only if a state accepts federal funds and if federal conditions of aid are clearly and unambiguously stated. In *Youngberg v. Romeo*,[74] the U.S. Supreme Court ruled that even when a right to treatment exists, it should be operationalized by qualified professionals, not judges.

Thus, accountability battles between federal district court judges and state politicians have given way to battles between federal district court judges and federal appeals court judges. On questions of constitutional rights, the appeals court judges generally have deferred to federal district courts, to the chagrin of the states. On questions of remedies, however, the appeals courts have cautioned lower courts against excessive specificity that stretches the limits of judicial expertise.

Conclusion

State administrative agencies once enjoyed considerable autonomy. Ignored by virtually everyone but clientele groups, they were "semi-sovereign" entities. In the early 1970s, that began to change. As state budgets grew and state bureaucracies increased in importance, this era came to a close. To make state agencies more accountable, politicians and judges institutionalized a wide variety of reforms. Through direct and indirect means, they attempted to bring state bureaucracies under control.

Ironically, this occurred at precisely the same time as the growing professionalization of state agencies. Thanks to civil service reforms, budget increases, rising education levels, and growing pressure for specialization, state bureaucracies acquired greater experience and expertise. They now are more adept at problem solving than ever before and arguably more deserving of discretion. Thus, they chafe at external pressure, particularly when it is highly coercive.

General agreement exists that state agencies ought to be accountable. Even state bureaucrats cheerfully concede that point. However, consensus on the need for bureaucratic accountability has given way to "dissensus" on lines of authority. If governors and state legislators both claim an electoral mandate, who is right? If presidents and governors both cite constitutional prerogatives, who is correct? If federal judges and state politicians disagree on spending priorities, who deserves the power of the purse?

In the 1990s, state agencies are living in a different world—one characterized by growing emphasis on hierarchy, oversight, and judicial review. State agencies are more accountable to their sovereigns than they used to be. Yet accountability has become a murky concept. Principal-agent theories of politics[75] work only when the principal's identity is clear to the agent. In numerous policy areas, state bureaucratic agents face dual principals or even multiple principals.

Thus, accountability battles rage, as competing sovereigns press their claims. As one might expect in a federal system, different actors have won accountability battles in different settings and at different times. Increasingly, however, federal judges are settling the most difficult of these battles. In the process of resolving disputes, federal judges have themselves become interested parties. Ultimately, federal judges decide how accountability shall be defined, how authority shall be structured, and how power shall be wielded in a federal system. If accountability battles persist, the judicialization of state administration is the most probable result.

Notes

1. *Immigration and Naturalization Service v. Chadha*, 462 U.S. 919 (1983).
2. L. Harold Levinson, "The Decline of the Legislative Veto: Federal/State Comparisons and Interactions," *Publius* 17:1 (Winter 1987): 115-132.
3. Thad L. Beyle, "The Executive Branch: Organization and Issues, 1988-1989," in Council of State Governments, *The Book of the States, 1990-1991* (Lexington, Ky.: Council of State Governments, 1990), 76.
4. Lydia Bodman and Daniel Garry, "Innovations in State Cabinet Systems," *State Government* 55:3 (Summer 1982): 93-97.
5. Thomas Lauth, "Zero-Base Budgeting in Georgia State Government: Myth and Reality," in *Perspectives on Budgeting*, ed. Allen Schick (Washington, D.C.: American Society for Public Administration, 1980), 114-132.
6. Larry J. Sabato, *Goodbye to Good-time Charlie: The American Govenorship Transformed* (Washington, D.C.: CQ Press, 1983).

7. Susan King, "Executive Orders of the Wisconsin Governor," *Wisconsin Law Review* 2 (1980): 333-369.

8. Justin Kopca, "Executive Orders in State Government," unpublished manuscript, Madison, Wis., May 1987.

9. E. Lee Bernick, "Discovering a Governor's Power: The Executive Order," *State Government* 57:3 (1984): 97-101.

10. Matthew McCubbins and Thomas Schwartz, "Congressional Oversight Overlooked: Police Patrols versus Fire Alarms," *American Journal of Political Science* 28:1 (February 1984): 180-202.

11. William Gormley, Jr., "The Representation Revolution: Reforming State Regulation through Public Representation," *Administration and Society* 18:2 (August 1986): 179-196.

12. Involuntary bill inserts later were ruled unconstitutional in a California case that effectively invalidated a key provision of the Wisconsin law. See *Pacific Gas and Electric v. Public Utilities Commission of California*, 106 S. Ct. 903 (1986).

13. Beth Givens, *Citizens' Utility Boards: Because Utilities Bear Watching* (San Diego, Calif.: Center for Public Interest Law, University of San Diego Law School, 1991).

14. Howard Schutz, "Effects of Increased Citizen Membership on Occupational Licensing Boards in California," *Policy Studies Journal* 2 (March 1983): 504-516.

15. Regulatory federalism also may be used to describe the relationship between state and local governments. For more on the growing burdens placed by state governments on local governments, see Catherine Lovell and Charles Tobin. "The Mandate Issue," *Public Administration Review* 41:3 (May/June 1981): 318-331. See also Joseph Zimmerman, "Developing State-Local Relations: 1987-1989," in Council of State Governments, *The Book of the States, 1990-1991*, 533-548.

16. Advisory Commission on Intergovernmental Relations, *Regulatory Federalism: Policy, Process, Impact and Reform* (Washington, D.C.: Advisory Commission on Intergovernmental Relations, 1983).

17. Timothy Conlan, "And the Beat Goes On: Intergovernmental Mandates and Preemption in an Era of Deregulation," *Publius* 21:3 (Summer 1991): 43-57.

18. Ibid., 50.

19. James Gosling, "Transportation Policy and the Ironies of Intergovernmental Relations," in *The Midwest Response to the New Federalism*, ed. Peter Eisinger and William Gormley (Madison: University of Wisconsin Press, 1988), 237-263.

20. Sanford Schram, "The New Federalism and Social Welfare: AFDC in the Midwest," in *The Midwest Response to the New Federalism*, 264-292.

21. *Massachusetts v. U.S.*, 435 U.S. 444 (1978); and *Connecticut Department of Income Maintenance v. Heckler*, 105 S. Ct. 2210 (1985).

22. *Hodel v. Virginia Surface Mining and Reclamation Association*, 452 U.S. 264 (1981); and *FERC v. Mississippi*, 456 U.S. 742 (1982).

23. *South Dakota v. Dole*, Slip Opinion No. 86-260, U.S. Supreme Court, June 23, 1987.

24. *EEOC v. Wyoming*, 460 U.S. 226 (1983); *Garcia v. San Antonio Metropoli-*

tan Transit Authority, 105 S. Ct. 1005 (1985); *City of New York v. FCC,* 108 S. Ct. 1637 (1988); and *Mississippi Power and Light v. Mississippi,* 108 S. Ct. 2428 (1988).

25. *Wyatt v. Stickney,* 324 F. Supp. 781 (M.D. Ala., 1971).
26. *Newman v. Alabama,* 349 F. Supp. 278 (M.D. Ala., 1972).
27. *James v. Wallace,* 406 F. Supp. 318 (M.D. Ala., 1976); and *Pugh v. Locke,* 406 F. Supp. 318 (M.D. Ala., 1976).
28. *Youngberg v. Romeo,* 102 S. Ct. 2452 (1982).
29. *Ruiz v. Estelle,* 503 F. Supp. 1265 (S.D. Tex. 1980).
30. Joel Rosch, "Will the Federal Courts Run the States' Prison Systems?" in *State Government: CQ's Guide to Current Issues and Activities 1987-1988,* ed. Thad L. Beyle (Washington, D.C.: Congressional Quarterly Inc., 1987), 165-168.
31. Robert Bradley, "Judicial Appointment and Judicial Intervention: The Issuance of Structural Reform Decrees in Corrections Litigation," in *Courts, Corrections, and the Constitution,* ed. John DiIulio, Jr. (New York: Oxford University Press, 1990), 249-267.
32. John DiIulio, Jr., "Conclusion: What Judges Can Do to Improve Prisons and Jails," in *Courts, Corrections, and the Constitution,* 288-289.
33. William Gormley, Jr., *Taming the Bureaucracy: Muscles, Prayers, and Other Strategies* (Princeton, N.J.: Princeton University Press, 1989).
34. David Godschalk and Bruce Stiftel, "Making Waves: Public Participation in State Water Planning," *Journal of Applied Behavioral Science* 17:4 (October-December 1981): 597-614.
35. Judy Rosener, "Making Bureaucrats Responsive: A Study of the Impact of Citizen Participation and Staff Recommendations on Regulatory Decision Making," *Public Administration Review* 42:4 (July/August 1982): 339-345.
36. Administration on Aging, U.S. Department of Health and Human Services, *National Summary of State Ombudsman Reports for U.S. Fiscal Year 1982* (Washington, D.C.: U.S. Government Printing Office, 1983).
37. Abraham Monk et al., *National Comparative Analysis of Long Term Care Programs for the Aged* (New York: Brookdale Institute on Aging and Adult Human Development and the Columbia University School of Social Work, 1982).
38. William Gormley, Jr., *The Politics of Public Utility Regulation* (Pittsburgh, Pa.: University of Pittsburgh Press, 1983).
39. Paul Teske, *After Divestiture: The Political Economy of State Telecommunications Regulation* (Albany: SUNY Press, 1990), 63-85.
40. Ibid.
41. Gerald Thain and Kenneth Haydock, *A Working Paper: How Public and Other Members of Regulation and Licensing Boards Differ: The Results of a Wisconsin Survey* (Madison, Wis.: Center for Public Representation, 1983).
42. James Q. Wilson, ed., *The Politics of Regulation* (New York: Basic Books, 1980).
43. Cheryl Miller, "State Administrator Perceptions of the Policy Influence of Other Actors: Is Less Better?" *Public Administration Review* 47:3 (May/June 1987): 239-245.
44. Glenn Abney and Thomas Lauth, *The Politics of State and City Administra-*

tion (Albany: SUNY Press, 1986).

45. David Rafter, "Policy-Focused Evaluation: A Study of the Utilization of Evaluation Research by the Wisconsin Legislature," Ph.D. dissertation, University of Wisconsin, Madison, Wis., 1982.

46. Kenneth Meier, "Executive Reorganization of Government: Impact on Employment and Expenditures," *American Journal of Political Science* 24:3 (August 1980): 396-412; and Karen Hult, *Agency Merger and Bureaucratic Redesign* (Pittsburgh, Pa.: University of Pittsburgh Press, 1987).

47. Doug Roederer and Patsy Palmer, *Sunset: Expectation and Experience* (Lexington, Ky.: Council of State Governments, June 1981).

48. Evelyn Brodkin and Michael Lipsky, "Quality Control in AFDC as an Administrative Strategy," *Social Service Review* 57:1 (March 1983): 1-34.

49. Eric Black, "Why Regulators Need a Don't-Do-It-If-It's-Stupid Clause," *Washington Monthly* 16:12 (January 1985): 23-26.

50. Richard P. Nathan, "The Role of the States in American Federalism" (Paper delivered at the annual meeting of the American Political Science Association, Chicago, September 3-6, 1987).

51. Richard Elling, "Federal Dollars and Federal Clout in State Administration: A Test of 'Regulatory' and 'Picket Fence' Models of Intergovernmental Relations" (Paper delivered at the annual meeting of the Midwest Political Science Association, Chicago, April 17-20, 1985).

52. Douglas Stencel, "Analysis of Joint Committee for Review of Administrative Rules Caseload 1985-1986," unpublished manuscript, Madison, Wis., April 1987.

53. Tinsley Yarbrough, *Judge Frank Johnson and Human Rights in Alabama* (University: University of Alabama Press, 1981).

54. James Marquart and Ben Crouch, "Judicial Reform and Prisoner Control: The Impact of *Ruiz v. Estelle* on a Texas Penitentiary," *Law and Society Review* 19:4 (1985): 557-586.

55. Aric Press, "Inside America's Toughest Prison," *Newsweek*, October 6, 1986, 46-61.

56. Levinson, "The Decline of the Legislative Veto," 121.

57. *Enourato v. New Jersey Building Authority*, 448 A. 2d 449 (N.J. 1982).

58. *General Assembly v. Byrne*, 448 A. 2d 438 (N.J. 1982).

59. Gary Warner, "Despite Ruling, Future of Liquor Stores Up in Air," *Pittsburgh Press*, December 30, 1986, 1.

60. Charles Friederich, "Lawmakers to Sue Thompson over Budget Vetoes," *Milwaukee Journal*, September 2, 1987, B3; and Doug Mell, "Thompson Vetoes Win in Court," *Wisconsin State Journal*, June 15, 1988, 1.

61. *National League of Cities v. Usery*, 426 U.S. 833 (1976).

62. *Hodel v. Virginia Surface Mining and Reclamation Association*, 452 U.S. 264 (1981).

63. *FERC v. Mississippi*, 456 U.S. 742 (1982).

64. *Garcia v. San Antonio Metropolitan Transit Authority* 105 S. Ct. 1005 (1985).

65. 105 S. Ct. 1018 (1985).

66. 105 S. Ct. 1016 (1985).

67. Robert Whereatt, "State Loses Guard Suit," *Minneapolis Star and Tribune*,

August 5, 1987, 1.

68. *Perpich et al. v. Department of Defense,* Slip Opinion No. 89-542, U.S. Supreme Court, June 11, 1990.

69. Linda Harriman and Jeffrey Straussman, "Do Judges Determine Budget Decisions?" *Public Administration Review* 43:4 (July/August 1983): 343-351.

70. *Newman v. Alabama,* 559 F. 2d 283 (5th Cir., 1977).

71. *Ruiz v. Estelle,* 679 F. 2d 1115 (1982).

72. *New York State Association for Retarded Children v. Carey,* 631 F. 2d 162 (1980).

73. *Pennhurst State School and Hospital v. Halderman,* 101 S. Ct., 1531 (1981).

74. *Youngberg v. Romeo,* 102 S. Ct. 2452 (1982).

75. Jonathan Bendor and Terry Moe, "An Adaptive Model of Bureaucratic Politics," *American Political Science Review* 79:3 (September 1985): 755-774.

9 ▬▬▬

The Persistence of State Parties

Samuel C. Patterson

Democracy does not work well on a large scale without competition among political parties. At their best, political parties mobilize and manifest citizens' interests, preferences, and needs. They permit voters to make effective choices from among teams of politicians seeking election to public offices. Political parties help make democratic politics responsible and accountable. When citizens stop identifying with a political party and vote as independents, knowingly or unknowingly they create an incentive for political party organizations to strengthen themselves and behave more competitively because support no longer can be taken for granted. Today, parties are weaker in the electorate than they once were, but they are stronger and more coherent as organizations. Accordingly, the state political parties are more important than ever.

Political parties are pervasive in American state politics. As of 1991, forty-eight of the fifty governors were either Democrats or Republicans. The other statewide elected officials were unanimously adherent to one of the two major parties. All of the 7,461 state legislators were Democrats or Republicans, except for the members of Nebraska's unicameral legislature and a handful of independents. Democrats and Republicans dominate local politics where they are not legally nonpartisan. In national politics, splinter party presidential electors occasionally have succeeded, but citizens almost always elect only Democrats or Republicans to represent them in Congress.

What logically follows is that lying behind the Democratic and Republican monopoly on political offices are highly organized and well-oiled party organizations. But this is not the case and never has been. In general, a political party may be thought of as "any group, however loosely organized, seeking to elect governmental office-holders under a given label." [1]

American party politics are broad in the scope of their coverage. Almost all elected public officials and the vast majority of voters call themselves Democrats or Republicans. The Democratic and Republican parties are about the only organized parties in America. However, party politics are shallow. As organizations, parties often are not robust; in government, party cleavage may be episodic and ephemeral; among voters, loyalty may evanesce during elections.

Party politics, however, are not inconsequential. American parties may not compare unfavorably with parties in other Western democracies, as so often is assumed.[2] American electoral politics are not merely shadow and symbol, with no grounding in political party organization. Organized parties operate in every state, more-or-less endowed with leadership, managerial resources, staff, budgets, local organization, and loyal followers. What are these state party organizations like?

The Organized State Parties

State party organizations vary in size and shape, but they are similar enough to permit a general analysis. Their distinguishing features are found in their organizational formats, their purposes, their decentralization, their tenacity, and their regulation by government.

Organization

The states have organized their parties in a remarkably similar fashion. Each party has a governing committee presided over by the state party chair. This Democratic or Republican State Central Committee is made up of party activists who oversee party efforts at the state level. The state party chairs, elected by the state committees in three-fourths of the states and by the state party conventions in the rest, provide leadership and management for their state organizations. These state chairs may be the state's principal political leaders, or they may be agents of, and perhaps even handpicked by, the governor.

In the smallest political unit of the state reside the grass-roots party leaders—the precinct committee members. Between the precinct leadership at the base of the organization and the state committee at its peak lies a range of party committees. Typically, party committees are established in congressional districts, state legislative districts, counties, towns, cities, and wards. The county chairs provide a crucial echelon of leadership for state parties. Party committees are not laid out in the form of a hierarchy. They are not centralized in the state capital, with orders flowing from the top down, like a bureaucracy or a firm. Instead, the organizational committees form autonomous layers, connected together, but each layer maintains its own structure and functions. This layering feature of American parties has been called "stratarchy" to denote the presence of "layers, or strata, of control rather than one of centralized leadership from the top down." [3]

In the early 1980s, a team of scholars conducted interviews and collected mailed questionnaire data from state and local party leaders throughout the country. They gathered data on state parties from about three-fourths of the sitting state chairs, from two-thirds of the 560 men and women who served as state chair from 1960 to 1978, and from about 4,000 of the 7,300 local party leaders.[4] The state parties mainly are defined by the individuals who fill their leadership and committee posts. The parties are called cadre parties, or skeletal organizations, because they feature small groups of leaders and activists and lack a "regularized, dues-paying membership commonly found among parties in other nations and among almost all nonparty organizations." [5]

Purpose

The state parties serve a variety of purposes, most importantly (1) giving meaning within the political system to individuals' preferences about policy issues or their ideological predispositions, (2) facilitating the transformation of public opinion into governing policy, and (3) providing avenues for social activity. The thousands of people involved in state party politics may wish to do a variety of things, operate on the basis of diverse motives, or have divergent axes to grind.

State party organizations primarily are concerned with elections. The party organization embraces "a group of persons who consciously coordinate their activities so as to influence the choice of candidates for elective office." [6] Or, more succinctly, a party is "a team seeking to control the governing apparatus by gaining office in a duly constituted election." [7] In seeking to win elections, however, parties are not single-minded and do not always make the right choices. They often are best described as "forms of organized trial and error." [8]

Resiliency and Decentralization

"Organizations," said James Q. Wilson, "tend to persist." [9] The American state parties, certainly, are resilient. They have adapted to changes in resources, political fortunes, electoral realignments, campaign technology, and influence. Rarely has the extent of state party organizational tenacity been the focus of empirical inquiry. One exception is Mildred A. Schwartz's analysis of the Illinois Republican party. She concludes:

> The lesson to be learned from examining the life of the Illinois
> Republican Party is one of robust organization. . . . In its robustness, the

party displays an overall vigor . . . that enables it to continue despite recurring defeats. It is robust in the roughness of its structure, shrinking and expanding under changing environmental conditions without being bound to a set pattern.[10]

The resiliency and persistence of the state parties lies partly in the decentralization of American party organization. The parties are mainly organized to capture state and local offices. Only the president, vice president, and 535 members of Congress are elected to national office; thousands of elective offices are available in the states. Accordingly, the political parties have taken on an organizational structure mirroring that of the federal system of government. Centralization of the parties has been advocated,[11] and some party nationalization has taken place since 1968: in the Republican party, largely through funding to the states; in the Democratic party, mainly through adoption of rules regulating the selection of national party convention delegates.[12] Despite the importance of these nationalizing tendencies, their effect has been limited. The state parties remain autonomous in most activities, and the aggregate system remains primarily federated.

The state party's resiliency, its adaptability, and thus its persistence also may have resulted from its skeletal character. Without a large number of paid employees, or a body of politicians dependent upon the organization for their livelihoods, the parties have more freedom to compromise. They are much less tied to the protection of vested interests.[13]

Regulation

Scholars often note that political parties were eschewed by the founders of the republic and that they nowhere are mentioned in the Constitution. They are, however, controlled by law. State parties are highly regulated, so much so that political scientist Leon D. Epstein refers to them as public utilities.[14] For approximately one hundred years, the state parties have not been considered private, voluntary associations under state laws. On the contrary, like the electric company or the water works, political parties are conceived in state laws as agencies providing public services, serving a public interest, and subject to state regulation.

State laws define what constitutes a political party. Ohio's law is typical in its legalistic detail and long-windedness:

A political party . . . is any group of voters which, at the last preceding regular state election, polled for its candidate for governor in the state or nominees for presidential electors at least five percent of the entire vote cast for such office or which filed with the secretary of state, subsequent to any election in which it received less than five percent of such vote, a petition signed by qualified electors equal in number to at least one percent of the total vote for governor or nominees for presidential electors at the last preceding election, declaring their intention of organizing a political party, the name of which shall be stated in the declaration, and of participating in the next succeeding primary election, held in even-numbered years, that occurs more than one hundred twenty days after the date of filing. . . . When any political party fails to cast five percent of the total vote cast at an election for the office of governor or president it shall cease to be a political party.[15]

The scope of state regulation of parties varies among the states, but all except five (Alaska, Delaware, Hawaii, Kentucky, and North Carolina) have regulations dictating how the state parties are to be organized, how their membership is defined, and how their internal operations are to be conducted. In 1984, the Advisory Commission on Intergovernmental Relations (ACIR) conducted an analysis of state statutes regulating political parties, revealing the extent of influence the laws have (see Table 9-1).

In addition to regulation of party organizations, the states also oversee the involvement of parties in the electoral process. These legal constraints include requiring nomination of candidates by primary elections, determining whether parties may engage in preprimary endorsements of candidates, regulating who can vote in party primaries, deciding whether primary losers can run in the general election under the label of another party, and establishing whether the ballot will permit straight party voting. Moreover, federal and state regulation of campaign finance practices has had a major impact upon state party organization.

In some states, regulation leads to a strong party role in the electoral process. For example, states in which laws allow preprimary endorsement, provide for closed primaries, or facilitate straight-ticket voting foster strong parties. But the ACIR study concluded that "most states do not provide a legal environment conducive to the development or maintenance of strong state and local party roles in the electoral process." [16]

At the same time, state regulation of parties in recent years has been challenged successfully in the courts. For instance, in the case of *Tashjian v. Connecticut* (1986), the U.S. Supreme Court held that the state of Connecticut could not bar registered independents from voting in a Republican primary election when that party explicitly permitted them to do so. And, in *Secretary of State of California v. San Francisco Democratic Central Committee* (1989), the Supreme Court held invalid a series of California regulations of political parties, including that state's ban on preprimary party endorsements.

Table 9-1   State Regulation of Political Parties

Regulation	Number of states with regulation
Composition of local party committees	34
How local party committee members are selected	35
How state central committee members are selected	36
Local party committees' internal rules, procedures, and activities	45
Party internal rules and procedures	28
State central committee's meeting dates and location	15
Who may serve on state central committees	32

Source: Advisory Commission on Intergovernmental Relations, *The Transformation in American Politics: Implications for Federalism* (Washington, D.C.: Advisory Commission on Intergovernmental Relations, 1986), 128-144.

Strengths and Weaknesses of State Parties

A substantial amount of uninformed speculation exists about the strength of state party organizations. Claims about party effectiveness, and more common assertions about party decline, are usually strident, impressionistic, and inclined to exaggerate the impact of technology. These notions are presumptive of a golden age of strong parties based on the model of a few urban political machines or the disciplined socialist parties of western Europe.

Recently, a few scholars undertook empirical investigation of state and local party organizations, gathering data and observing party performance firsthand.[17] Their findings belie the view that the state parties have been enervated—nationalized, swamped by political action committees (PACs), decimated organizationally, overcome by media technology or modern "snake oil" public relations, or even altogether nonexistent.

The balanced assessment is that state party organizational strength has not been impressively high for many decades and was never high for most states. Much diversity exists today among states in the strength of their party organizations.

> There is mounting evidence that political parties, far from becoming doddering relics on the verge of extinction, are undergoing a complex process of adaptation to new electoral conditions and are emerging in many states as vigorous entities capable of performing a mix of both modern and traditional tasks.[18]

Resources of the Party Organizations

The resources available to the state party organizations can be described from the data gathered by two major investigations, one led by political scientist Cornelius P. Cotter, and the other by the staff of the Advisory Commission on Intergovernmental Relations. These two field studies showed that

• Most state parties have permanent headquarters offices in the state capital, about a fifth of the county party organizations have permanent headquarters, and more than half the county parties have offices during the campaign season.

• Most state headquarters are staffed by at least one full-time staff member and about 15 percent have ten or more staff. Republican state parties are substantially better staffed than Democratic state parties.

• The state parties now have significant, though modest, budgets for operations, which are considerably more than they had two decades ago. In 1984, nearly two-thirds of Democratic state parties had budgets that were less than $250,000; more than half of Republican state parties had budgets that were more than $500,000. The disparity occurs partly because state Republican parties get more help than the Democratic parties from the national party and partly because the state Republicans have effectively exploited modern fund-raising methods such as direct mail and telephone solicitations.

Resources in office facilities, staff, and budgets allow the state parties to engage more fully in campaign politics. A sizeable majority of the parties provide money and fund-raising assistance to state and congressional candidates (see Table 9-2). Moreover, most can provide a range of technical assistance to state candidates, such as assistance with polling, media use, or coordination of contributions from PACs.

The Republican parties on average have a substantial edge over the Democratic parties in receipt of state party services. Only in fund-raising assistance for congressional candidates do state Democratic party leaders report levels of activity equal to that of Republicans.

Diversity of Party Strength

A 1984 study showed wide variation among the states in the organizational strengths of their state and local parties (see Table 9-3). Two sets of indicators were used to measure party organizational strength: organizational complexity and programmatic capacity. Organizational complexity was measured through indicators of accessibility to party headquarters, staffing, and budgets; programmatic capacity was measured through indicators of institutional support, such as fund raising, electoral mobilization, polling, providing information, and candidate-directed activity, which included financial contributions to candidates, providing services, and preprimary endorsements.[19]

According to the data in Table 9-3, state Republican parties in general were organizationally stronger than state Democratic parties. Of

Table 9-2   State Party Contributions to Candidates, 1984

Type of assistance or service	Percentage receiving assistance or service	
	Democrats	Republicans
Campaign contributions		
Congressional candidates	56	70
State candidates	70	90
Campaign seminars	76	100
Coordinating political action committee		
contributions	31	52
Fund-raising assistance		
Congressional candidates	63	63
State candidates	63	95
Media consulting	46	75
Polling services	50	78

Source: Advisory Commission on Intergovernmental Relations, *The Transformation in American Politics: Implications for Federalism* (Washington, D.C.: Advisory Commission on Intergovernmental Relations, 1986), 115.

the ten strongest state parties, eight were Republican. Both parties were more-or-less equally strong in only four states—California, Michigan, Minnesota, and Pennsylvania. In these states, the county party organizations were rated "strong" as well. That the California parties were rated as relatively strong parties perhaps reflects the loose character of state party strength in the United States. Students of the California parties often speak of the formal party organizations as weak and ineffectual but attribute considerable strength to voluntary party organizations and influence on the state's politics to the legislative parties.[20]

Massachusetts had the weakest pair of party organizations; most of the other weak parties were Democratic parties in southern states and both parties in the mountain west.[21] Studies of party organizations in Florida and South Carolina indicated significant growth in organizational strength, especially in light of their traditional partisan torpidity.[22]

Although some correlation exists between party strength at the state and local levels, parties strong at one level are not necessarily strong at the other. For instance, Ohio Republicans were rated strong at both state and local levels, but Ohio Democrats were organizationally weak at the state level while maintaining relatively firm local control. In some southern states, the Republicans developed impressive, centralized state party organization without grass-roots party organization of parallel strength.[23]

State parties appear to be organizationally stronger in states where the legal environment is supportive and where minimal party regulation exits. Where state laws support parties and regulation is light, the parties (62 percent) tend to be organizationally strong. But, where the legal

Table 9-3   Strength of State Party Organizations

	State party strength			
	Strong		Weak	
	Democratic	Republican	Democratic	Republican
Strong local parties	California	Arizona	Alaska	Hawaii
	Florida	California	Connecticut	Rhode Island
	Michigan	Connecticut	Delaware	West Virginia
	Minnesota	Illinois	Idaho	Wyoming
	North Dakota	Indiana	Illinois	
	Pennsylvania	Iowa	Indiana	
	Rhode Island	Maine	Maine	
		Michigan	Maryland	
		Minnesota	New Hampshire	
		Nevada	New York	
		New Mexico	North Carolina	
		New York	Ohio	
		North Carolina	Tennessee	
		North Dakota	Utah	
		Ohio	Washington	
		Pennsylvania		
		Tennessee		
		Washington		
		Wisconsin		
Weak local parties	Georgia	Alabama	Arizona	Idaho
	Kentucky	Colorado	Arkansas	Kentucky
	Nebraska	Florida	Colorado	Louisiana
	South Dakota	Georgia	Iowa	Massachusetts
	Virginia	Kansas	Kansas	Utah
	Wisconsin	Mississippi	Louisiana	Vermont
		Missouri	Massachusetts	
		Montana	Mississippi	
		Nebraska	Missouri	
		New Hampshire	Montana	
		Oklahoma	Nevada	
		Oregon	Oregon	
		South Carolina	South Carolina	
		South Dakota	Texas	
		Texas	Vermont	
		Virginia	West Virginia	
			Wyoming	

Source: Cornelius P. Cotter, James L. Gibson, John F. Bibby, and Robert J. Huckshorn, *Party Organizations in American Politics* (New York: Praeger, 1984), 28, 52.

Note: These state parties could not be classified because of insufficient data: Democrats in Alabama, Hawaii, New Jersey, New Mexico, and Oklahoma; and Republicans in Alaska, Arkansas, Delaware, and Maryland.

climate is unsupportive and regulation of parties is heavy, the state parties (57 percent) tend to be organizationally weak.

Financing the Parties

Research is only beginning to be conducted on state political campaign spending that would allow firm generalizations about the sources of political money and its effectiveness. The state parties have been increasingly active in fund raising and in investment decisions. Party campaign spending runs a poor third to individual contributions and PAC expenditures. Nevertheless, it is not insignificant. State parties have shown "they were able to maximize their financial role in the campaign process through skillful management of party resources."[24]

A number of states provide for financing parties and candidates through some system of public funding. Eleven states developed a tax-checkoff system. Taxpayers indicate on their income tax return whether or not they want a contribution of state funds to go to the state Democratic or Republican party (in Iowa, a taxpayer could choose "both," in which case half of the designated dollar goes to each party), to candidates, or both. Eight states have an "add-on" system of public funding. Here, the taxpayer must accept an additional tax liability to make a contribution to a party or candidate.

State public funding systems vary widely. In the nineteen states operating with public funding, ten channel the funds to the state political parties:[25] Alabama, California, Idaho, Iowa, Kentucky, Maine, North Carolina, Rhode Island, Utah, and Virginia. Public funding has had only a small effect upon campaign efforts by the state parties, partly because the amounts have been modest and partly because the parties have tended to use the funds for operational or organizational maintenance purposes. Moreover, taxpayer participation is declining. The future of public funding practices may be in doubt. Nevertheless, public funding is one technique for supporting and strengthening the state parties, and in some states this effect has been considerable.

A recent striking development in state political financing has been the growth of campaign fund raising through the legislative parties. This phenomenon was pioneered by California assembly Speaker Jesse Unruh in the early 1960s. Today, in at least half the states, the legislative party leaders raise campaign warchests and distribute funds to legislative candidates.[26] In Ohio, where House Speaker Vernal G. Riffe, Jr., replenishes his large campaign coffer at his annual birthday party, the Speaker's legislative campaign committee had about $2.7 million at its disposal to support Democratic candidates in the 1990 election. Ohio senate president Stanley Aronoff raises Republican campaign money in a similar fashion.[27] To a considerable extent, this development embraces the channeling (or "laundering," to some) of PAC money. Major state interest groups find contributing to legislative parties more permissible or more effective than making direct donations to candidates.

The national parties used to levy monetary assessments against the state parties as a way of raising money. Times have changed. By the 1990s, political money raising had been centralized, with massive amounts of national party money transferred to the state parties. Republicans led the way in national party fund raising and in investment of national party funds in the state parties. For example, in 1983-1984, a large majority of Republican state party chairs reported they had gotten financial help from the national Republican party. Seventy percent said the state party or state candidates had received national party financial aid; three-fourths reported getting fund-raising assistance from the national party. Democratic state chairs reported national party financial assistance was given to the state party as well, but on a much smaller scale. Only 7 percent reported national party financial aid to the state party, although 13 percent said national funds had gone to state candidates and 20 percent reported fund-raising assistance from the national party.[28]

Another source of national party funding for campaign efforts in the states is provided by the Federal Election Campaign Act of 1971. This legislation provided for coordinated expenditures and the so-called agency agreements, which permit the national parties to fund congressional and senatorial campaigns on behalf of the state parties. Coordinated expenditures are neither counted as contributions to candidates nor considered expenditures by the candidates. They are party expenditures coordinated with a candidate's campaign and spent on behalf of the candidate. Each of the national parties in 1988 transferred between $30 million and $50 million to state and local party organizations.[29]

Although the organizational strength of the state parties can be enhanced by the financial support of the national parties, exactly how much this support has helped the state parties is not known. Because the national Republican party so far has taken advantage of strategies for intergovernmental party finance, much more than the Democrats have, the effects on the state parties have been felt mainly by the Republicans.[30]

The 1979 amendments to the Federal Election Campaign Act incorporated putative efforts to assist the state parties, or at least stem the tide of party financial nationalization. These amendments allowed the state parties to buy campaign material (for example, buttons and bumper stickers) and conduct voter registration drives unfettered by limits on campaign expenditure for national offices. The effects have been highly debatable; some think they have helped the state parties, others think the state parties have been weakened. General agreement exists, however, that the reporting and accounting provisions of the federal law are so complex that they have further encouraged the state parties to stay away from national candidates and concentrate on races for governor and state legislature.[31]

What the Parties Do

An array of state parties could be imagined that have an organizational structure but perform no significant political role or engage in no relevant activities. They would be shadows of their former selves, the functions they once fulfilled forgotten. Some come close to speaking of the parties in this fashion now, as if they had been superannuated by candidate-centered campaigning, the powerful media, and manipulative political consultants. But party organizations at the grass roots do perform politically relevant activities, and party activists are engaged in state and local party politics.

Campaign Activities

Scholars who gather empirical evidence about state and local party efforts find, sometimes surprisingly, that a good deal of party activity goes on. Conventional wisdom directs that they should have discovered little party effort. A study about state parties in 1980 showed party activists impressively engaged in party organizational maintenance activities, despite the personalized, nonbureaucratic structure of the local parties, as well as substantial campaign activity on the part of state and local parties.[32]

Perhaps the most striking was the level of campaign activity performed by the state parties as revealed by 1984 data on county party leaders gathered by political scientists James L. Gibson, John P. Frendries, and Laura L. Vertz.[33] Comparing the 1980 data with the 1984 data, significant increases took place in party activity in the states. In 1984, well over 90 percent of county parties had a complete set of officers, with most having precinct chairs filled; more than 80 percent of both Democratic and Republican county chairs reported spending six hours or more a week engaged in party business; two-thirds indicated that their county committee met twice a month or more during the election season; and about 70 percent maintained a campaign headquarters. Meanwhile, almost no county chairs received a salary, and only a minority had a staff or a regular annual budget. For a sampling of local party activities reported by party leaders in 1984, see Table 9-4.

In the aggregate, the two parties differ little in conducting local party activity, but the data indicate variations among states. A significant increase took place in the level of activity among southern Democratic parties, presumably to catch up with the Republicans. Local parties were

Table 9-4 Local Party Activities

Local party activity	Percentage of county party leaders engaged in local party activity	
	Democrats	Republicans
Arranged fund raisers	84	85
Bought radio or television time	36	35
Canvassed door-to-door	67	68
Conducted public opinion polls	23	25
Conducted registration drives	78	78
Contributed money to candidates	69	77
Distributed campaign literature	89	91
Involved in recruiting candidates for Congress	61	66
Involved in recruiting candidates for state legislature	76	81
Organized telephone campaigns	78	78
Sent mailings to voters	66	75
Worked with congressional candidates on campaign planning and strategy	87	84
Worked with state legislative candidates on campaign strategy	93	92

Source: James L. Gibson, John P. Frendreis, and Laura L. Vertz, "Party Dynamics in the 1980s: Change in County Party Organizational Strength, 1980-1984," American Journal of Political Science 33 (1989): 73-74.

more intensively and pervasively engaged in recruiting candidates, planning campaigns, and mounting traditional campaign efforts than they were in buying and using mass media or opinion surveys. Although a proportion of local parties were inert and some local party leaders were not actively involved in campaigning, the reported levels of overall local party activity were substantial and impressive. The findings were confirmed in recent studies of party activism conducted in Middlesex County, New Jersey, in Cuyahoga County, Ohio, and in five major cities.[34]

Party Activists

Who are the activists who provide the core of state and local party organizations? Two responses can be given to this question: One has to do with the types of people who become activists; the other with their attitudes.

Invariably, studies show that party activists are drawn from the higher reaches of the socioeconomic scale. They are mostly college graduates and have relatively high incomes. They are about equally divided by gender. Racial and ethnic minorities in general are poorly represented, but their representation is better in Democratic parties and in states with large minority populations.[35] The two parties do not differ significantly in the socioeconomic status of their party activists; the two parties recruit their local party activists from about the same social classes.

Party activists tend to be ideologically more committed than the average citizen and much more strongly identified with their party.[36] The ideological difference between Republican and Democratic party activists is especially striking. According to studies of grass-roots party leaders, Republicans are markedly conservative while Democrats are decidedly liberal. For instance, a study of more than seventeen thousand state convention delegates in eleven states in 1980 showed "the consistent liberalism of the Democrats and the consistent conservatism of the Republicans," irrespective of the state in which the activists resided.[37] Even in Indiana, a state conventionally reputed to have notoriously job- or patronage-oriented politics, a study of party activists showed sharp ideological differences between Republicans and Democrats.[38] Moreover, in Indiana and elsewhere, Republican activists appear as ideologically homogeneous, while Democratic activists often exhibit an ideological mix.[39] The same sharp ideological differences are to be found among state party activists who become national convention delegates.[40]

Evidence abounds that these grass-roots party activists are deeply involved in mobilizing voters. The activists of the two parties think of themselves as rival teams seeking control of political offices. Competitive activists appear, on the whole, to be thriving in many states—and in such contrasting contexts as traditionally partisan Michigan or reputedly organizationally weak California.[41]

Do State Parties Matter?

The case for the persistence of the state parties is weakened if, even with local party organizations active in campaign politics, their party efforts make no difference.

Impact on Nominations

State parties have an effect on the nomination of candidates, despite the advent of the direct primary. Informally, party leaders may channel competition for primary nominations, in essence slate-making within the context of the direct primary system.[42] In a number of states, the parties officially may endorse candidates in primaries. When endorsed by state party conventions, candidates reap advantages in garnering the support of activists and developing an effective organization.

In states where the parties endorse candidates, the primary election may become a formality. A study of 1982 gubernatorial nominations showed that "when endorsements are made, there are fewer contested gubernatorial nominations and, if there is a contest, the endorsee wins about three-fourths of the time." [43] Even if preprimary endorsement is not officially sanctioned, state parties may endorse candidates, such as in Minnesota.[44]

Effect on Elections

The effectiveness of the state parties is dependent upon the outcome of elections. "The relationship between electoral success and party organizational strength is," as John F. Bibby stated, "exceedingly complex." [45] In states where one party historically has enjoyed electoral dominance, little incentive exists for either party to organize. But where competition is present, where opportunities for electoral successes are available, organizational efforts by the state parties can bear handsome rewards, as the recent experience of the southern Republican parties attests.

The study of the impact of the state parties on electoral outcomes supports two assertions. First, state-level party organizational strength substantially affects state elections for governor and legislator but has a much smaller impact on presidential and congressional contests.[46] Presidential and congressional races usually follow national party campaigns. Second, when party organizations gain strength, their electoral clout is greater. Cornelius Cotter, James Gibson, John F. Bibby, and Robert J. Huckshorn established in their study that the state-level organizations had a significant effect on the outcomes of gubernatorial races in the 1975-1980 period.[47] Gibson, Frendries, and Vertz demonstrated in their investigation of county party organizational changes and election outcomes from 1980 to 1984 that, although party strength was not great, it was large enough to affect election results.[48]

Engendering Competitive Politics

State parties also contribute to competitive politics by stimulating political participation.[49] On the whole, patterns of party competition for state offices—for governor and state legislature—have been stable in the post-World War II era. However, variations in partisan competitiveness across the states have been substantial. States differ according to their socioeconomic circumstances. In states with socioeconomic diversity, partisan competitiveness is keen. Competitiveness also varies because of urbanization and population size. The largest metropolitan states have tended toward relatively uncompetitive politics. Cross-state differences in competitiveness also reflect the traditional political differences between North and South.[50]

One analysis of the variables affecting state party competition from 1970 to 1980 concluded:

> No one doubts for a moment that partisan competition has a profound grounding in socio-economic complexity, in the sheer size of political units such that the probability of opposing coalitions is enhanced, and in the politico-cultural differences between regions. What is equally important and often overlooked . . . is that active effort by organized political parties contributes extensively to the generation of competitive politics.[51]

State politics and elections can become more competitive by enhancing the organizational strength of the state political parties.

Conclusion

Some American state parties are strong and vigorous; some are sluggish; and some others, moribund. But on balance, the state parties appear remarkably vibrant. Party strength has waned in the electorate—fewer Americans think of themselves as "strong Democrats" or "strong Republicans" than in the 1950s, and more say they are political "independents." How can it be that the state party organizations—and the national parties—are stronger when, at the same time, party identification among voters is weaker? The answer may lie in the incentives that the less committed electoral marketplace presents to those who seek to capture political offices.

If the voters' response to candidacies is preordained, as in the classic "safe seats" or in the old "solid South," parties have little incentive to organize; the candidates of the dominant party will win without organization, and the candidates of the minority party cannot win through organization. But with greater uncertainty in the electoral response, parties have an incentive to organize and behave competitively. Ironically, diminution of party strength may have a fairly powerful role to play in stimulating parties to get organized, recruit competitive candidates, find adequate financial resources, mobilize voters, and compete vigorously for the control of offices.

The state parties are in need of much encouragement and improvement. Their organizational strength is still unevenly distributed. Further organizational development should be encouraged. Laws conducive to party effectiveness should be passed in the states. The state parties should adapt, where they have not already done so, to the new campaign technologies. All state party chairs should take as a model the report of Indiana Republican party chairman Gordon Durnil:

> We decided to teach ourselves the new campaign technology. The Republican organization developed a capacity for direct mail and

handling demographics and other aspects of modern campaigning. As a result, politics in Indiana has remained party-oriented.[52]

Public funding of electoral politics should be reinvigorated and renewed. State public funding laws should provide public funds to the parties, instead of to the candidates. State and federal laws should encourage party channeling of private money and stimulate PACs to contribute to the parties. Candidate-centered politics need not be diminished; partisan campaigning can and should be candidate-oriented. Candidate- and party-centered politics are not inimical to one another; candidate-centered politics also should be party-centered. State parties are becoming more, not less, capable of supporting effective candidacies. Running for office in the states is a more professional endeavor than it used to be. State parties should be encouraged and expected to do a professional job in electoral politics.

If the state parties were to become professionalized and competitive campaigning and governing organizations, then E. E. Schattschneider's dream of "party reconstruction," at least in part, would come true.[53] Certainly the state parties can be stronger organizationally.

Conditions for the development of party organizational strength vary. In the twentieth century, the state parties in general never have been particularly strong. They are not, and never have been, close to the model for responsible party government found in the socialist parties of western Europe. The skeletal organizations that constitute most state parties, nevertheless, are important to the American political process.

To the foreign eye, the United States may seem to be engaged in nonparty politics, because the parties look so weak. But the state parties play an important role. Their nonbureaucratic organization belies their effectiveness. They engage in a remarkable array of electoral activities and have an independent and potentially decisive impact on political outcomes. Furthermore, a good chance exists that they can become considerably stronger. In this sense, American state parties persist.

Notes

1. Leon D. Epstein, *Political Parties in Western Democracies* (New Brunswick, N.J.: Transaction Books, 1980), 9. See also Anthony Downs, *An Economic Theory of Democracy* (New York: Harper and Row, 1957), 25; and Joseph A. Schlesinger, *Political Parties and the Winning of Office* (Ann Arbor: University of Michigan Press, 1991), 5-10.
2. Epstein, *Political Parties in Western Democracies*, 122-129.
3. Samuel J. Eldersveld, *Political Parties in America* (New York: Basic Books, 1982), 99.

4. Cornelius P. Cotter, James L. Gibson, John F. Bibby, and Robert J. Huckshorn, *Party Organizations in American Politics* (New York: Praeger, 1984), 171-184.
5. Leon D. Epstein, *Political Parties in the American Mold* (Madison: University of Wisconsin Press, 1986), 144.
6. James Q. Wilson, *Political Organizations* (New York: Basic Books, 1973), 95-96.
7. Downs, *An Economic Theory of Democracy*, 25.
8. Joseph A. Schlesinger, "On the Theory of Party Organization," *Journal of Politics* 46 (1984): 369-400; and Joseph A. Schlesinger, "The New American Political Party," *American Political Science Review* 79 (1985): 1152-1169.
9. Wilson, *Political Organizations*, 30.
10. Mildred A. Schwartz, *The Party Network: The Robust Organization of Illinois Republicans* (Madison: University of Wisconsin Press, 1990), 283-284.
11. E. E. Schattschneider, *Party Government* (New York: Rinehart and Co., 1942); James MacGregor Burns, *The Deadlock of Democracy* (Englewood Cliffs, N.J.: Prentice-Hall, 1963); and Austin Ranney, *Curing the Mischiefs of Faction: Party Reform in America* (Berkeley: University of California Press, 1975).
12. William Crotty, *Party Reform* (New York: Longman, 1983); and Gary D. Wekkin, "Political Parties and Intergovernmental Relations in 1984: The Consequences of Party Renewal for Territorial Constituencies," *Publius: The Journal of Federalism* 15 (1985): 19-37.
13. Schlesinger, "On the Theory of Party Organization," 369-400.
14. Epstein, *Political Parties in the American Mold*, 155-199.
15. Ohio Revised Code, 3517.01.
16. Advisory Commission on Intergovernmental Relations, *The Transformation in American Politics: Implications for Federalism* (Washington, D.C.: Advisory Commission on Intergovernmental Relations, 1986), 128.
17. Ibid.; Cotter, Gibson, Bibby, and Huckshorn, *Party Organizations in American Politics*; and Malcolm E. Jewell, *Parties and Primaries: Nominating State Governors* (New York: Praeger, 1984).
18. Timothy Conlan, Ann Martino, and Robert Dilger, "State Parties in the 1980s: Adaptation, Resurgence and Continuing Constraints," *Intergovernmental Perspectives* 10 (1984): 6-13.
19. Cotter, Gibson, Bibby, and Huckshorn, *Party Organizations in American Politics*.
20. Charles G. Bell, "Is Party Allegiance Growing in California?" *Comparative State Politics Newsletter* 5 (1984): 5-7; and Richard Zeiger, "Future Uncertain for State's Democrats," *California Journal* 18 (1987): 120-123.
21. Alexander P. Lamis, *The Two-Party South* (New York: Oxford University Press, 1984); and John G. Francis, "The Political Landscape of the Mountain West," in *The Politics of Realignment: Party Change in the Mountain West*, ed. Peter F. Galderisi, Michael S. Lyons, Randy T. Simmons, and John G. Francis (Boulder, Colo.: Westview Press, 1987), 19-32.
22. Lewis Bowman, William E. Hubary, and Anne E. Kelley, "Party Organization and Behavior in Florida: Assessing Grassroots Organizational Strength" (Paper delivered at the annual meeting of the American Political Science

Association, Chicago, September 3-6, 1987); and Robert P. Steed, Laurence W. Moreland, and Tod A. Baker, "The Nature of Contemporary Party Organization in South Carolina" (Paper delivered at the annual meeting of the American Political Science Association, Chicago, September 3-6, 1987).

23. Stella Z. Theodoulou, *The Louisiana Republican Party, 1948-1984: The Building of a State Political Party* (New Orleans: Tulane University Studies in Political Science, 1985).

24. Ruth S. Jones, "Financing State Elections," in *Money and Politics in the United States*, ed. Michael J. Malbin (Chatham, N.J.: Chatham House Publishers, 1984), 193.

25. Herbert E. Alexander and Mike Eberts, *Public Financing of State Elections* (Los Angeles: Citizens' Research Foundation, 1986).

26. Malcolm E. Jewell, "A Survey of Campaign Fund Raising by Legislative Parties," *Comparative State Politics Newsletter* 7 (1986): 9-13.

27. David C. Saffell, "Happy Birthday, Speaker Riffe," *Comparative State Politics Newsletter* 12 (1991): 16-18. For Illinois, see Richard R. Johnson, "Partisan Legislative Campaign Committees: New Power, New Problems," *Illinois Issues* 13 (1987): 16-18.

28. Advisory Commission on Intergovernmental Relations, *The Transformation in American Politics*, 120.

29. John F. Bibby, Cornelius P. Cotter, James L. Gibson, and Robert J. Huckshorn, "Parties in State Politics," in *Politics in the American States*, 5th ed., ed. Virginia Gray, Herbert Jacob, and Robert B. Albritton (Glenview, Ill.: Scott, Foresman, 1990), 110-111.

30. Gary C. Jacobson, "The Republican Advantage in Campaign Finance," in *The New Direction in American Politics*, ed. John E. Chubb and Paul E. Peterson (Washington, D.C.: Brookings Institution, 1985), 154-160.

31. Advisory Commission on Intergovernmental Relations, *The Transformation in American Politics*, 271-278.

32. Cotter, Gibson, Bibby, and Huckshorn, *Party Organizations in American Politics*, 20-26, 43-49.

33. James L. Gibson, John P. Frendreis, and Laura L. Vertz, "Party Dynamics in the 1980s: Change in County Party Organizational Strength, 1980-1984," *American Journal of Political Science* 33 (1989): 67-90.

34. Kay Lawson, Gerald Pomper, and Maureen Moakley, "Local Party Activists and Electoral Linkage: Middlesex County, N.J.," *American Politics Quarterly* 14 (1986): 345-375; Ronald J. Busch, "Ambition and the Local Party Organization" (Paper delivered at the annual meeting of the Ohio Association of Economists and Political Scientists, Columbus, Ohio, May 2, 1987); and William Crotty, *Political Parties in Local Areas* (Knoxville: University of Tennessee Press, 1986).

35. Ronald B. Rapoport, Alan I. Abramowitz, and John McGlennon, *The Life of the Parties: Activists in Presidential Politics* (Lexington: University Press of Kentucky, 1986), 44-58.

36. Malcolm E. Jewell and David M. Olson, *Political Parties and Elections in American States*, 3d ed. (Chicago: Dorsey Press, 1988), 56-62.

37. Rapoport, Abramowitz, and McGlennon, *The Life of the Parties*, 50. For results from the 1984 state convention delegates in twelve states, see Barbara

Burrell and James Carlson, "Issue Coalitions and Cleavages among Party Activists" (Paper delivered at the annual meeting of the Midwest Political Science Association, Chicago, April 9-11, 1987).

38. Robert X. Browning and William R. Schaffer, "Leaders and Followers in a Strong Party State," *American Politics Quarterly* 15 (1987): 87-106.

39. Alan Ware, *The Logic of Party Democracy* (New York: St. Martin's Press, 1979), 130-152.

40. Warren E. Miller and M. Kent Jennings, *Parties in Transition: A Longitudinal Study of Party Elites and Party Supporters* (New York: Russell Sage Foundation, 1986), 161-188.

41. Samuel J. Eldersveld, "The Party Activist in Detroit and Los Angeles: A Longitudinal View, 1956-1980," in *Political Parties in Local Areas*, ed. William Crotty (Knoxville: University of Tennessee Press, 1986), 89-119.

42. Paul M. Green, "The Democrats' Biennial Ritual: Slatemaking," *Illinois Issues* 12 (1986): 12-14, 39.

43. Jewell, *Parties and Primaries*, 273.

44. Joseph A. Kunkel III, "Party Endorsement and Incumbency in Minnesota Legislative Nominations," *Legislative Studies Quarterly* 13 (1988): 211-213; and David Lebedoff, *The 21st Ballot: A Political Party Struggle in Minnesota* (Minneapolis: University of Minnesota Press, 1969).

45. John F. Bibby, *Politics, Parties, and Elections in America* (Chicago: Nelson-Hall, 1987), 107.

46. James L. Gibson, "The Role of Party Organizations in the Mountain West: 1960-1980," in *The Politics of Realignment: Party Change in the Mountain West*, ed. Peter F. Galderisi, Michael S. Lyons, Randy T. Simmons, and John G. Francis (Boulder, Colo.: Westview Press, 1987), 206-213.

47. Cotter, Gibson, Bibby, and Huckshorn, *Party Organizations in American Politics*, 100-103.

48. John P. Frendreis, James L. Gibson, and Laura L. Vertz, "The Electoral Relevance of Local Party Organizations," *American Political Science Review* 84 (1990): 225-235.

49. Timothy Bledsoe and Susan Welch, "Patterns of Political Party Activity among U.S. Cities," *Urban Affairs Quarterly* 23 (1987): 249-269.

50. Samuel C. Patterson and Gregory A. Caldeira, "The Etiology of Partisan Competition," *American Political Science Review* 78 (1984): 691-707; and Frank B. Feigert, "Postwar Changes in State Party Competition," *Publius: The Journal of Federalism* 15 (1985): 99-112.

51. Patterson and Caldeira, "The Etiology of Partisan Competition," 703-704. See also James D. King, "Interparty Competition in the American States: An Examination of Index Components," *Western Political Quarterly* 42 (1989): 83-92.

52. *Brookings Review* 5 (1987): 24.

53. E. E. Schattschneider, *The Struggle for Party Government* (College Park: University of Maryland Program in American Civilization, 1948), 27-43.

10 ▬▬▬

The New Storm over the States

Carl E. Van Horn

In the influential book *Storm over the States*, Terry Sanford, former governor of North Carolina and later a U.S. senator, described profound changes that swept state governments in the 1960s as they adjusted to federal statutes and Supreme Court rulings that forced them to modernize.[1] New storms now are brewing, caused by soaring state government activism in the 1980s, the crash of the American economy in the early 1990s, and the withdrawal of the federal government from domestic policy leadership. The storms are battering the foundation of state political institutions and are threatening not only incumbent officeholders but also the representative functions of governors and state legislatures.

Political Reform

The origins of greater state activism were changes in representation, governmental organization, and professionalization spawned in the late 1960s. The states' activism was tested when federal officials began cutting aid to states and local governments in the late 1970s. Interest groups shifted their focus from Washington, D.C., to the state capitals, repeating a phenomenon that has occurred before in American history.

Rewriting state constitutions, restructuring political institutions, and assembling professional expertise enabled state governments to design and implement far-reaching public policies.[2] Furthermore, the policy-making circles—in legislatures, courts, bureaucracies, and governors' mansions— no longer exclusively were filled with the upper-middle class, white males that dominated government for most of American political history.

Landmark reapportionment decisions and changes in social attitudes transformed state governments from unrepresentative, homogeneous institutions to more representative bodies.[3] The U.S. Supreme Court in *Baker v. Carr* and *Reynolds v. Sims* removed barriers to direct representation of voters and reapportioned legislatures according to the principle of "one person, one vote." The Voting Rights Act of 1965 eliminated obstacles to full political participation by black Americans. Black registration in the deep South grew by more than 1 million between 1964 and 1972, an increase from 29 percent to 57 percent of eligible voters.[4]

State legislatures and administrative agencies today have greater numbers of women and minorities than twenty years ago but still far fewer than men or Caucasians. Women holding legislative office, for example, increased from 4 percent in 1969 to 17 percent in the early 1990s.[5] In Colorado, Maine, New Hampshire, Vermont, and Washington, women hold more than 25 percent of the seats in the legislature. Women's participation in state government positions also has risen at the appointive policy-making levels. Women have been less successful in obtaining statewide elected office. In 1992, only two women were serving as governors; only eleven women have been elected governor in the nation's history.[6]

Minority participation in elected and appointed policy-making positions in state government also has grown, but very slowly. Blacks, which account for 12 percent of the U.S. population, held one governorship—L. Douglas Wilder of Virginia—and 5 percent of the state legislative positions in 1992. In 1970, none of the governors was black and less than 2 percent of legislators were black.[7] Hispanics increased their share of elected positions in several states where they make up a significant part of the population—Arizona, California, Colorado, and New Mexico. Florida and New Mexico have elected governors of Hispanic origin.

Representatives of these newly empowered groups demanded greater government intervention to ameliorate social and economic problems in their communities. Elected officials' policy priorities reflect their life experiences and professional training. More teachers and working women in elected and appointed positions encouraged greater attention to family leave programs, child care, and women's and children's health care.[8]

Business, labor, local governments, school boards, and other traditionally powerful groups still wield the most influence in state politics, but environmentalists, consumer advocates, and senior citizens have become more effective. Citizen participation in state policy making has exploded since the early 1970s. State agencies now routinely allow citizens to voice concerns through public boards and commissions, ombudsmen, public advocates, and public hearings. Newly active groups raise money and contribute to candidates, advertise in the mass media, and exert considerable influence over governors and legislatures.[9]

The initiative process has been employed with increasing frequency by political leaders, interest groups, and citizens groups. Ballot initiatives doubled between 1976 and 1990. Sometimes the initiative is used as a method of circumventing the legislative process. In other cases, the mere threat of mounting such a campaign is used to spur the legislature to act.

In 1990, 236 ballot questions appeared in forty-three states—the largest number since 1914. Sixty-seven proposals were launched by citizens groups. In recent years, voters weighed important and controversial proposals, including the regulation of pornography, acid rain, abortions, drug use, and the length of time legislators may remain in office.[10] Some state officials have concluded that joining initiative battles is better than fighting them. For example, California governor Pete Wilson lead a drive in 1992 to curb welfare programs via a ballot initiative.

Political institutions also have expanded their staffs to achieve their policy agendas and to compete with rival institutions in the struggle for power. Governors expanded staffs overseeing the bureaucracy, monitoring developments in Washington, D.C., and shepherding the flock of legislative proposals in the statehouse. Legislatures bolstered staffs to keep a watchful eye on the executive branch and to provide more effective service to the folks in their districts.

The cumulative impact of state governments acquiring more expertise and the renewed focus on state government has been dramatic. State officials now are able to fulfill their ambition and to meet the expectations of others in carrying out their responsibilities in the federal system. States now plan and execute complex policy initiatives: water supply and quality improvement programs, pollution prevention programs, welfare reform, science and technology development, and energy conservation initiatives.[11]

State courts matched the activism of legislators and governors. The courts hired more judges, law clerks, and administrative officers to meet the rising demands for court review of policy and administrative cases. They took aggressive action on several public policy fronts, including expanding the rights of women, minorities, and criminal defendants. In doing so, state judges often relied upon state constitutions to establish rights that the U.S. Supreme Court has not found in the U.S. Constitution. State courts also expanded the rights of individuals to recover for personal injuries and imposed strict liability rules for faulty products. Once regarded as the obstacles to civil liberties, many state courts now are the champions of change.

From Entrepreneurship to Crisis

During the 1980s, state governments brimmed with an entrepreneurial spirit. No longer passive partners in the federal system, states eagerly became a driving force in American politics. They levied and spent vast sums of money, hired hundreds of thousands of new employees, managed tough public problems, sought out new policy frontiers to conquer. The states aggressively set policy agendas for the nation and fashioned innovative solutions for some of the most important policy problems.

State governments were imperialistic in the 1980s. Governors and legislators clamored for new ideas and expanded government spending and regulation. State officials displayed no sustained interest in controlling government's spiraling costs. State leaders were more concerned with improving public education, reforming welfare, protecting the environment, and rebuilding roads, bridges, and sewers.

The rosy fiscal picture became clouded when the U.S. economy lapsed into a long and deep recession in early 1990s. Because the federal government was unable to prime the state government pump with new dollars, the burden of the recession fell squarely on the states. Following the path taken in the 1982 recession, states responded by raising $16 billion in additional taxes and by cutting $10 billion in state programs. States scaled back their plans for greater government intervention. Unlike the federal government, which can defy fiscal gravity by borrowing money, state budgets are tethered to the reality of declining revenues. States cannot spend what they do not collect.

The need to fund basic services, such as education, prisons, health care, and transportation, sent state officials down a pragmatic path and blurred partisan differences. The policy positions that divided Republicans and Democrats are far fewer today than they were twenty-five years ago, when Democrats advocated activist government policies and Republicans called for less government.

Many Republicans elected to statewide office in the 1980s and 1990s were likely to favor strong government intervention, while Republican presidents Ronald Reagan and George Bush generally eschewed such policies. Former Republican governors Thomas H. Kean of New Jersey, James R. Thompson of Illinois, and Lamar Alexander of Tennessee reflected pragmatic, pro-government positions long advocated by Democrats.[12]

State leaders seldom hold on to rigid ideological positions as they go about the business of governing. This pragmatic orientation helps explain why the conservative policies of the Reagan administration never took hold in state capitals. Even when Reagan was governor of California, he often followed a middle-of-the-road course instead of adhering to the conservative principles that later defined his presidency.

When state officials deal with AIDS, homelessness, environmental protection, and economic growth, they typically opt for solutions that involve government regulation and spending. For example, Democratic and Republican governors and legislatures developed similar strategies for reforming welfare programs for the poor. Federal welfare reform legislation incorporating principles advocated by a bipartisan group of governors eventually was adopted after considerable wrangling between Democrats and Republicans in Congress.[13]

State government programs are paid for by taxpayers. State officials have not escaped the public's ambivalence about fiscal policy. Most voters want lower taxes and higher spending. State officials constantly are buffeted by the need to reconcile competing priorities. When revenues declined, as they have in the 1990s, the pressures on state officials grew more intense.

In the early 1980s, tax-limitation initiatives, most notably California's Proposition 13, were adopted by several states. The reigning government buzzwords were zero-based budgeting, executive reorganization, and cutback management. But the "limited government" movement, the love affair with curbing government growth, turned out to be a brief flirtation.

State government spending soared at rates faster than inflation through the 1980s. Ironically, this spurt of government growth was rooted in the economic crisis of 1982. Faced with the prospects of greater social welfare spending and reduced tax collections, twenty-eight states increased their income taxes, and thirty increased sales taxes.[14] Even without additional tax increases, these actions eventually would have yielded a fiscal bonanza. But nineteen states raised either their income or sales taxes again in 1984 and 1985. In addition, the 1986 federal tax reform law brought millions of additional dollars rolling into state treasuries.

The 1980s-style budgets could not be balanced with the revenues collected during the depressed economy of the 1990s. Facing a rising tide of red ink, more than thirty-five states turned to tax increases and program cuts to bring their budgets into balance. Despite those drastic measures, states had difficulty achieving equilibrium. Within six months of enacting the largest tax increases in decades, more than half the states still were facing budget deficits in their current year budgets.[15]

Partisan differences on state fiscal policy have not disappeared, but they have been muted. Republicans are reluctant to raise taxes, but they do. Although they usually oppose higher personal income or business taxes, they raise them, too. Republicans and Democrats alike have been raising taxes and increasing their budgets.

The sustained economic recovery of the mid-1980s contributed to reduced spending on some government services, such as unemployment insurance and welfare, and increased revenue collections. When the state treasuries bulged, most states spent the windfall instead of giving it back to the taxpayers. Several states established so-called rainy-day funds to cushion the shock of another recession, but typically the increased state revenues were quickly committed to new or expanded programs.[16]

The economic troubles of the 1990s reversed the trends of the 1980s and resulted in more demands for government spending and in less revenues. As the recession deepened, states spent more to meet the swelling demand for social services. Revenues dropped sharply as unemployment rose and as the corporate bottom line changed from profit to loss.

New Jersey policy makers, for example, raised sales and income taxes in 1982 so that the state could balance its budget. The state's budget more than doubled and built up a $1 billion surplus by the mid-1980s. At no point during this period did political leaders propose rolling back any major tax increases. By 1990, however, the surplus vanished and the state cut programs and raised taxes to cope with a $3 billion deficit.

Power Struggles

Reforms fashioned to strengthen the competence of state government simultaneously encouraged governors, legislators, judges, and bureaucrats to boldly assert power. As power fragmented, state politics became more conflict-ridden. Policy makers who wanted to tackle tough problems struggled to find consensus for specific actions. Distrust deepened as governors, judges, legislators, and administrators jealously guarded their prerogatives.

Unfortunately, the positive developments that made state governments more democratic and responsive also caused some troubling problems. Personal conflicts often escalated into battles for institutional control and the agenda of government. Fragmented policy making sometimes blurs clear lines of responsibility and thus decreases institutional accountability.

The reforms that fostered modern political institutions carved up power into bits and pieces and undermined the ability of any one institution or political leader to dominate state politics. Individualism was encouraged at the expense of institutional responsibility. With more at stake in the governance of states, everyone has a greater incentive to seek power and control.

Prevailing attitudes about the responsibilities of legislators also changed during the 1980s. Modern legislators are much more likely to pursue their own agendas instead of those dictated by party leaders. Legislators feel they must aggressively champion their districts' interests even if they come in conflict with county party organizations, governors, and legislative leaders.[17] With their antennae tuned to the voters back home and campaign contributors, legislators often feel free to ignore appeals for party discipline.

Fragmented, competitive politics promotes the convergence of policy agendas. Legislators, governors, and agency executives are eager to advance new policies and distribute benefits to constituents. This dynamic of competing power centers adds to the existing political and economic pressures that engender more spending and higher taxes.

The dispersion of power within political institutions has resulted in fierce battles for the control of policy agendas and outcomes. More intense competition is apparent in all phases of state political life from elections to state budget decisions. More legislators, judges, bureaucrats, and interest groups have sufficient clout to engage in the struggle, but few have enough power to rule.

The desire to hold on to power strongly shapes the political process within institutions, especially in legislatures where electoral considerations are paramount. The quest for power is hardly a new phenomenon, but career-oriented politicians are more intent on winning because they are more intent on remaining in office for a long time. "Permanent" legislators must constantly deliver benefits, claim credit for accomplishments, and attack opponents in the executive branch or elsewhere.[18] They undertake new legislative initiatives, examine administrative rules and regulations, scrutinize the state budget, and investigate government agencies. Clearly, these strategies serve their intended purpose; incumbents rarely lose.[19]

Incumbents and challengers also have stepped up the intensity of campaigns. Costs are rising because people are willing and able to spend huge sums of money to gain elective office. The staples of modern campaigns—media consultants, pollsters, and television advertising—are expensive. Statewide candidates must collect substantial sums of money or have a large personal fortune. Even legislative candidates now are required to assemble substantial resources, except in the smaller states.

A candidate that cannot afford to participate in high-cost elections is less likely to be heard. Those who form political action committees and contribute money or political support or both get special attention from the candidate and from officeholders who want to keep their jobs. Educators, dentists, senior citizens, labor leaders, builders, and others are effective advocates for their interests because they supply the campaign funds and the reliable voters that keep incumbent politicians around to serve them another day.

State politics is locked in a spiraling institutional "arms race." Governors, legislators, bureaucrats, judges, and interest groups are employing new techniques and strategies to achieve their goals. Governors assert greater control over the bureaucracy. Legislatures step up efforts to oversee executive government agencies. Interest groups bypass representative institutions and pursue goals through the initiative process. State courts adjudicate disputes between legislators and governors and make policy independently.

Nothing is inherently wrong with conflict. Representative government and deliberation are well served by sharp clashes of strongly held views. Few observers of American politics are nostalgic for a return to an era when a handful of party bosses and top ranking elected officials called the shots. But, unfortunately, many political conflicts result from ambiguous authority and personal political ambition instead of from disputes over competing policy visions. Institutional conflicts have sidetracked the policy process into a round robin policy game as the court, legislature, and governor fight with one another for leadership.

The more strident politics of the 1990s has soured many incumbent officeholders and led to a rash of early retirements. Consider the remarks of Democratic governor Bruce Sundlun of Rhode Island:

> It's not fun to be governor. You can't have fun shutting the state down, abolishing positions, laying off personnel, and balancing the budget by cutting expenditures. Nobody likes any of these those things.[20]

Divided party control of the legislature and governorship exacerbates institutional conflict. Voters in most states do not seem to be bothered, however. A remarkable increase in split-ticket voting has taken place in the last thirty years. Split control of state legislatures has increased from four states in 1961 to fifteen states in 1990. In half the states in 1990 where one party dominated the entire legislature, the governor was from the other party.

As battles for power intensify, others are drawn into the fray. When legislators and governors cannot reach clear decisions, they often delegate hard choices to the bureaucracy or create new administrative entities. This policy-making-by-other means has caused a proliferation of commissions and "independent" authorities created through legislative and gubernatorial appointments. State courts, as a result, frequently are forced to mediate between the other branches of government. For example, courts have ruled recently on the authority of governors to exercise their line-item veto and extent of gubernatorial appointment and removal powers.

By entering into disputes between representative institutions, the courts allocate political power, shed the role of referee, and become policy makers.[21] For example, the state courts have handed down dozens of liberal decisions in civil rights cases and other fields. But this activism has come with a price. Many legislators, governors, and voters perceive that courts have thwarted majority preferences. And they have sought to reverse the courts by amending the constitution, passing new laws, or removing judges from office.

State courts have become a battle ground for competing ideologies and policy agendas. Interest groups, legislators, and governors have tried to overturn court decisions. The courts successfully have fended off challenges to their authority in the interpretation of constitutional law. But their power to interpret common law has not been so well defended. For example, state legislatures have narrowed the rights of injured parties, but they have been less successful in curbing the state courts' support for the civil liberties of criminal defendants and the rights of women in sex discrimination cases.

Recently, liberal judges have been challenged in judicial confirmation elections as a way of reining in the courts. Decisions on hot-button issues, such as the death penalty, frequently are central issues in campaigns to oust judges. Spending on judicial elections and the number of direct challenges have risen substantially. Ballot initiatives have overturned liberal court decisions affecting criminal defendant rights. While the defeat of incumbent judges and anti-court initiatives still are rare, the fear of defeat may curb the courts' liberal leanings. In California, the defeat of three Supreme Court justices in the mid-1980s resulted in new appointees who affirmed more death penalty sentences—the outcome sought by voters in statewide referendums.

Bureaucracies also are embroiled in disputes over their activities, purposes, and performance. Legislatures have sharpened their oversight of agency decisions through sunset laws and reviews of administrative rules and regulations. Governors have exerted greater control through executive reorganizations, a reduction in the number of boards and commissions, centralization of budgeting techniques, and executive orders mandating direct accountability to the governor.

Federal bureaucrats and judges also have asserted greater control over the states. For example, federal courts ordered sweeping changes in state actions regarding the mentally ill and state prisoners on the grounds that the U.S. Constitution guarantees due process of law.[22] Governors and the federal government have gotten in battles over interpretations of federal statutes, such as environmental laws.

Governing in Hard Times

State governments are facing unprecedented challenges in the 1990s. The unfriendly environment of economic recession placed governors and legislators in the center of a political storm over the size and purpose of state government. Their survival skills are being tested as they try to meet the conflicting demands of taxpayers, recipients of government services, and interest groups.

The rise of governmental, institutional, and individual entrepreneurship makes meeting these new challenges more difficult. Institutional accountability has been overshadowed by individual accountability. When incumbent governors and legislators deny responsibility for the actions of their own governments or institutions, they are trying to avoid responsibility. When no one is willing to accept responsibility, people are less willing to act responsibly.

Legislators have tried to insulate themselves from executive domination, party leaders, and legislative leaders. Governors increasingly portray themselves as the clarion of the people, not the head of state government. They play to the press and go over the heads of party and legislative leaders. Political parties have been shoved aside by candidate-centered politics, where the incumbent, not the party, is judged. Partisanship is on the rise, but responsible party governance is on the decline. Even judges now are more wary of voter reactions to their judicial decisions.

When political officials act like independent agents in the political system, leadership becomes difficult. Leaders serve at the pleasure of their members. So they wield influence by distributing campaign funds instead of through the art of persuasion. Legislators and governors used to be primarily concerned with governing. Now, they more likely are preoccupied with power. And they are dismantling local party organizations and taking over electoral functions through leadership caucuses and political action committees.

The high price tag of elections means that elected officials are more accountable to those with money and less accountable to the public at large. The deep public resentment of special interest politics helps explain why proposals to limit the terms of officeholders have caught fire in more than a dozen states.

Political fund raising diverts time from governing responsibilities and compromises elected officials. Legislators and governors commonly hold large fund-raising events while important policy issues are under consideration. Elected officials regularly solicit and receive campaign contributions from companies that either have contracts with the state or want to do business in the future. Partisan staff in the executive and legislative branches are routinely deployed to work on election activities.

Warfare between legislatures and governors enhances the power of bureaucracy and courts and thus reduces accountability to the public. More decisions are delegated from democratic institutions to administrative agencies. While these agencies are somewhat more responsive to the public than before, they are less responsive than governors or legislatures. And bureaucracies often obscure clear lines of responsibility and make establishing who is in charge difficult. Ultimately these conflicts may generate more contradictions, delay, rigidity, and uncertainty. As more decisions are thrown into the courts, the "judicialization of state administration" may result.

The new state politics also also put its stamp on public policy. As the power of narrow, special interests rises, policies serving the public interest suffer. Policy makers concerned with their political survival are likely to choose the safest course and are less likely to confront the difficult choices.

When governors and legislators are driven by short-run political needs, they may ignore the long-term needs of their state. Electoral expediency crowds out other important values. State officials may ensure their reelection but undermine their state's future and further cripple democratic institutions.

If more fiscal restraint had been exercised in the 1980s when the economy was booming, the 1990s recession would not have wreaked so much havoc on state budgets. Unlike the federal government, the states cannot borrow their way out. So they have been raising taxes, cutting programs, and angering voters. Incumbent officeholders now are paying the political price for the loose-money politics of the 1980s; they are declining to run for reelection or they are getting beat.

The reliance on statewide initiatives to resolve public policy disputes represents a troubling development. In some of the nation's more populous states, such as California and Florida, state elected officials are passing the responsibility for tough decisions to initiative campaigns. These "issue elections" seldom are grass-roots citizens movements. They instead are dominated by interest groups that spend lavishly on television advertising, direct mail, and tracking polls. For example, the insurance industry spent $60 million attempting to defeat a proposal to cut insurance premiums in California. The opponents succeeded, in part because they were able to raise $20 million.

The erosion of accountability raises serious implications for the ability of political institutions to effectively handle public policy problems. Expansion, distribution, and innovation are popular, but power struggles within and across institutions reduce the possibilities for reaching consensus on matters involving difficult trade-offs. The fragmentation of power and the reluctance to assume responsibility produce policy gridlock and delegation of the hard choices to administrative agencies.

But hard times create opportunities. Basic assumptions about the size and standard operating procedures of state governments are ripe for challenge and change. The quest for more effective and efficient state government has found new urgency in the dark days of economic recession. The struggle for economic security means that state policy makers must make critical contributions to the well being of the nation. State governments are going to endure this latest storm, but not without sustaining some serious damage to the reputations of state officials and the institutions they run. How skillfully state leaders will manage the harsh realities of the 1990s and whether they will emerge in a stronger position to serve the needs of their states and the nation remain to be seen.

Notes

1. Terry Sanford, *Storm over the States* (New York: McGraw-Hill, 1967).
2. Ibid.; and Larry J. Sabato, *Goodbye to Good-time Charlie: The American Governorship Transformed* (Washington, D.C.: CQ Press, 1983).
3. Timothy G. O'Rourke, *The Impact of Reapportionment* (New Brunswick, N.J.: Transaction Books, 1980).
4. Charles S. Bullock and Charles M. Lamb, eds., *Implementation of Civil*

Rights Policy (Monterey, Calif.: Brooks/Cole, 1984), 20-54.

5. Cathleen Douglas Stone, "Women and Power: Women in Politics," *New England Journal of Public Policy* 6 (Spring/Summer 1990): 157-161.

6. Center for the American Woman and Politics, National Information Bank on Women in Public Office, Eagleton Institute of Politics, Rutgers University, November 1992.

7. Personal communication from the Joint Center for Political Studies, Washington, D.C., December 5, 1992.

8. See, for example, Alan Ehrenhalt, "In Alabama Politics, The Teachers Are Sitting at the Head of the Class," *Governing*, December 1988, 22-27.

9. William T. Gormley, Jr., " The Representation Revolution: Reforming State Regulation through Representation," *Administration and Society* 18:2 (August 1986): 179-196.

10. Patrick B. McGuigan, *The Politics of Direct Democracy in the 1980s* (Washington, D.C.: Free Congress Research and Education Foundation, 1985); Patrick B. McGuigan, ed., *Initiative and Referendum Report* (Washington, D.C.: Free Congress Research and Education Foundation, December 1986/January 1987); and Carol Matlack, "Where the Big Winner Was the Status Quo," *National Journal*, November 10, 1990, 2748-2749.

11. See, for example, Advisory Commission on Intergovernmental Relations, *The Question of State Government Capability* (Washington, D.C.: Advisory Commission on Intergovernmental Relations, 1985).

12. Tom Kean, *The Politics of Inclusion* (New York: Free Press, 1988).

13. Julie Rovner, "Welfare Reform: The Issue That Bubbled Up from the States to Capitol Hill," *Governing*, December 1988, 17-21.

14. David S. Broder, "States Make Hard Decisions as Reagan Fantasies Wane," (Raleigh) *News and Observer*, August 5, 1987, A17.

15. National Association of State Budget Officers, *Looking for Light at the End of the Tunnel: States Struggle with Another Difficult Budget Year* (Washington, D.C.: National Association of State Budget Officers, January 1992), 2.

16. Steven D. Gold, ed., *Reforming State Tax Systems* (Denver, Colo.: National Conference of State Legislatures, 1986).

17. See, for example, Malcolm Jewell, *Representation in State Legislatures* (Lexington: University of Kentucky Press, 1982).

18. See, for example, Joel A. Thompson, "Bringing Home the Bacon: The Politics of Pork Barrel in the North Carolina Legislature," *Legislative Studies Quarterly* (February 1986): 91-108.

19. Richard Niemi and L. R. Winsky, "Membership Turnover in State Legislatures: Trends and Effects of Redistricting," *Legislative Studies Quarterly* 12 (1987): 115-124.

20. David Sherman, "Governors of Fiscally Strapped States, Seeing No Sign of Relief, Yearn for the Good Old Days," *Wall Street Journal*, August 19, 1991, 12.

21. Dave Frohnmayer, "The Courts as Referee" (Paper delivered at the State of the States Symposium, Eagleton Institute of Politics, Rutgers University, December 15-16, 1988).

22. Linda Harriman and Jeffrey Straussman, "Do Judges Determine Budget Decisions?" *Public Administration Review* 43:4 (July/August 1983): 343-351.

INDEX

future prospects, 46-47
governors' role in, 33-35, 83, 84
lower income groups and, 45, 46
mandates from federal government
and, 36-37
national economy, states' depen-
dence on, 45
rainy-day funds, 34, 35, 217
recession of 1990s and, 31-32, 36,
42-45, 216-218
revenue system, 5, 32-33, 34, 39, 40
STABLE and DISTRESS states,
comparison of, 37-42
structural budget deficits, 34, 37
surpluses of 1980s, 36
trends (1960-1992), 5-6
zero-based budgeting, 173-174
See also Taxes
Florida
federalism and, 24
legislative elections, 133-134
legislature, 121, 124
Supreme Court, 165
Florio, James J., 7, 58, 59, 60, 102,
131, 164
Ford, Gerald R., 35
Frendries, John P., 204, 207

*Garcia v. San Antonio Metropolitan
Transit Authority* (1985), 22, 184
Gibson, James L., 204, 207
Gold, Steven D., 18, 25
Governors, 11, 79-80, 106-107
"accidental" governors, 96
accountability battles, 182-183
appointment powers, 82, 85-87,
174
bureaucracy, management of, 173-
174
CEO role, 80-81
courts, conflicts with, 93-94
divided government and, 91, 220
entrepreneurial government and,
103
executive branch, conflicts within,
91-92
executive orders, 174, 182
"first" governors, 96-97, 101

fiscal policy, role in, 33-35, 83, 84
"good job" governors, 97-98
illegal and unethical actions by, 99-
100
issue campaigns and, 96
legislatures, conflicts with, 92-93,
106
media coverage of, 56
multiple-term governors, 97, 99
piecemeal approach to governing,
103, 106
policy-planning process and, 83-84
political changes affecting, 79
powers of governors, comparative
studies of, 89-91
power struggles, 218-221
pragmatic orientation, 216
presidential politics and, 98
public dissatisfaction with, 102-
103, 104-105
reelection eligibility, 55, 81-82
reforms affecting, 3
removal powers, 87-89
reorganizations of governments, 84
staff available to, 82-83, 215
tax increases and, 102
terms of office, 55, 81
veto powers, 34, 82, 93, 182
See also Gubernatorial elections;
Gubernatorial legacies
Grants-in-aid, 19-21, 26
Grasso, Ella T., 97
Gray, Virginia, 24
Great Society programs, 22
Gregg, Judd, 58
Grodzins, Morton, 15, 19, 26
Gubernatorial elections, 51
campaigning and governing, relationship between, 95-97
candidate-centered campaigns, rise
of, 51-52
contributions by recipients of official state patronage, 59
direct primaries, 54-55
expenditures of campaigns, 59
federal and state elections,
decoupling of, 57-58
financing of campaigns, 59-61, 222